ETHICAI

C000148082

Marian Eide argues that the central concern of James Joyce's writing was the creation of a literary ethics. Eide examines Joyce's ethical preoccupations throughout his work, particularly the tension between his commitment as an artist and his social obligations as a father and citizen during a tumultuous period of European history. Eide argues that his narrative suggestion that ethics, which etymologically signifies both "character" and "habitat," might be understood best as an interaction between immediate and intimate processes (character) and more external and enduring structures (habitat). Drawing on feminist theory, Eide focuses on the ideas of alterity and difference. The literary ethics developed in this book proceed from a textual focus in order to examine how our assumptions about what it means to read and interpret produce within each reader an implicit ethical practice. This is the first study devoted to Joyce's ethical philosophy as it emerges in his writing.

MARIAN EIDE is Assistant Professor of English at Texas A&M University. She is the author of several articles on twentieth-century literature.

ETHICAL JOYCE

MARIAN EIDE

Texas A&M University

CAMBRIDGE UNIVERSITY PRESS
Cambridge, New York, Melbourne, Madrid, Cape Town, Singapore, São Paulo, Delhi

Cambridge University Press
The Edinburgh Building, Cambridge CB2 8RU, UK

Published in the United States of America by Cambridge University Press, New York

www.cambridge.org
Information on this title: www.cambridge.org/9780521814980

First published 2002
Reprinted 2004
This digitally printed version 2008

A catalogue record for this publication is available from the British Library

ISBN 978-0-521-81498-0 hardback
ISBN 978-0-521-10010-6 paperback

In memory of
Ellen Olsen Eide
& Stephen Vincent Gilligan

Once the realization is accepted that even between the closest human beings infinite distances continue to exist, a wonderful living side by side can grow up, if they succeed in loving the distance between them which makes it possible for each to see the other whole and against a wide sky.

Rainer Maria Rilke (*Letters to a Young Poet*)

Contents

Acknowledgments

It has become a common-place to say that an academic book is a collaborative effort. But like many other writers, I find writing a solitary activity. And while I generally bask in the particular quality of that solitude, I am grateful for the interruptions that have been so generously provided by friends and colleagues who agreed to read and comment on these pages, who often inspired me, always encouraged me, and occasionally interrogated me with just the right questions.

My kind and wise friend Vicki Mahaffey helped me to start this project and has accompanied me throughout its composition; my life and my work are immeasurably enriched by her friendship. Larry Reynolds stepped in just when I most needed him with a generous, gentle, and intelligent reading. From the distance of half a country and often an ocean, Jean-Michel Rabaté has supported me in my research from its earliest days. I began my friendship with Katharine Conley in a series of letters from the northeast of America to France, and our continued friendship of letters made this writing itself more pleasurable.

I am blessed with the most extraordinary group of colleagues in the English Department at Texas A&M. Each of them has been a generous reader and a thoughtful critic. I would like to express my gratitude to Dennis Berthold, Susan Egenolf, Kate Kelly, Pam Matthews, Howard Marchitello, David McWhirter, Mary Ann O'Farrell, Patricia Phillippy, Sally Robinson, Susan Stabile, Janis Stout, and Lynne Vallone. My thanks also to Shelden Brivik, Vincent Cheng, Barbara Lonnquist, and Nicholas Miller for their encouragement. Mikel Parent was invaluable in his tireless work checking details for a final revision of the manuscript, and for being one of the manuscript's first readers. I would also like to thank my students at the University of Pennsylvania, the Rosenbach Museum and Library, and Texas A&M University for inspiring conversations.

Research in the archive of Joyce / Léon letters was supported by a travel grant from the University of Pennsylvania. Further travel for research has been supported by Texas A&M's Center for Humanities Studies Research and Program for Scholarly and Creative Activities.

I would like to thank the *James Joyce Quarterly* for permission to reprint a revised version of "The Language of Flows: Fluidity, Virology, and *Finnegans Wake*" (Vol. 34, no. 4, summer 1997). Thanks also to Louis le Brocquy and Pierre le Brocquy for permission to reproduce "James Joyce."

Finally, I would like to thank my family for the habitat they have always provided, Richard DeVaul for years of ethical conversation, and especially Uwe Moeller for loving me on my umbrella, and for standing by my side against an expanse of sky.

Abbreviations

Works frequently cited are listed parenthetically using the following abbreviations:

CW Joyce, James. The *Critical Writings of James Joyce*, ed. Ellsworth
      Mason and Richard Ellmann. New York: Viking, 1959.

D   Joyce, James. *Dubliners: Text, Criticism, and Notes*, ed. Robert
      Scholes and A. Walton Litz. New York: Viking, 1969.

E   Joyce, James. *Exiles: A Play in Three Acts, including Hitherto
      Unpublished Notes by the Author, Discovered after His Death, and an
      Introduction by Padraic Colum*. New York: Viking, 1951.

FW Joyce, James. *Finnegans Wake*. New York: Viking, 1939.
      References are indicated by page number followed by the
      line number.

GJ Joyce, James. *Giacomo Joyce*, ed. Richard Ellmann. New York:
      Viking, 1968.

P   Joyce, James. *A Portrait of the Artist as a Young Man: Text,
      Criticism, and Notes*, ed. Chester G. Anderson. New York:
      Viking, 1968.

OTB Levinas, Emmanuel. *Otherwise than Being: or, Beyond Essence*.
      Trans. Alphonso Lingis. Pittsburgh: Duquesne University
      Press, 1998.

TI Levinas, Emmanuel. *Totality and Infinity: An Essay on Exteriority*.
      Trans. Alphonso Lingis. Pittsburgh: Duquesne University
      Press, 1969.

U   Joyce, James. *Ulysses: The Corrected Text*, ed. Hans Walter
      Gabler with Wolfhard Sheppe and Claus Melchior.
      New York: Random House, 1986. References are identified
      by chapter and line number.

Introduction

I will provide you with the available words and the available grammar. But will that help you to interpret between privacies?

Brian Friel, *Translations*

If Europeans had read James Joyce's *Finnegans Wake*, World War Two need never have happened. Or such, at least, is the legendary claim Joyce is said to have made for his final book. The legend is as indicative as it may be apocryphal. Certainly it is possible to read this claim as a marker of the author's often noted pride (the same pride that led him to tell the elder, established poet W. B. Yeats that he had met Yeats too late to really help him).[1] It is also possible for a frustrated reader to see the legend comically: who indeed would have time to launch a major military offensive while trying to read this obsessive book written for the ideal insomniac.[2] But I prefer, at least provisionally, to take this story at its face value, as a tragic statement of the *Wake*'s ambitious and admirable goals. If read according to Joyce's claim, the *Wake* emerges as a radically anti-totalitarian book which is not only descriptive but also performative in its effects.[3] In other words, this experimental text engages the reader in acts of interpretation that will, of necessity, affect that readers' ethics not by instruction or influence (which are potentially coercive modes) but through the agencies of interpretive exchange, which in Joyce's works demands reciprocity. These are the claims I will make for Joyce's literary, ethical project, a project that, I will argue, began with his first writings and is most sustained in his final work.

I

"I looked on her face as she lay in her coffin – a face grey and wasted with cancer – I understood that I was looking on the face of a victim and I cursed the system which made her a victim." James Joyce wrote these words describing his mother to Nora Barnacle on August 29, 1904 in the first summer of their courtship. Paradoxically, in this encounter with his mother's corpse, an experience of absolute alienation, Joyce came to understand her situation clearly for the first time. He wrote to Nora that she had been killed slowly by a system in which she was confined to an inadequate home, sentenced to provide for a family of seventeen, subjected to her husband's alcoholic "ill-treatment," and his own "cynical frankness of conduct." Responding to his mother's untimely death and acknowledging the systems that had caused it, he wrote to Nora to justify his emerging ethical investments; he indicated the necessity of experiencing sympathy with another, and from the core of that sympathy rejecting any system that would make the other a victim. For Joyce, then, the first ethical obligation is to experience and express sympathy while preserving the differences between oneself and another. Even in the alienated encounter with his mother's corpse described in this letter, he emphasized that the ethical subject is responsible for that other no matter how incommensurable the differences between them. Joyce elaborated the ethics reflected in this encounter throughout his literary career. In *Ethical Joyce*, I will argue that the central concern of his writing was the creation of a literary ethics responsive to the particularities of the culture to which his mother fell victim.[4]

In each of his works, Joyce maps the complex relations within a domestic setting or immediate context onto exterior processes in the social and political realms. *Ethical Joyce* reflects his repeated textual suggestion that ethics, which etymologically signifies both "character" and "habitat," might be best understood as an interaction between immediate and intimate processes (character) and more external and enduring structures (habitat). For example, his realization that his mother had provided him with his first habitat and sustained his life through adolescence and yet fell victim to the very system that nurtured his own success, altered Joyce's understanding of his obligation to women both in his literary representations and in his private relations with Nora Barnacle and later with his daughter, Lucia. The literary ethics I develop in this book proceed from a local, formal or aesthetic textual focus in order to examine how our assumptions about what it means to read and interpret produce within each reader an implicit ethical practice. Contrary to prevailing assumptions that aesthetic concerns are in some way divorced from or even allergic to ethical responsibility, I argue that Joyce's aesthetic choices constituted his performative ethics and suggest an ethical practice for his readers.[5]

Following Joyce's literary cue, my own method in the chapters that follow will be to focus on specific textual moments throughout his works that present particular ethical dilemmas or opportunities. Rather than surveying the vast range of possible instances, I will model the ethical suggestion and response by a process of interpretive dilation intended to present the encounter with an other in all of its ambivalence. While it may be possible to survey the range of ethical possibilities in the works, I prefer the kind of ethical interpretation that Joyce's complex texts make possible: to examine the character – or textual moment – in its habitat – or context – with all the vast implications, distinctions, and connections Joyce makes available to the reader. My approach is not to be exhaustive, or even exhausting, but perhaps insomniac: eyes open against darkness or obscurity (in other words, dilated), alert to the range of possibilities produced in Joyce's textual web.[6]

Joyce's texts locate readers between disparate subject positions, each of which makes an ethical demand. Drawing on the literal meaning of interpretation – putting between – I argue that reading Joyce's texts requires an ethical investment in which a reader maintains a suspended position between opposing claims. Stephen argues this case explicitly when in *Portrait* he defines "proper" art (as opposed to the "pornographic" or "didactic" arts) as static: "The esthetic emotion," he claims "is a face looking two ways."[7] While didactic arts impel the reader in a specific direction, demanding a particular, and predetermined reaction, "proper" arts compel ambivalence. In using the term "static" to describe fine art, Stephen does not suggest a paralytic or frozen response; rather, the reader's face looks two ways; the response, then, is a dynamic ambivalence.[8] Following Stephen's cue and recognizing the impossibility of conjoining oppositions, the reader performs the impossible yet imperative task of "interpreting between privacies."

Ethics, as I am defining it, is an engagement with radical alterity, or difference, within the context of ultimate responsibility (which encompasses responsiveness) to the other in his or her habitat. The alterities that Joyce addresses in his fictions include the differences between text and reader, text and author, between genders in a marriage, generations in a family, nations in a colonial empire, and races in conflict.[9]

At the close of Joyce's *Portrait of the Artist as a Young Man*, the young writer Stephen Dedalus inscribes the following, much quoted, entry in his diary as he prepares for his creative life in exile: "I go to encounter for the millionth time the reality of experience and to forge in the smithy of my soul the uncreated conscience of my race" (*P* 252–253). While Stephen is, as Joyce emphasizes, "a young man," and while his objectives are perhaps more dramatically articulated than those of his author, the idea that ends *Portrait* might yet be read as the crucial impetus for Joyce's artistic project: the forging of an uncreated conscience. Joyce's central concern as a writer was the creation of a literary ethics (or conscience) responsive to the particularities of Irish national culture, to the particularities of his character's context or habitat. He forged that ethics in the smithy of the encounter, in the place of meeting an other in which the situation demands that a subject communicate ethically across incommensurable difference.[10] For Joyce the first ethical consideration is the experience and expression of sympathy within the preservation of difference. In other words, ethical response makes possible a communion that does not obscure necessary separation.

II

Joyce's ethical theory may be elucidated by comparison with contemporary ethical thought. The second half of the twentieth century saw a major revolution in ethical theory founded primarily in response to the work of philosopher Emmanuel Levinas. Levinas makes a case for philosophical ethics very similar to Joyce's in many respects when he critiques the classical tradition as totalizing, noting the tendency of ontological thought to subsume the claims of the other under the rubric of the one. In *Totality and Infinity*, for example, Levinas writes of Martin Heidegger's ontology that its focus on the concept of "Being" tends to "neutralize" that which exists in the real in order to comprehend or understand it. There is no attempt in this ontology, according to Levinas, to form a relation with an other; rather, this philosophy reduces the other to a version of the self or same.[11] In Heidegger's philosophy, even "freedom" depends on this reduction, maintaining the primacy of the self in any relation with an other to ensure the "autarchy of an I." The effort of conceptualizing according to ontological premises depends on the "suppression or possession of the other" (*TI* 45–46). Levinas argues that when philosophy begins with the question of Being as its Archimedes lever,[12] the philosopher risks reducing or "neutralizing" everything outside his or her consciousness in order to know it. Ontology begins with the (perhaps unethical) assumption of the supreme philosophical importance of one being or consciousness. If this assumption is the foundation of philosophical inquiry, Levinas elaborates, then all subsequent thought will be, by definition, reductive, attempting to reduce multiplicity and difference to a theme or concept that can be understood in its totality, that can, in other words, be totalized.

Like Joyce who saw his final work as an act of resistance to the rise of European fascism and increasing militarization at the beginning of World War Two, Levinas devoted his philosophical writings to resisting the totalitarianism he experienced during that same war when he was incarcerated in a military prisoners' camp.[13] While his work is primarily philosophical and theological, like Joyce's, it rests on a fundamental belief that an ethical disposition would be the only effective means for preventing the destructive politics of totalitarian regimes.

In "Difficult Freedom," Levinas argues that "Political totalitarianism rests on ontological totalitarianism."[14] Ontology, according to these terms, is the effort to span, mediate, or compress the difference between subject and other in order to reduce otherness to a recognizable same (see also *Totality and Infinity* 42–43). The political programs that would arise from these assumptions rest on the importance of universal truths and put all manifestations of difference at risk. As an alternative to the totalitarian impulses of ontology, Levinas argues that ethics is first philosophy and emphasizes the subject's responsibility in the primal encounter with the naked face of the *Autrui*.[15] "The face in which the other – the absolutely other – presents himself does not negate the same, does not do violence to it . . . It remains commensurate with him who welcomes; it remains terrestrial. This presentation is preeminently nonviolence, for instead of offending my freedom it calls it to responsibility and founds it. As nonviolence it nonetheless maintains the plurality of the same and the other" (*TI* 203). While the nonviolence of a subject's ethical encounter with the face of the other might tempt a reader to sentimentalize Levinas's philosophy, one must remember that this encounter with the specific other is also a repetition of the primordial meeting with the *Autrui* from whom we are commanded "Thou shalt not murder" and in whom we potentially see our own annihilation. "The identifying of death with nothingness befits the death of the other in murder. But at the same time this nothingness presents itself there as a sort of impossibility. For the Other [*Autrui*] cannot present himself as Other [*Autrui*] outside of my conscience, and his face expresses my moral impossibility of annihilating . . . The Other [*Autrui*], inseparable from the very event of transcendence, is situated in the region from which death, possibly murder comes" (*TI* 232–233).

Joyce's approach might be compared fruitfully to that of Levinas in their mutual emphasis on the decentralization of the subject and the openness of the subject to an "other." Levinas's "other" (*autre*) might be more accurately referred to as "*the* Other" (*Autrui*), in the sense of the transcendent, the abstract, and the absolute. In *Totality and Infinity*, Levinas writes that the "Other [*Autrui*] is not other with a relative alterity as are, in a comparison, even ultimate species, which mutually exclude one another but still have their place within the community of a genus – excluding one another by their definition, but calling for one another by this exclusion across the community of their genus. The alterity of the Other [*Autrui*] does not depend on any quality that would distinguish him from me, for a distinction of this nature would precisely imply between us that community of genus which already nullifies alterity" (*TI* 194).[16]

Luce Irigaray calls Levinas's conception of the *Autrui* into question to the extent that this *Autrui* is defined as absolute and incommensurably different from the subject. She notes that in Levinas's work the distance from an other is always maintained, even in love. "This autistic, egological solitary love does not correspond to the shared outpouring, to the loss of boundaries which takes place for both lovers when they cross the boundary of the skin into the mucous membranes of the body, leaving the circle which encloses my solitude to meet in a shared space, a shared breath. . . ."[17] Irigaray prefers to offer a model of the subject's responsibility to the other that relies on interactions of difference and connection. Drawing on the metaphors made possible in the body's mucosity she proposes a model for ethics to be found in acts of love. Her metaphor does not assume a connection between disparate species based on shared genus, a connection Levinas warns against, rather she suggests the possibility of connection even in the context of absolute difference. Anna Livia Plurabelle's fluid interventions between her warring sons in *Finnegans Wake* offer just such a model for an ethical relation between others that balances alterity with connection (see chapter three).

While Levinas's *Autrui* is absolute, incomparable, Joyce's other is more immediate and plural, a series of "others."[18] However, the tendency of both Joyce and Levinas to understand the subject in relation to an other, and to cast difference as incommensurable rather than relative, roots their very different discourses within a common concern for the ethical. Both writers also resist any totalizing philosophical or theoretical impulse because such an ontology reduces difference to the same, subsumes the other under the principles of the One.

To be responsible, the subject must recognize the extent to which in encountering an other from whom one experiences an essential difference, the encounter is understood to be singular, separate from the assumptions of group identity. As Derek Attridge argues in "Innovation, Literature, Ethics: Relating to the Other," this term, "other," "implies a wholly new existent that cannot be apprehended by the old modes of understanding and could not have been predicted by means of them; its singularity, even if it is produced by nothing more than a slight recasting of the familiar and thus of the general, is absolute."[19] In its singularity, an encounter with the other reconfigures the subject even as the subject begins to apprehend or even understand that other.

The change implied by this singular occurrence can be seen in Joyce's *Dubliners* story "An Encounter" in which, as the title indicates, there may be many meetings, but only one encounter. In the boy narrator's play, in his school, and in the disquieting incident with the "queer old josser," there is a consistent pattern of domination: of one character taking another as his object and imposing on that other his own preoccupations and desires. The pederast's imposition is the most obvious and egregious example, of course. However, in the final moments of the story, the narrator recalls one authentic encounter between the two boys who have spent their day "miching." The narrator calls to his friend, Mahony, in his desperation to escape from the pederast and recollects that "my heart beat as he came running across the field to me! He ran as if to bring me aid. And I was a little penitent; for in my heart I had always despised him a little."[20] In this final moment, the narrator recalls what I have been describing as an ethical encounter: Mahony responds to his call and, responsible to the need the narrator's call implies, Mahony inadvertently effects a change within his friend who becomes, in this ethical encounter, other to himself. He realizes that he has despised his school friend, and, apprehending Mahony for the first time in all his difference from the narrator's assumptions, he is penitent.

For Joyce the first ethical consideration is the preservation of difference within a context of response or responsibility. Reduction of the other to the principle of the same, of the one, or the self is a form of unethical colonization (or, to quote Levinas, "ontological imperialism," [*TI* 44]) whether it happens at the level of the nation, the group, or the individual. For example, in the "Cyclops" episode of *Ulysses*, the citizen's interrogation of Leopold Bloom indicates not a recognition of an other but an attempt to create a unified truth (or to draw on Joyce's punning invocation of the *Odyssey*'s Cyclops: one-(eye)idea) that would expel Bloom's difference. "What is your nation if I may ask? says the citizen."[21] Implying that Bloom's Jewish heritage taints his Irish nationality, the citizen identifies relative difference in order to solidify his own identity; his position is totalitarian in that he sees difference as dangerous and potentially threatening. Through rhetorical flourishes in which he denigrates Bloom's idealism and draws bigoted attention to his Jewishness, he attempts to reduce or expel Bloom's subjectivity by the power of his own nationalist unification. "That's the new Messiah for Ireland! says the citizen. Island of saints and sages!" (*U* 12:1642–1643). The citizen's unethical position stems from his perception of otherness as threat to which he reacts violently rather than responsively or, to use Levinas's language, responsibly. For Levinas, as for Joyce, the other to whom we are called to respond is not necessarily welcome or even benign, and yet we must be in responsible relation to that other.[22]

Joyce adapted Homer's *Odyssey* to record his literary ethics in which the exiled traveler constantly encounters alterity and difference and is called to respond and connect even when that difference threatens his happiness or even safety. In adapting the *Odyssey* he presents a crucial change from Homer's example in that Bloom can never return home; his return to 7 Eccles Street is a return to a home that has changed, been adulterated with his wife's adultery. Odysseus returns to the familiar in Ithaca, to a home and wife that have remained faithful and that he can bring back under his control in a brutal extermination of suitors. Levinas reads Odysseus's journey as exemplary of a failed ethics because this hero insists on the totalizing recurrence of the same. Odysseus "through all his peregrinations is only on the way to his native land." As such Odysseus is exemplary of a strain in western philosophy "struck with a horror of the other that remains other."[23] Levinas's own work insists on the subject's responsibility to the other in all his or her alterity by reference to another myth. "To the myth of Ulysses returning to Ithaca, we wish to oppose the story of Abraham who leaves his fatherland forever for a yet unknown land" (*ibid* 348). Joyce's Jewish Ulysses bears the trace of this diasporic Abraham whose exile necessitates responsibility to the other. Bloom, like Abraham, accepts exile without return. He leaves his home without keys to insure his return, and when he gains entrance by unorthodox means in "Ithaca," he catalogues the changes in his home and in his wife, accepting, albeit with pain, a kind of internal exile comprised in her difference, her essential otherness to him.

Levinas's philosophical ethic pursues the enduring and transcendent truth, whereas Joyce invests his literary ethic in the immediate and imma-nent. For example, Levinas advocates a return to metaphysical questions that provide possible alternatives to ontology, referring back to Plato's notion of the Good and Descartes's "Idea of the Infinite."[24] Joyce's

What same? unless she means the desire
to resemble ideals of birthing
— but this is contested in J & in
Ireland

Introduction 9

emphasis on the other might be understood to derive from sources that were as personal as they were philosophical. Though his early religious training might have predisposed him to think ethically toward an absolute Other in the form of the Roman Catholic God, it was catholicity of another kind that motivated his thinking as an adult. Living in a colonial environment and raised among Republicans and Nationalists (as the Christmas dinner scene in *Portrait*, if read autobiographically, might indicate), Joyce saw his environment as one in which incommensurable differences (cultural, philosophical, religious, ethical, and political) were violently yoked together under the guise of the sameness that is colonial culture. Encountering his mother's gray face in her coffin, falling in love with his very forceful partner, Nora Barnacle, and raising his daughter, Lucia, with whom he was strongly identified, he began to see the ways in which cultural differences yoked together as sameness in colonial culture are paralleled in gender differences, which are yoked into the sameness of patriarchal culture.[25] The result is his enduring ethical investment, in all of his fictions, in an understanding of the subject as an unstable entity formed in relation to an other from whom that subject is incommensurably different.[26] In contrast, for Levinas that incommensurable difference is neither unstable nor relative but absolute and primordial.

III

While Joyce presents his ethical theory primarily through the auspices of experimental narrative and representation, Levinas, especially in his early career, describes esthetic representations as totalizing forms, subsuming the other under the principles of the same: "For the moment let us note that the structure of representation as a non-reciprocal determination of the other by the same is precisely for the same to be present and for the other to be present to the same. We call it 'the same' because in representation the I precisely loses its opposition to its object; the opposition fades, bringing out the identity of the I despite the multiplicity of its objects, that is, precisely the unalterable character of the I" (*TI* 126). For Levinas, then, the insistent presence of representation subsumes the difference of the text's subject and its reader (that representation's others) under the presence of the representation itself (the same).

Robert Eaglestone provides an extremely accessible summary of Levinas's reservations about art in *Ethical Criticism*. He notes that "*Totality and Infinity* was open to criticism on the ground that it had difficulties over the issue of representation in general and the issue of aesthetic representation in particular."[27] Eaglestone locates Levinas's reservations in the question of the face: in the philosopher's writing of the early period that culminates with *Totality and Infinity*, ethics derive from the face-to-face encounter which assumes the *presence* of an other. "To suggest that presence is only re-presented in material forms, to confuse the issue of presence with the issue of how presence is represented, is to challenge the actual face-to-face relationship with the Other, one of Levinas's most central ideas. It is because of this that Levinas is suspicious of the idea of representation, in art or otherwise, and either ignores representation or attempts to circumvent it."[28] However, this theory of representation relies on a Platonic assumption of literature as essentially mimetic rather than elaborating on the esthetic as itself a practice of intersubjective ethics, as I will argue.[29]

Jacques Derrida, in "Violence and Metaphysics," argues that Levinas's insistence on the materiality and immediacy of the face in an encounter merely prefers empiricism to philosophy, assuming that that empiricism can get beyond representation or the mediations of language, whereas, as Derrida points out, empiricism would actually be another philosophical gesture, performed within mediating language. Eaglestone glosses this philosophical conversation, noting that for "Derrida, ethics cannot exist save in language . . . which will underlie any 'pure' ethical moment: the ethical . . . is a result of language."[30] *Otherwise than Being* is Levinas's response to Derrida's essay in which he posits a theory of the Saying and the Said which suggests that an ethical gesture may reside in language (and especially in philosophical language) and resist the totalizing tendencies of representation. I will return to the theory of the Saying and the Said in the third chapter.

While Levinas resists literary representation as ethical expression, many of his examples of ethical interchange are actually derived from literary examples including Shakespeare, Dostoevsky, Celan, and Blanchot among others.[31] Jill Robbins argues that this allusive practice co-opts the alterity of the literary text, "the fact of allusion threatens to effect a return to a shared literary or textual heritage."[32] Rather than understanding "this divided perspective as a transformation of his view," it is possible to "approach this tension as one operative *within* each of his texts about art" (*ibid* 75). Levinas pays homage to textuality from Biblical to secular examples, but for his purposes, as Robbins notes "the art that makes an ethical difference can no longer be conceived as aesthetic" (*ibid* 134).

I would like to argue against Levinas that esthetic representations provide an ideal ground for ethical theorizing not simply because esthetic texts may model morally desirable behavior, but because representation provides an ethical ground for the practice of responsibility between self and other. Drucilla Cornell also insists on the centrality of esthetics especially for a feminist theory and practice of ethics. She notes an historical alliance between some forms of esthetic modernism and feminism (citing Joyce's *Finnegans Wake* most specifically and extensively), and turns to these esthetics practices as providing the ground on which it is possible to "'rite' different ways of being with our sexuality."[33]

Levinas does not, indeed could not, provide this book with a method or framework for interpreting Joyce's literature. Not only would this adaptation of Levinas's work be disrespectful of his critique of esthetics, but it would also distort considerably the way in which his ethics are developed through his texts. Eaglestone notes that there "cannot be a Levinasian ethical criticism *per se*, because as soon as a way of reading becomes a methodology, an orthodoxy or a totalising system" it fails as ethical response. Rather than presenting a Levinasian reading of Joyce, my aim is to present Joyce's own ethics made explicit by comparison both with Levinas's ethical writings and with the rich contemporary field of feminist ethics with which Joyce's own writings bear striking similarities.

IV

While Levinas himself notes a connection between ethical philosophy and the feminine, the specific connections he draws tend to transform actual women into objects without consciousness, the occasion for men's ethical response. In *Totality and Infinity* and perhaps more explicitly in *Time and the Other* Levinas describes alterity and otherness in specifically feminine terms: "alterity is accomplished in the feminine. This term is on the same level as, but in meaning opposed to consciousness."[34] Thus Levinas clearly illustrates that in writing of the ethical subject he assumes a masculine entity to whom he grants consciousness that is in stark contrast to the feminine who provides the habitat or dwelling in which masculine consciousness and responsibility take place.[35]

Though Levinas has provided feminist philosophers with the fruitful ground from which to develop a feminist ethic, his comparison of the feminine and the habitat has been, as one would expect, quite controversial. Simone de Beauvoir, an early reader and critic of Levinas, in constructing her own ethical theory in *The Second Sex*, notes Levinas's conflation of women with the inert and the unconscious. She writes: "I suppose that Levinas does not forget that woman, too, is aware of her own consciousness, or ego. But it is striking that he deliberately takes a man's point of view, disregarding the reciprocity of subject and object. When he writes that woman is mystery, he implies that she is mystery for man. Thus his description, which is intended to be objective, is in fact an assertion of masculine privilege."[36] The assertion of a singular, masculine privilege at the heart of Levinas's ethics damages his investigation of responsibility by robbing the other, or in this particular case, woman, of her own conscious response. De Beauvoir prefers to emphasize the reciprocity and mutuality of the subject in her or his relations with a conscious other. She recognizes that if the other is taken to be mute and unconscious then the *Mitsein* (to use the Hegelian term which can be imprecisely translated as Being with) emerging between subjects could not be based on "solidarity and friendliness" (to adopt de Beauvoir's terms). On the contrary, de Beauvoir indicates, one would "find in consciousness itself a fundamental hostility toward every other consciousness; the subject can be posed only in being opposed – he sets himself up as the essential, as opposed to the other, the inessential, the object."[37] In preference to this structure that builds hostility within it as an essential element, de Beauvoir proposes a structure based on intersubjectivity or mutuality.

Luce Irigaray in her "Questions to Emmanuel Levinas" criticizes the philosopher on similar grounds. While she credits him with developing a philosophy based on responsibility to the other, she notes that he "abandons the feminine other, leaves her to sink, in particular into the darkness of a pseudo-animality, in order to return to his responsibilities in the world of men-amongst-themselves."[38] The feminine other does not merit his respect, she is robbed of her specific "face." "On this point his philosophy falls radically short of ethics. To go beyond the face of metaphysics would mean precisely to leave the woman her face, and even to assist her to discover it and to keep it" (*ibid* 116). In *Ethics of Sexual Difference*, Irigaray provides her own philosophical exploration of the womb as initial habitat, noting that each subject is born into "dereliction" by expulsion in birth from this original home, however, men recompense that loss at women's expense. In the masculine imaginary, she argues, one will always find a nostalgia for the original home, an attempt to own and control that habitat in order to be able to return to it.[39] This fantasy of return is made actual, she argues, in the desire to keep women in the home, in a role of economic or social dependence, so that women increasingly serve a function for men rather than being granted their actual, separate being.[40]

Irigaray elaborates on this critique in her "Questions to Emmanuel Levinas" through the idea of the caress. Drawing on the idea of an erotic caress to describe a philosophical encounter or conversation she accuses Levinas of using the caress only for the "elaboration of a future for himself..." Incorporating the feminine as a philosophical metaphor useful only in developing an exclusively masculine position, Levinas transforms the "flesh of the other into his own temporality" and "the masculine subject loses the feminine as other."[41]

Feminist ethics offers a mediated response compatible with the compromises of literary representation and deeply invested in maintaining a recognition of difference at the same time that it opens avenues of identification and responsibility. Feminist ethics, like Joyce's, regards difference as the point of departure or basic assumption and proceeds interactively, often through models of sympathy or mutuality toward an other who is radically and even incommensurably different from the self who addresses him or her. This ethical investment departs from classical ethics (in the tradition of Aristotle, Locke, or Kant) in that it resists universal codes or ideals for moral belief and right behavior, investing instead in the essential undecidability of morality and demanding nonetheless provisional models for ethics based on interactive contact between irreducibly different subjects.[42]

Seyla Benhabib articulates this position in "The Generalized and the Concrete Other" in which she distinguishes between *substitutional* and *interactive* universalisms. I would describe substitutional universalisms as moral code and interactive universalisms as ethics. Benhabib's interactive model is founded on the immediate dilemma encountered in particular differences between subjects. Classical philosophy, she argues, relies on substitutional universalisms through which an immediate ethical conflict may be understood by substituting the specific instance with the relevant generality outlined in a philosopher's thought. Distinguishing between morality and ethics presents a departure from classical modes of addressing these questions. Paul Ricoeur notes that "Nothing in their etymology or in the history of the use of the terms requires such a distinction."[43] Creating this distinction for the first time is among the contributions made in twentieth-century ethical philosophy.

Arguing that "difference" is "a starting-point for reflection and action," Seyla Benhabib labels her own position "interactive universalism," a feminist mode of ethical thought which she defines as a system that "acknowledges the plurality of modes of being human, and differences among humans, without endorsing all these pluralities and differences as morally and politically valid."[44] Julia Kristeva, herself advocating a version of interactive ethics, notes the extent to which moral absolutism can become a form of violence in its attempts to construct predetermined forms of subjectivity. In *Desire in Language*, she writes, "Ethics used to be a coercive, customary manner of ensuring the cohesiveness of a particular group through the repetition of a code – a more or less accepted apologue. Now, however, the issue of ethics crops up where a code (mores, social contract) must be shattered in order to give way to the free play of negativity, need, desire, pleasure, and jouissance, before being put together again, although temporarily and with full 'knowledge' of what is involved."[45] Ethics, according to Kristeva, might be understood as a study of the indeterminate region of interaction between subjects which can be neither legislated nor predicted and which is, at the same time, the greatest ethical responsibility of each subject within a community, the subject's defining encounter. Gayatri Spivak, addressing both feminist and postcolonial issues, comes to similar conclusions regarding the ethical relations between self and an incommensurably different other when she adopts Jacques Derrida's *aporia* to argue that "ethics is the experience of the impossible."[46]

In contrast to Levinas's return to metaphysics in constructing his ethics, philosopher Susan Bordo has traced the subjection of traditionally feminine attributes and the preference for those associated with masculinity to metaphysical thought, and more specifically to the influence of Descartes's *Meditations*. Bordo proposes an alternative possibility of "sympathetic" thought which counters the dominant "Cartesian masculinization of thought." Her phrase, "Cartesian masculinization of thought," summarizes a set of assumptions that emphasize objectivity as the absolute separation of thinking subject and object of thought; at the same time this thought subsumes that object under the processes of the thinking subject, in effect, reducing the other to the principles of the same. As an alternative to this objectification, Bordo explores "sympathy," a thought process that locates itself *between* subjects. Rather than describing intellectual understanding as grasping or colonizing, Bordo suggests that knowledge comes from "merging" "that which is to be known," in a process in which "interior movement replace[s] clarity, interior closeness replace[s] objectivity." Knowing through sympathy requires that the thinking subject give epistemological value to processes such as personal experience and intuitive response. In spite of the fragmentary and contradictory information collected through these methods, the knowledge gained may have increased epistemological currency. According to

Bordo, sympathetic thought "is the only mode which truly respects the object, that is, which allows the variety of its meanings to unfold without coercion or too-forced interrogation."[47] Bordo's epistemological model does not rely on absolutes but rather allows understanding to evolve in a process of exchange between the thinker and the object or person she or he contemplates. This model is necessarily intersubjective or mutual. At the same time, however, this identification resists coercion. Sympathy, then, should not be misunderstood by applying an exclusively emotional definition that would lead to associations with pity, patronage, or even condolence. These responses risk subsuming another under the assumptions of one's own emotions (that risk has been seen as one of the problems with the care model for ethics proposed by many North American ethical philosophers).[48] Bordo's sympathy might be understood more fruitfully through the models provided by physiology. The sympathetic systems of the human body allow for an increase or diminution of the activities of one organ based on the conditions of another organ; this shared activity, which nonetheless preserves the different physiological responsibilities of each organ, is described as sympathetic. Like Joyce's ethics, Bordo's sympathy proceeds interactively while preserving difference.

Kelly Oliver, in *Family Values*, examines the value of difference in the processes of sympathetic thought, which she describes as "identification." According to Oliver, identification should not be understood only as a merging of self and other, but must incorporate differentiation as a part of connection and understanding.[49] Commenting on contemporary debates concerning cultural and gendered difference, Oliver develops "a notion of identification that can navigate between the two extremes that plague contemporary attempts to theorize difference: at one pole, the position that I can understand anyone by just taking up their position, and at the other, that I can understand no one because of radical alterity which prevents me from taking up their position. . . ."[50] In the first case, one sees communication as simple and transparent, it is only necessary to be direct or honest; in the second case, any understanding between groups would be impossible. "The first assumes we are absolutely identical, which erases our difference, and the second assumes that we are absolutely different, which erases our communion. I maintain that we can communicate or commune only because of our radical difference" (*ibid* 96). When I suggest, in response to Joyce's work, that the difference between the subject and his or her other is incommensurable, I wish to underscore the idea that communication will not be transparent or immediate because the differences between subjects are so radical.

However, following Oliver's incisive argument that communion is made possible by difference, I argue difference makes possible the emergence of an ethical subject. In other words, it is not the case that a subject will be unable to communicate with the other but rather that the incommensurability of this other calls the identity of the subject into question, undermining basic assumptions and causing the subject to be remade in the encounter. This basic difference, however, the difference at the heart of ethical response, might be understood not merely as a hindrance but rather as an opportunity.

Oliver's compelling suggestion is that we might consider desire as a form of identification that promotes difference. She suggests that desire is the "excess of identification." Desire is not a process that makes the other the same as the self or that converts you into me; rather, desire, a form of identification, allows the self to spill out of its borders and come closer to the other, I am taken "beyond myself toward you." Desire is not premised on similarity, nor does difference within desire merely serve the purposes of re-establishing the borders of one's own subjectivity. On the contrary, because of the differences that provoke desire, the subject can move away from stagnant or overly stable versions of identity to make contact with another. Oliver argues that desire is the "excess of the other in one's own identification. . . . Desire and identification are not polar opposites, neither are they the same. To say that there is no desire without identification is not to say that desire is the annihilation of difference. Rather, desire is the difference in excess of any identification" (*ibid* 95).

At the heart of Joyce's literature is an exploration of ethical desire; it is a desire that refuses to take another as an object but rather desires because the other cannot be wholly subsumed by the subject's conceptualization. In experiencing desire as an interplay of identification and difference, the subject of Joyce's texts is in a constant process of becoming.

V

Drawing also on the literal meaning of ethics as habitation, Levinas locates human subjects in the home, in the relation between subjectivity and habitat. The home, as he writes in *Totality and Infinity*, is directly associated with the feminine: "And the other whose presence is discreetly an absence, with which is accomplished the primary hospitable welcome which describes the field of intimacy, is the Woman. The woman is the condition for recollection, the interiority of the Home, and inhabitation" (*TI* 155). Hospitality, a central concept for Levinas's ethics depends on "woman" and yet that woman is described as a present absence, an inert context within which "man" is able to enact his ethical subjectivity. Elaborating on this point, Levinas admits that the actual presence of a living woman is completely unnecessary to hospitality, the home, or ethics. "The feminine has been encountered in this analysis as one of the cardinal points of the horizon in which the inner life takes place – and the empirical absence of the human being of 'feminine sex' in a dwelling nowise affects the dimension of femininity which remains open there, as the very welcome of the dwelling" (*TI* 158). Though she is associated with the home (in which she is imprisoned in this philosophy, having no other characteristic space), she is extraneous to the ethical man's experience of ethical hospitality.[51]

It is possible to elaborate on Levinas's association of the woman with habitation and ethics without robbing women of their "empirical" presence or particular subjectivities. The two strands of the ethical theory I have been outlining thus far – the encounter with the other and the responsibility to context – may be joined together if one follows the theoretical explorations of Hélène Cixous, Julia Kristeva, and Luce Irigaray who locate the first instance of subjectivity in the relation of children with their mothers who provide those children with an initial context or habitation both literally in the womb and more figuratively in the development of ethical relations that recognize both connection and differentiation. Accordingly, ethics might be founded on the human subject's first habitat, the womb and the mother's home.[52] The subject's ethics develop from that initial relationship to encompass relations in increasingly centrifugal contexts (such as nation or "race" in Stephen's call for a developing "conscience").

By focusing on the womb as the initial habitat and situation for an emerging ethical subjectivity, I do not wish either to imply or to give hospitality to any simplistic reading that would conclude that abortion would then be "unethical." Rather, I wish to emphasize the obligation each of us incurs at birth for the hospitality we were afforded by a woman who allowed us to make her body our home.[53] Locating ethical philosophy, in part, in a model provided by the womb risks repeating a western cultural preoccupation with the idealized mother, an idealization that Joyce held partly responsible for his own mother's victimization in her habitat. Julia Kristeva notes this risk in "Stabat Mater" when she observes that "we live in a civilization where the *consecrated* (religious or secular) representation of femininity is absorbed by motherhood."[54] She notes also that this idealized motherhood is a cultural "*fantasy* that is nurtured by the adult, man or woman, of a lost territory" (*ibid* 308). This idealization is founded on a primary narcissism, the child's inability to register the difference between self and other in early developmental stages, a narcissism that, when extended into adulthood subsumes the mother under the cultural and particular needs of the adult child.[55] However, Kristeva insists on the irremediable otherness that separates mother and child and that refutes the idealized connection associated with primary narcissism. "Then there is this other abyss that opens up between the body and what had been its inside: there is the abyss between the mother and the child. What connection is there between myself, or even more unassumingly between my body and this internal graft and fold which, once the umbilical cord has been severed, is an inaccessible other? My body and . . . him. No connection. Nothing to do with it. And this, as early as the first gestures, cries, steps, long before *its* personality has become my opponent. The child whether *he* or *she*, is irremediably an other."[56] Despite the metaphor of complete union provided by the image of the pregnant body, the umbilicus, or the mother and newborn child, Kristeva asserts the opening between the two, spanning the distance of an abyss. While that difference is more obvious when the child begins to assert a personality, it is also present in gestation itself in which Kristeva describes the embryo as a "graft," an entity added to the subject's body rather then completely integrated within it.[57]

Balanced against the irremediable difference between mother and child, Kristeva asserts the possibility of connection which may occur when either subject goes beyond the borders of what constitutes identity. She locates that connection in "laughter where one senses the collapse of some ringing, subtle, fluid identity or other, softly buoyed by the waves" (*ibid* 323). She also notes that the act of birthing, in which the separation between subjects becomes immediately apparent with the cutting of the umbilical cord, also provides the condition for ethics. "Although it concerns every woman's body, the heterogeneity that cannot be subsumed in the signifier nevertheless explodes violently with pregnancy (the threshold of culture and nature) and the child's arrival (which extracts woman out of her oneness and gives her the possibility – but not the certainty – of reaching out to the other, the ethical)" (*ibid* 327–328). Kristeva argues against the cultural idealization of mother and child as one, and also against the language that would attempt to mask heterogeneity in favor of an imagined union.[58] Instead she notes that in pregnancy the boundaries of the body that would allow an individual to imagine herself as singular, autonomous, and unified within herself are ruptured with the grafting of another body. The occasion of birth allows the individual to understand herself at base through relation to another, and that understanding sets the occasion for the ethical.

In conversation with biologist Hélène Roach, published in *Je Tu Nous*, Luce Irigaray also explores the biological relation between woman and child in patterning a philosophy of ethics and devotes particular attention to the formation of the placenta during pregnancy.[59] The placenta provides one possible model for ethical relations between self and other. A tissue created by the embryo during gestation, the placenta forms a lining within, and closely joined to, the uterus; this lining, at the same time, creates a separate space for the developing embryo so that embryo and uterus are not actually fused into one entity. The placenta regulates exchanges between woman and fetus, acquiring nutrition and expelling waste. It also modifies a woman's metabolism to accommodate fetal development and to promote a woman's increased provision of nutrients without exhausting her resources in the process. Or to examine this tissue more metaphorically, the placenta creates a habitation or dwelling that is also a barrier protecting both mother and child while allowing for communication between them. Thus the placenta regulates neither an economy of fusion nor one of pure parasitism.

In the course of their conversation, Hélène Roach notes that the placenta is not merely a structure designed for protection of the fetus which would suppress a mother's immune system or prevent her body from recognizing the fetus as foreign to it. Rather, to be produced, the placenta, like the communication of desire described by Kelly Oliver, depends on the body's recognition of the fetus as different. The fetus, in turn, depends on that process of recognizing difference and producing a responsive habitat for its survival. With the placenta as mediating space within the body, the "difference between the 'self' and other is, so to speak, continuously negotiated. It's as if the mother always knew that the embryo (and thus the placenta) was other, and that she lets the placenta know this, which then produces the factors enabling the maternal organism to accept it as other" (*ibid* 41). A woman's immune system remains active during pregnancy because the placenta allows the body to recognize the embryo as different without exciting an immune response that would devour or expel that foreign entity. This balance allows the woman's body to remain protected from disease while providing a safe environment for the embryo. The placenta is the subject's first production and it is an ethical production of connection and separation, coming into being in relation to another.

Roach and Irigaray both note the importance of a concrete biological understanding of pregnancy in discussing its moral or ethical implications. The misunderstanding of pregnancy as either absolute fusion or horrifying parasitism is at the heart of many controversial discussions about the ethics of pregnancy and the responsibilities inherent in it. It is interesting to note the biological responsibility the fetus takes for regulating relations with a woman from its initial stages of development. (I want to emphasize here that I am speaking only of *biological* responsibility. I am not attributing consciousness or agency to the fetus. Rather I am suggesting that the bodily processes that take place between fetus and womb might provide a model for ethics in subjects who, after birth, do definitely have consciousness and, often, agency.) That biological response presents a model for developing ethics, one in which a memory of childhood responsiveness, of the mutual subjectivity that the fetus regulates in her or his combined separation and reliance on another, might form a basis for adult ethical responsibility. Irigaray's conceptual discussion of the placenta, then, is theorized through the perspective of the embryo who produces the tissue and reminds each of us of our initiation into ethical mutuality. The placenta provides evidence that each human subject comes into being in the first instance in relation to another on whom that subject relies and from whom he or she must recognize an essential difference. The first relation is an ethical relation.

Irigaray's focus on the placenta in understanding procreation provides a welcome antidote to more prevalent versions of the maternal relation that assume an initial fusion which must be rejected for the child to gain autonomy and individuation. The misogynist implication inherent in this theory is that the devouring mother must be rejected, or even abjected, for the subject to emerge. As Kelly Oliver argues in *Family Values*: "If abjection of the mother or maternal body is described as a normal or natural part of child development, then one consequence is that without some antidote to this abjection, all of our images of mothers and maternal bodies are at some level abject because we all necessarily rejected our own mothers in order to become individuals" (*ibid* 99). And even more threatening to a formation of ethical mutuality, this initial gesture may justify more broad-ranging social versions of the maternal abjection such as "discrimination, exclusion, and oppression. If our identities are necessarily formed by rejecting and excluding what is different, then discrimination is inherent in the process of identification" (*ibid* 99). It is crucial, then, that our understanding of the maternal rests on the sympathetic exchange suggested by Bordo and by the placental examples investigated by Roach and Irigaray. According to these models, difference also provides the opportunity for mutuality, and following Kristeva's discussion of abjection in *Powers of Horror*, the subject recognizes otherness within: the abject which revolts me and which I try to expel is coextensive with, a part of myself. Identity as separate and sovereign selfhood is, according to each of these models, impossible; instead the subject is part of a complex web of other and same; abjection gives way to mutuality and "[m]eaning is created in the space between social bodies."[60]

Like Irigaray, Hélène Cixous relies on a bodily process in developing an ethical model. In "The Laugh of the Medusa," she writes of the essential relatedness inherent in *écriture féminine* (which might also be understood as ethical writing according to the terms I am developing here). "Even if phallic mystification has generally contaminated good relationships, a woman is never far from 'mother' (I mean outside her role functions: the 'mother' as nonname and as source of goods). There is always within her at least a little of that good mother's milk. She writes in white ink."[61] Writing with the white milk of the mother "a woman is never far from" may be the most crucial metaphor in Cixous's thought. On one level, its implications are troubling: the image seems prescriptive of a maternal role, as if all women must become mothers to produce the milk with which to create *écriture féminine*. And should women choose to become mothers and to write from their maternal experience (which is culturally inscribed, Cixous herself points out, as "nonname" and "source of goods") and with the products of their nurturing bodies, their writing will be illegible: white ink on white paper produces invisible script and serves to silence women's already conventionally suppressed *écriture*.

However, I would like to suggest another, and possibly more accurate, reading of this metaphor. Cixous does not necessarily demand that each writer become a mother; rather, she encourages the writer to remember his or her birth from the mother's body and the mother's milk that each child has ingested and "always" has "within her at least a little of" in later life. The milk with which she encourages women to write is the milk received in nurturing at the breast. If the writer remembers the mother's milk still held within him or her as the experience of sustenance and bonding, each person has an opportunity to imagine his or her subjectivity anew. The subject is both separate, thus the need for milk from the mother's nutritional store, and connected, having shared the body of the mother and exchanged fluids with her. Cixous's metaphor is only enriched in the women's time (to use Julia Kristeva's term) of repetition and cyclicality for women who become mothers and can layer on another experience of mother's milk with which to write.

The metaphorical white ink with which the writer inscribes thought is not immediately legible or lucid. It requires an intervention on the part of the reader. A page written on with white milk must be heated for the writing to emerge: the milk scorches slightly with heat and becomes visible as brown traces on the white page. Ink that consists of a colorless or pale liquid which remains invisible until it is developed by the use of heat or a chemical reagent can also be referred to as sympathetic ink (according to the *Oxford English Dictionary*). The active process of reading demanded by sympathetic ink recalls Bordo's concept of knowledge that is developed sympathetically, in conjunction with the subject of that knowledge. Cixous's metaphor inscribes both the mutuality of writing in the original inscription and also the mutuality of interpretation in which the writing only becomes visible through active reception. Additionally, this writing might be understood as more tactile; the milk puckers the paper on which it is written and might be read like Braille with the facilities of the touch.

Cixous's *écriture féminine* provides an image of writing as ethical in its literalization of difference, which is not exactly opposition. Writing with blue or black ink that contrasts starkly with the white page, the writer emphasizes the distinction between the imposition of inscription and the blank, existent page. Writing with milk employs nuanced alterations, shadings of difference that at the same time emphasize connection and similarity by virtue of the comparable colors of ink and page.

While Cixous's *écriture* is clearly gendered, it is not exclusively attributed by virtue of the writer's sex. Rather, one of the earliest examples of *écriture féminine* that Cixous described was Molly Bloom's monologue at the close of Joyce's *Ulysses*. That monologue is written sympathetically, with a little of the white milk the author had still within him, with the memory of difference and communion which that milk allows. As such, the monologue emphasizes both the fluids of the body (Molly meditates on breast milk, menstrual blood, urine, and perspiration) and the difficult negotiation of separation and connection between ethically attached subjects. It may be worth remembering, in drawing this connection, that Cixous's first sustained research was on Joyce. Her doctoral dissertation and first published book were titled *The Exile of James Joyce*. Throughout her theoretical writings one can see the influence of Joyce's associative logic and his emphasis on the body as the locus for ethical understanding.

Cixous's image of milky ink may be written in response to a comparable image in Joyce's *Finnegans Wake* in which Shem writes on his body with his own excrement.

. . . when the call comes, he shall produce nichthemerically from his unheavenly body a no uncertain quantity of obscene matter . . . through the bowels of his misery, flashly, faithly, nastily, appropriately, this Esuan Menschavik and the first till last alshemist wrote over every square inch of the only foolscap available, his own body, till by its corrosive sublimation one continuous present tense integument slowly unfolded all marryvoising moodmoulded cyclewheeling history. . . . (FW 185.28–186.2)

Like Joyce, Cixous emphasizes the embodiment of writing, its fundamental relation to our physical experience. But she diverges from Joyce's image, which emphasizes autonomy and self-sufficiency (all the materials for Shem's writing are produced by his own body). Cixous's image is imbued with the associations of physical connection, nurturance, and mutuality. While Joyce's image suggests the productive and creative potentials of waste, Cixous's image is perhaps more purified, emphasizing instead generativity, nutrition, and touch. However, Cixous's metaphor when applied to the progeny, who still has some inherited mother's milk, reminds the subject that her contribution to the generative dyad of mother and child was waste. Joyce's image also recognizes the abjection of waste and otherness that evolves from within and which the subject may long to expel and even deny. However, Shem's writing is a reminder that the abject is as much a part of the subject as the skin on which he writes; his writing, then, celebrates otherness within. Recognizing the foreign material within the body and claiming that recognition as part of creativity, in both these images, raises the chances of recognizing connection to others who in more totalizing concepts are abjected, rejected because of their difference. If one writes from the intersubjectivity or mutuality suggested by Cixous's metaphor, one writes from a place of responsibility as an agent who understands both distinction from and relatedness to an other. In both Cixous's conception and Joyce's, writing is an essentially ethical act. A reminder of difference within and of the interdependence of the subject with his or her others, these writings inscribe the mutuality of the ethical subject.

VI

Ethics, as I am defining it in response to the works of Emmanuel Levinas, to feminist ethicists, and most centrally to Joyce, is an engagement with radical alterity or difference within the context of ultimate responsibility (in the sense of responsiveness) to the other. The alterities I will engage in this book include the differences between text and reader, text and

author, between genders in a marriage, generations in a family, nations
in a colonial empire, and between races. In each of these pairings, the
opposites are differently powered, with one side of the dyad far more
vulnerable.

Perhaps the least obvious, though most immediate, example of this
paradigm is the relation between text and reader. However, the vulnerability of text to interpretive control becomes more clear when we consider
that predominant models for reading in our learning institutions, crys-
tallized by the work of New Criticism but present also in traditional
exegesis, proceed from an implicit objective of mastery over the text.
The metaphors conventionally presented to describe the interpretive
process are culled from the language of domination and control. One
refers to penetrating a difficult passage or mastering a complex text as
if the book were either an enemy territory or a servant in the household
of our imagination. Despite their recourse to concepts of domination,
these models are not ultimately empowering for the reader. Rather, the
text is the all-powerful center of meaning that the reader must mine by
violent and invasive acts of interpretation. A powerful act of interpretation may temporarily change the way a text is understood. Harold
Bloom has advocated this possibility when describing how an author's
"anxiety of influence" leads (usually) him to create a powerful revision
of a precedent text. Roland Barthes, in describing the death of the author, celebrates the reader's power to reinvent a text through the act of
interpretation. However, more recently, interpretive theories based on
literary ethics have suggested a mode of reading based on partnership.
Lawrence Buell notes that in this "Levinasian view, the work is an other
in the form of a creative act for which readers are called to take responsibility, to allow themselves to become engaged even to the point of being
in a sense remade."[62] To the same extent as the reader is remade by the
text, the text comes alive through the responses of the reader.

Coming to a theory of interpretation within a postcolonial historical
context such as that provided by Joyce's Ireland (the locus of all his
published fictions), the inadequacies of models based on competition
or invasion become increasingly apparent. Joyce's fiction, for example,
explores the politics of pacifism and of Irish decolonization.[63] How can
readers successfully apply models based on aggression when reading his
texts? Joyce poses the same question when, in *Finnegans Wake*, he puns
on reading as "raiding." A reader's goal of intellectual conquest is at
odds with the shifting complexities of Joyce's writing practice, which
embraces change and mutability. A reader who shares these heterodox

preferences will have nothing to gain from the "raiding" paradigm of textual interpretation. To fix and conquer any of Joyce's works in order to master them, if it were possible, would be reductive and distorting.

My aim in *Ethical Joyce* is to offer an explicit ethical alternative to models of interpretive control or to the idea that reading is at heart an expression of or struggle for power. Based on a literal understanding of interpretation as placement between, ethical interpretation relies on a communal approach to reading, one that admits to the permeable border between text and reader, text and conditions of production or reception, and between various readers and their multiplying interpretations. Vicki Mahaffey cogently expresses this emphasis on relinquishing control and relying on chance associations with the literary text in "Intentional Error: The Paradox of Editing Joyce's *Ulysses*." She notes that Joyce's particular approach to representation demands that "we give up some of our illusion of control over the act of reading itself, not knowing what our interaction with the text may produce, but only that its products are potentially unexpected, incongruous, unstable, and abundant, and that in another sense the interaction produces nothing."[64] In a practice of reading that I would call ethical, Mahaffey suggests that the reader can create the conditions for a dialogue with the text which has not been prescribed by formulaic expectations for literature. "Instead of colonizing or using or subordinating the text, we have to grant it a limited power to remake us to the extent that we remake it" (*ibid* 224). Jill Robbins makes a similar case for the interpretive process, noting that while a text does not have alterity in the same way that a person does, "reading alters the very economy of the same that the other interrupts."[65] It is in that interruption that literary criticism becomes an ethical experience. J. Hillis Miller's *Ethics of Reading* focuses more on the text's facility to remake the reader in an ethical moment of interpretation in which there is of necessity, he argues, an imperative, some "I must" or *Ich kann nicht anders* [I cannot do otherwise.]"[66] He argues that the ethical moment leads to ethical activity. In my own reading the interpretive exchange is understood more as a partnership. Joyce himself suggests, in his fictional accounts of interpretation throughout his works, the complex interactions between text and reader and the facility with which a text changes readers and is itself changed by their reading.

In chapter five of *Finnegans Wake*, for example, a section Joyce referred to as "the Hen," he describes a letter, dug up from a refuse heap, that both indicts and defends Humphrey Chimpden Earwicker (HCE) in his possibly transgressive encounter with a cad in the park. Describing this letter and how it might be considered in judging HCE, Joyce addresses questions of ethical interpretation. He argues that to read a work ethically one must consider not just the literal content of the document but the surrounding circumstances as well. Metaphorically, he suggests that the envelope must be considered when interpreting a letter; to read the letter without first examining its envelope would be as unethical as imagining a woman without her clothes and contemplating her sexual parts on first acquaintance.[67]

Admittedly it is an outer husk: its face, in all its featureful perfection of imperfection, is its fortune: it exhibits only the civil or military clothing of whatever passionpallid nudity or plaguepurple nakedness may happen to tuck itself under its flap. Yet to concentrate solely on the literal sense or even the psychological content of any document to the sore neglect of the enveloping facts themselves circumstantiating it is just as hurtful to sound sense (and let it be added to the truest taste) as were some fellow in the act of perhaps getting an intro from another fellow turning out to be a friend in need of his, say, to a lady of the latter's acquaintance, engaged in performing the elaborative antecistral ceremony of upstheres, straightaway to run off and vision her plump and plain in her natural altogether, preferring to close his blinkhard's eyes to the ethiquethical fact that she was, after all, wearing for the space of the time being some definite articles of evolutionary clothing. . . . (*FW* 109.8–23)

Drawing on the literal meaning of ethics as both character and habitat or dwelling, Joyce refers to a woman's clothing as "ethiquethical fact," or the fact of ethics qua ethics; her clothes are her habitat, her circumstance and her surroundings, and they are partially indicative of her character. Thinking of this woman without her dress reduces her to an object by negating her context and character, her choices, the ideas about herself that she chooses to convey in clothing.[68] To acquaint himself with her ethically, Joyce's fellow must meet her in her own habitat, address her based on an understanding of her context as she expresses it herself. Unlike Levinas's association of woman and dwelling, Joyce's ethical woman is neither passive, absent, nor inert. She voices the claims of habitation and context both in her physical presence and in language.

The practice of interpretation – in this case the reading of a letter – is ethical insofar as it recognizes and is responsive to context. To interpret the letter properly, the reader must first know, both literally and figuratively, where the letter is coming from: not only its point of origin (as stamped on the envelope) but also its ethics – its habitat or context. Ethical interpretation, then, takes place between context and text, between origin and destination, and between author and reader. Further, the methods through which one interprets text are at least parallel to and perhaps even indicative of the methods or ethics through which one addresses other subjects and indeed other people.

The questions Joyce raises in comparing a woman in her clothing with a letter in its envelope suggest the importance of considering how a text intervenes in the social field. While literary representations do not have simple correspondences to or effects on the real, our habits of processing information in the steps between perception and response, the processes of interpretation, apply concurrently to both literary or social fields. In other words, habits of interpreting a text have much to tell us about perceptions of and responses to the wider culture.

Joyce interprets ethics as an interaction of macro- and micrological processes. In each of his works, the complex and intimate relations within the domestic setting are explicitly mapped onto more external processes between a patriarchy and its discontents, between nations and their colonized counterparts. *Ethical Joyce* reflects his narrative suggestion that the concepts and practices of ethics might be best understood as interactions between the most immediate and intimate processes with more global or enduring structures. The literary ethics I develop in this book proceed from just such a local focus in order to examine how our assumptions about what it means to read and interpret produce an implicit ethical subject.

VII

My intention in this introduction has been to form a context or habitat for understanding Joyce's ethics through an explicit review of contemporary ethical theory. However, in the chapters that follow, that context will recede into the background in order to foreground the character of Joyce's own ethical practice throughout his literary career.

In chapter one, "Ethical Interpretation and the Elliptical Subject," I argue that Joyce defines the ethical subject as incomplete, requiring the community of others and in return, responsible to that community. In *Dubliners*, for example, Joyce defines subjectivity through the figure of the *gnomon*, a parallelogram from which a smaller figure of the same proportions has been extracted. Gnomon literally means a judge or interpreter, indicating a necessary relationship to an other (who may be judged or interpreted and who in turn judges and interprets). Implicit in the stories is Joyce's definition of the subject as one who, as gnomon, is unstable, decentered, and open to an other. He elaborates this figure in *Exiles* with the rhetoric of *aporia*, the impassable passage, in which the moral rectitude adopted by such characters as Richard Rowan fails in response to the ethical demands of his family and of his readers. Interpretation emanates from these *aporia* in Joyce's work, the moments in which a reader is asked to suspend decision, entertain ambivalence, and occupy a position between habitual options. In this stasis, *aporia* presents itself as the rhetorical equivalent of what Stephen Dedalus calls proper art, art that stills kinesis, and that is responsible for "creating the uncreated conscience."

Based on the premise that knowledge has moral significance, chapter two, "Ethical Knowledge and Errant Pedagogy," raises the question: how is it possible to encourage or share knowledge ethically? Joyce suggests that methods of conveying knowledge have ethical implications: to learn by rote (as is the case in Stephen's early education described in *Portrait*) may have a blinding effect on a subject's ability to learn in other contexts, and the knowledge gained by rote may also be misused or used primarily for the subjugation of others. Resisting the authoritarian pedagogy exemplified in his own education, Joyce suggests other methods of knowing that rely on encountering an other in his or her context or habitat. In *Ulysses*, Stephen practices this ethics as pedagogical method: he engages student responses that would be considered erroneous according to more traditional or authoritarian pedagogies. Admitting the knowledge his students have already achieved, he finds ways to provoke and expand both their intellectual capacity and their access to and retention of information. Joyce also indicates in Stephen's encounter with his headmaster, Garrett Deasy, that this errant pedagogy has the potential to address ethical conflicts.

Chapter three, "Ethical Opposition and Fluid Sensibility," presents Anna Livia Plurabelle as an ethical agent, a figure (sometimes quite literally, as when she becomes a geometrical figure) through whom ethical relations might be understood and engaged. ALP presents in her own interactions and in the habitat she provides for her children, an ethical understanding formed by her assumption that oppositional categories are interdependent though never interchangeable.[69] Addressing the two warring and yet mutually dependent brothers, Shem and Shaun, ALP indicates both their connection to each other and their responsibility to their context. But she does not, cannot, resolve their oppositions into unity or erase their differences. Rather, her influence places difference under erasure. Difference is scored through in its present condition only to underscore, to highlight and embrace, an ethical logic of dissimilarity based on an understanding of the presence of the other in the same.

The final chapter, "Ethical Representation through Lucia's Looking Glass," focuses on the last years of Joyce's life, during which he faced perhaps the most difficult ethical dilemma in his experience, the care and treatment of his disturbed daughter. In *Finnegans Wake*, Joyce records a vexed version of his relationship with Lucia Joyce through the story of Humphrey Chimpden Earwicker's troubled relations with his daughter, Issy. This chapter draws on a collection of Joyce's unpublished correspondence housed at the National Library of Ireland and composed during the period of Lucia Joyce's decline to trace the creation and composition of Issy in *Finnegans Wake* based on Joyce's identification with Lucia. He presents this identification in figures of mirroring such as narcissism and inversion, and suggests the potentially damaging results of over-identification in metaphors of incest. Representing Lucia in his final work raised ethical questions for Joyce concerning the potential of characterization to usurp a person's voice or self-definition, and also concerning the possible failure of that representation to acknowledge the gap or difference between his own concerns and desires and those of his subject. Joyce's representation resisted the impulse to claim Lucia as a shadow of his own consciousness by delineating his sense of the difference between them, while at the same time registering his sympathy for and responsiveness to his intensely creative daughter.

CHAPTER ONE

Ethical interpretation and the elliptical subject

What am I to do, what shall I do, what should I do in my situation, how proceed? By aporia pure and simple? Or by affirmations
and negations invalidated as uttered or sooner or later? Generally
speaking. There must be other shifts. Otherwise it would be quite
hopeless. But it is quite hopeless. I should mention before going any
further, any further on, that I say aporia without knowing what it
means.

Samuel Beckett[1]

The *aporia* that is Beckett's mark of uncertainty, invalidation, and even
hopelessness is for Joyce a rupture in certainty that makes possible ethical
thought. *Aporia* signifies the breakdown of immediate or accessible
meaning, as Beckett indicates, because the word etymologically signifies a
pathless path or an impassable passage, suggesting difficulty and perplex-
ity. In rhetoric it is an indication of real or pretended doubt. For Joyce,
educated in a Jesuit tradition in which doubt and the intellectual impasse
are the very bases for Catholic faith and drawn to the Celtic philosophers
of uncertainty,[2] the figures of doubt and impossibility, the undermining
of determinate meaning, the path that gives way, all of these are intellectual opportunities for creativity, for path breaking, for the entertaining of
possibility from within the impossible.[3] Jacques Derrida notes that aporia as nonpassage is a form of arrest: "nonpassage because its elementary
milieu does not allow for something that could be called passage, step,
walk, gait, displacement, or replacement, a kinesis in general."[4] In this
stasis, aporia presents itself as the rhetorical figure of what Stephen
Dedalus calls proper art, art that arrests kinesis, and that, in his particular vision is responsible for "creating the uncreated conscience." *Aporia*,
the impassable passage, is the locus for Joyce's ethics.

Aporia, as a rhetorical figure with literary critical implications, has a complex history in theoretical discussions of literature and especially in the diverse critical works commonly grouped under the term deconstruction. However, an emphasis on undecidability in textual study has commonly been understood to elide, negate, or even suppress ethical considerations.[5] This understanding conflates ethics with moral philosophy when it insists on determined codes. However, Geoffrey Galt Harpham notes that ethics, like poststructuralist theory, is concerned with the undecidable and "suffers determination by morality, a further imperative nested within the ethical whose business is to activate the chain of command, to pull the trigger. Morality both realizes and negates ethics . . ."[6] Additionally, as Derrida observes in *Limited, Inc.*, far from suspending ethical concerns, the emphasis on indeterminacy can itself be an ethical gesture. According to Harpham, "Far from licensing indifference or neutrality, Derrida said, he was trying to determine the conditions under which a reading became truly responsible by identifying a phase of undecidability through which reading must pass, a phase in which conclusions that had been taken for granted become subject to disinterested questioning" (*ibid* 391). J. Hillis Miller makes a similar case for "deconstructive" approaches in *The Ethics of Reading* in which he reviews the criticism directed at this interpretive method which was characterized as nihilist (using the philosophical term quite loosely). Critics argued that deconstruction allows the interpreter to adapt a text to mean whatever he or she chooses, that it annihilates the traditional use of classic texts as foundations for culture.[7] Miller counters that this criticism is "a basic misunderstanding of the way the ethical moment enters into the act of reading, teaching, or writing criticism. That moment is not a matter of response to a thematic content asserting this or that idea about morality. It is a much more fundamental 'I must' responding to the language of literature in itself. . . ."[8] In a similar vein, Adam Newton notes that deconstruction should not be understood as "an indifference to answerability; it is at its best a scrupulous hesitation, an extreme care occasioned by the treachery of words and the danger of easy answers."[9]

Within Joyce studies, deconstruction provided a welcome and powerful discourse through which to address the purposive undecidability (if such a thing were possible) of Joyce's literature. As early as 1962, Umberto Eco's *Opera Aperta* addressed Aquinas's esthetics and Joyce's stylistics with an emphasis on openness and indeterminacy. Jacques Derrida has been occupied with Joyce's writings throughout his career though perhaps most explicitly in the "*Envoi*" from *The Post Card*, in "Ulysses Gramophone," and "Two Words for Joyce."[10] Margot Norris's ground-breaking study *The Decentered Universe of Finnegans Wake* emphasizes the constant restructuring and reconsideration of basic terms through which this last text engages the possibilities of free play (in the Derridean sense) and *bricolage*.

Throughout the 1970s in France scholars concerned with Joyce's texts made use of the same techniques for approaching literature that Jacques Derrida engaged in addressing philosophical texts. Their work was presented to English speaking audiences in an influential collection of essays titled *Post-Structuralist Joyce* and edited by Daniel Ferrar and Derek Attridge. Poststructuralism provided an entirely revolutionary approach to Joyce's work which set itself apart from the "transcendental" approaches that fit his literature into larger patterns of cultural interest concerned with mythic structure or historic cycles and the "humanist" approach that domesticated Joyce's writing within a realist structure and highlighted human experience in its varying forms. Poststructuralism provided Joyce's readers with a revolutionary approach through which they might experience, as Attridge and Ferrer emphasize, "the infinite productivity of interpretive activity, the impossibility of closing off the processes of signification, the incessant shifting and opening-out of meaning in the act of reading and re-reading."[11]

My own response to Joyce relies on the work of poststructuralist critics in order to highlight a possibility within this work that has until now been largely overlooked in Joyce criticism: the ethical. From the beginning of his writings, Derrida initiated a philosophical conversation with Levinas's ethical theory.[12] However, Derrida's concern with the ethical has not been addressed by his English-speaking readers until the 1990s. This chapter brings to the fore the possibility of ethical theory latent in poststructuralist treatments of Joyce. In the varying figures of aporia, I locate not only a crucial undecidability, an open process of signification, but also the possibility that this shifting quality in Joyce's writing indicates the possibility of an ethics of interpretation. The impassable passage, the hesitation in language, invites an ethical engagement on the part of the reader.

From the beginning of his works, Joyce writes in ellipses producing in his readers the impression of aporia. Unexpectedly denied closure, the reader experiences a sense of not knowing, of not being able to arrive at an epistemological destination, watching the path wear out as the sentence trickles into its indefinite punctuation.[13] In *Dubliners*, for example,

while I would agree broadly, I think that, at least in Dubliners, the reader is flattered to deceive. Her prejudices are invited by a text in which aporia undermine their validity by stealth.

a reader is sometimes overwhelmed by the rhetoric of aposiopesis: the incomplete or unfinished sentence; each story reads, in structure, as aposiopesis written large. The ellipses in Joyce's work lead the reader to an interpretive aporia, to an impasse. In these ellipses the text demands that the reader both complete the thought and acknowledge that the thought cannot be completed. Readers are asked to suspend decision, to entertain ambivalence, to place ourselves in a position between two options; that "place between" options is the ethical space of interpretation and, as Joyce suggests in these elliptical moments, the ethical space of subjectivity itself.

The impassable (and yet imperative) passage that haunts Joyce's work is that of the difference between self and other that cannot be, and yet must be, bridged. The aporia confronts the reader with a form of ethical duty, or as Jacques Derrida notes in *Aporias*, the figure itself suggests an ethical duty that "dictates welcoming foreigners in order not only to integrate them but to recognize and accept their alterity." This duty also requires that the subject respect "differences, idioms, minorities, singularities, but also the universality of formal law, the desire for translation, agreement, and univocity, the law of the majority, opposition to racism, nationalism, and xenophobia."[14]

For Joyce the *aporia* is not only national but also relational: how can I know you? And mustn't I know you to be equitable in my treatment of you? And yet "knowing" you, do I not claim some version of ownership, as if I could subsume your difference to the constructed sameness that is my self? Not knowing you, not being able to know you, arrested in this dilemma between doubt and desire, between wondering and wanting, I am nonetheless obligated to you, obligated to be responsible to you, to be responsive to your call. I *am*, or rather I know myself as a subject, in this ethical aporia in which I face the other and am haunted by my response to that other.

Interpretation is, for Joyce, that very space between self and other in which the unknowable is desired, explored, understood and then lost or forgotten or complicated. Interpretation is a place of constant negotiation between self and other; it is figured most immediately, in the literary context, in the relation between text and reader. But that relation is applicable also to a series of differences and the interpretations between them: self and other, parent and child, citizen and foreigner, man and woman, and so on. Locating his ethics in the interpretive space between opposites, Joyce would of necessity, to paraphrase Derrida, oppose racism, nationalism, and xenophobias of various kinds.

The figure through which Joyce first suggests we understand his short stories, and through these narratives, the interpretive relation of self to other, is the geometric figure of the gnomon. This figure, an incomplete parallelogram that suggests a missing and yet present smaller parallelogram, is a model both of incompletion and also of the presence of the other in the same: the haunting of one figure (or square) in another figure (or larger square). Derrida suggests that this kind of haunting is intrinsic to the "plural logic" of the *aporia*. He notes that the "partitioning [*partage*] among multiple figures of *aporia* does not oppose figures to each other, but instead installs the haunting of the one in the other.... the nonpassage, the impasse or aporia, stems from the fact that there is no limit."[15]

The possibility of the ethical subject as engaged in sympathetic understanding with an incommensurably different other emerges in Joyce's work from the first pages of *Dubliners*, in which in "The Sisters" he defines subjectivity through the (now familiar) figure of the *gnomon*, a figure that suggests the autonomy of difference. According to the *Oxford English Dictionary*, gnomon literally means a judge or interpreter, indicating a necessary relationship to an other (who must be judged or interpreted and who in turn judges and interprets). In geometry, the gnomon is a parallelogram from which a smaller figure of the same proportions has been extracted. In "The Sisters," Joyce resists the narrator's uncle, who defines the complete subject as one who has learned to "box his corner," or complete the figure of the parallelogram.[16] Implicit in the story is Joyce's alternative definition of the subject as one who, as gnomon, is unstable, decentered, open to an other, a potentially ethical subject.[17]

Gnomon is among the three words the young narrator of "The Sisters" contemplates at the inception of the story. These words can provide the reader with cues or even techniques for reading each of the stories that follow. The paralysis of colonial Dubliners, for example, has been a traditional focus through which readers have understood the collection. Simony points others to the stories' ecclesiastic and economic concerns. And the image of Euclid's gnomon provides a complex introduction not only to the structures of "The Sisters" and *Dubliners* as a whole, but also to Joyce's ethical investment throughout his literature.

Hall and Stevens's *Textbook of Euclid Elements*, which Joyce owned, defines the gnomon:[18]

In any parallelogram the figure formed by either of the parallelograms about a diagonal together with the two complements is called a gnomon.

Thus the shaded portion of the annexed figure, consisting of the parallelogram EH together with the complements AK, KC is the gnomon AHF.

The other gnomon in the figure is that which is made up of AK, GF and FH, namely the gnomon AFH. (Hall and Stevens 120)

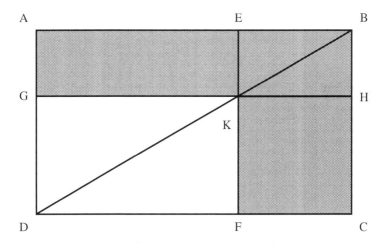

Gnomon has another literal meaning: something which enables another to be known or understood. Before Euclid applied the term to the incomplete parallelogram, gnomon signified the upright marker on a sundial which casts a shadow and indicates the time of day. By casting that shadow the marker indicates the place of the sun; thus it is an object that allows another to be known.

The term "gnomon" like the word "sisters" is relational and subordinate, existing only to interpret or direct attention to a more important entity, the sun in the sky, the brother in this family. Here, though, Joyce redirects attention to these interpreters themselves. For Joyce the task of narration is to put forward a position otherwise unrepresented. The Flynn sisters in the opening story of *Dubliners* are just such neglected subjects, deemed unworthy of representation in traditional narratives because of their reduced social status and their conventionality. An initial reading of Eliza and Nannie Flynn presents two stereotyped spinster sisters. Nannie is deaf and participates derisably in social intercourse; Eliza, though vocal and present, seems to speak in a combination of euphemisms and elisions. Yet a closer look at Eliza's conversation reveals her

remarkable honesty. She narrates with diplomacy the somewhat shameful story of her brother's clerical career, the discovery of his lapse (found
laughing in a confessional), and his ineffectual nostalgia. Her ellipses are
not misleading; the language around them gives shape and dimension to
these gaps indicating clearly the unpresentable, undignified information
that she both indicates and cloaks, providing her brother with a kind of
privacy while at the same time narrating his history honestly.

In presenting Eliza Flynn's narrative of her brother, Joyce reverses
the accustomed position of such subjects in literary and social traditions.
Female, unmarried, badly educated, and poor, Eliza Flynn is precisely
the kind of subject who more conventionally falls into the margins of a
narrative. Characters much like her provide the economic framework
and domestic comforts in a number of literary works of her time. Yet
their subjectivity is, for the most part, itself elided, merely providing a
stable, reliable backdrop for more notable and active characters. In titling
his story "The Sisters," and in narrating the closing pages through Eliza's
conversation, Joyce signals from the beginning of his oeuvre an ethical
investment in those subjects who are neglected and unpresentable.

Speaking habitually in ellipses, Eliza Flynn indicates that it troubles
her to mention anything fraught with conflict or social discomfort. Her
ellipses also indicate the gaps in representation, the places in which
these subjects call out to their others for interpretation which is a partial
completion. She tells the narrator's aunt just enough to allow her to
imagine the shape of omitted information and to sympathize with her
discretion in omitting what might damage the reputation of her deceased
brother. To society at large, and even to the boy narrator and their own
clerical brother, these women are, to adapt Oscar Wilde's ironic phrase,
"women of no importance." But Joyce titled his story in such a way as to
indicate an ethical narrative practice in which he will make this gnomon,
on a figurative level, or the unrepresented object, the sister, the subject
of his work, thus opening the narrative perspective to its dependence on
radical and incommensurable alterity. "The Sisters" presents a balance
between the explicit and present and the absent or implicit, the shape
and dimensions of which are framed and suggested by the narrative.
The rhetorical cue which signals the use of a narrative gnomon is that
ubiquitous aposiopesis, the unfinished sentence, used in recording the
character's dialogue.

The apparent focus of this story is the death of a Dublin priest, Father
James Flynn and the experience of that death by the young male narrator
who was his student and also, in a complex sense, his acolyte. Yet, while

the priest is almost entirely absent from the text, he seems to insist on his centrality in the narration, as if he were the parallelogram extracted from the gnomon. When the story begins he is about to die and we only know of his continued existence by an absence. "If he were dead, I thought, I would see the reflection of candles on the darkened blind for I knew that two candles must be set at the head of a corpse" (*D* 19). Flynn is separated from the reader's perspective by the window through which the boy looks; his present survival is indicated by the absence of the candles traditionally lit to mark death. Father Flynn is included in the story only by omission: as the narrative concludes he is physically present at his wake though already dead. However, he is the subject of much attention: the boy's thoughts, the sister's conversation. He is discussed both in the narrator's home and at the wake but always with a sense of mystery, of other characters' incomplete understanding.

Father Flynn's dimensions, his character, the events that shaped his life, are suggested by the presence of his two sisters. They are the human embodiment of the geometrical gnomon suggested on the first page. They are gnomon in multiple senses: they are gnomon in that they provide the frame that signals an absence; they are women and therefore no(t) men; and, like the upright markers on a sundial, they shadow forth the position of a (luminous) other. The focus of their conversation at the wake, in which they finally physically and verbally enter the story named after them, is, quite naturally, given his recent death, their dead brother and his disappointments as a priest, his fastidious approach to his office. It becomes clear from Eliza's conversation that she and Nan provide not only a literary frame (in that they narrate their brother's story) but they also provided James Flynn with the actual frame or framework within which he lived. Their modest and marginally successful drapery shop provides the unmarried sisters and their brother with economic support; they provide him the home attached to that shop in which he lives after his disgrace in the priesthood; his domestic needs are furnished by their labor. And just as is the case with a frame around a piece of visual art, the work of support and provision that the sisters perform is largely invisible to a cursory viewer's gaze. It is Father Flynn who takes up the center of attention even in his absence.[9]

In "The Sisters" the balance between gnomon and absent parallelogram is clearly gendered. Joyce indicates the extent to which women are perceived as merely no(t) men, as lack and absence. But he also indicates the extent to which masculinity itself is a constructed and carefully maintained subjectivity built up in great part in opposition to a feared and devalued femininity.[20] Worried about the boy narrator's relationship with Father James Flynn, the boy's uncle and his friend Mr. Cotter seem primarily concerned with the threat the fallen priest's friendship poses to the boy's masculinity. The identity they wish to enforce on him defines masculinity in terms of physical strength and endurance; they are suspicious of intimate connections between men which they perceive as feminine and describe as "queer."

Cotter, much to the narrator's disgust, initiates the discussion of masculinity:

My idea is: let a young lad run about and play with young lads of his own age and not be . . . Am I right, Jack?
– That's my principle, too, said my uncle. Let him learn to box his corner. That's what I'm always saying to that Rosicrucian there: take exercise. Why, when I was a nipper every morning of my life I had a cold bath, winter and summer. And that's what stands me now. Education is all very fine and large. . . . Mr Cotter might take a pick of that leg of mutton, he added to my aunt. (*D* 11, ellipses original)

What the two men fear from the narrator's association with the older priest is signaled by juxtaposition with the following story in the collection. (In "An Encounter," as I mentioned in the introduction, two truant boys encounter a "queer old josser" and are threatened by his oddly eroticized talk of flirtation and punishment.) The possibility of an erotic love between an older and younger man centered around knowledge is dumped into the ellipses in both the uncle's and Cotter's statements.[21] It is a possibility so dangerous as to be unmentionable. The uncle fears the secret or even private alliances between men he associates with the priest and "that Rosicrucian," the intellectual boy narrator. It is immediately apparent what kind of masculinity the boy's uncle prefers. He requires the silent attendance of a woman who is subservient to men (he suggests that his wife serve his friend with mutton) and whose mediating presence prevents any dangerous intimacy between men. The ideal man can "box his corner." He is strong, confident in his territory, and physically threatening. But more important, he is a man, not a gnomon. He is complete, a parallelogram with his corners boxed. His subjectivity signals no openness to the outside; no connection with an other will form his identity. He will take up the entire space of his own narrative, both frame and content, leaving no substantive room for any one else and certainly not for a woman.[22]

In this sampling of dialogue, Joyce indicates the extent to which the uncle's ideal masculinity must be elaborately constructed (with daily cold baths over the course of decades) and guarded (boxing his corner). The subjectivity Joyce clearly prefers and wishes to make the ethical focus of his narratives from this point onward is not specifically masculine, in the uncle's sense, but geometrical (Anna Livia Plurabelle, for example, is a "geomater"[23]): the figure of the gnomon (or no man). His ethical investment is in figures who are seen by Dubliners such as the uncle only as frames, who are shunted from the center of attention. He focuses on those figures who maintain an ethical investment in others (in Eliza's case by caring for her brother and his needs even after he has failed and been shamed), whose subjectivity leaves space for the influence, the presence, the collaboration of an other or multiple others: those subjects who recognize and accept their incompletion.

The narrative approach that Joyce adapts to this ethical investment in gnomon is the ellipsis that so distinguishes *Dubliners* as a collection: the sense many readers have that each story is unfinished; the punchline has not been told; the other shoe has not dropped.[24] In his narrative approach, Joyce mirrors the boy's geometrical preoccupation in an ethical commitment; by inscribing gaps within the text he signals the space of each reader's interpretation, and indicates a literary partnership in the creation of textual meaning. Joyce provides the reader with a frame, with (to use Brian Friel's language) the available grammar and the available words, and between us we make the impossible effort to interpret between privacies. Like the narrating boy who listens to his elder's elliptical definitions of masculinity, as a reader I must "puzzle my head to extract meaning from his unfinished sentences" (*D* 11).

The gnomon has another function as well. Joyce had planned to include in this short story collection his portrait of a modern, cosmopolitan Ulysses who would roam the streets of Dublin as Odysseus roamed the Mediterranean seas returning to Ithaca. Though that story exceeded its bounds (becoming, of course, Joyce's epic *Ulysses*), the traces of the plan for its inclusion remain in the neatness with which Joyce refers to that omitted story in "The Sisters." The gnomon of the first page might have been echoed in the "no man" called out later in the collection: the Cyclops's cry of pain and accusation when naming for his fellows the person who had injured him by poking out his eye ("Noman" was the alias Ulysses used when identifying himself to the Cyclops).[25] Joyce's ethical investment in this collection is in the undecidable region between the bully who threatens us and the victim whose injury must be and cannot be redressed. The interaction between Polyphemus and Ulysses is of particular ethical interest in that the two figures change roles between bully and victim. Defining ethical subjectivity thus, Joyce recurrently focuses on justice in the face of conflict, on radically alternative measures for negotiating the conjoining of difference, and on a fascination with and enduring concern for imbalances of power.

The space of the gnomon in Joyce's texts might be understood through Levinas's "*mauvaise conscience*" or bad conscience.[26] In *Ethics as First Philosophy* Levinas defines bad conscience as a fear of the violence and even murder that one's mere existence might occasion even if one's intentions or conscious efforts are innocent. "It is the fear of occupying someone else's place with the *Da* of my *Dasein*; it is the inability to occupy a place, a profound utopia."[27] The concern with usurping the place (*Da* or "there") of an other with one's subjectivity or consciousness (*Dasein*, literally "being there") is addressed by Joyce's figuring of the subject as gnomon. When the subject is conceived as incomplete, framing, opening outward to another, then the usurpation exemplified in both colonization and patriarchy is replaced by partnership and interdependence. Setting aside a preoccupation with ontology, with the construction of wholeness in subjectivity, Joyce makes ethics the first concern of his literature much as Levinas names ethics the first philosophy, the root of all other philosophical understanding. For Levinas, an ethical subject is required to set aside the ego in its sovereignty, the desire for meaning which may merely mask an appeal for justification. While ontology concerns the identification of an autonomous subjectivity, Levinas's ethics critiques that form of identity as a usurpation of the place of an other. Placing ethics as the first consideration in philosophical inquiry, Levinas investigates the subject as constitutively responsible to others; it is in ethical response to an other that the subject comes into being. For Joyce, as for Levinas, subjectivity is relational, formed in response to an other. Evoking the ethical dilemma, Joyce emphasizes interpretation, the relation between text and reader, by his creation of *aporia*, the impassable passages in the text.

III

In writing his only play, *Exiles*, Joyce was primarily concerned with the impassable passage that marks the difference between men and women. As Jacques Derrida notes, aporia is "the edge or borderline under the names of what one calls the body proper and sexual difference."[28]

Dramatizing questions of sexual difference, Joyce followed in the path of his admired predecessor Henrik Ibsen. In conversation with Arthur Power, Joyce indicated that he admired Ibsen for his attempt to imagine ethical relations between men and women. "The purpose of *A Doll House*, for instance, was the emancipation of women, which has caused the greatest revolution in our times in the most important relationship there is – that between men and women; the revolt of women against the idea that they are the mere instruments of men."[29] *Exiles* explores the multiple implications of that revolution by way of a series of *aporias*.

Joyce produces one such aporia with the gap between Acts 2 and 3 of *Exiles*. This lapse in fictive time, during which Bertha's sexual fidelity or sexual experimentation is decided, shifts the focus of the play from the moral question posed by Richard Rowan in exploring his partnership with Bertha, to the ethical dilemma posed to Joyce's audience by the couple's choices. Richard poses the question: how can a modern subject define love in a way that "liberates"[30] the lovers? Joyce, by cloaking the events in Robert's cottage, poses a slightly different question: how might an audience respond ethically to the moral dilemmas posed by a play?

Whether Bertha chooses chastity or license in no way changes the wound of doubt experienced by her partner or the wound of doubt instilled in the audience.[31] When the curtain is drawn between the acts, the predictable curiosity aroused by this mysterious treatment becomes the central issue in the play. In his notes preparing to write *Exiles*, Joyce inscribed his intention to produce doubt in the audience: "The doubt which clouds the end of the play must be conveyed to the audience not only through Richard's questions to both [Bertha and Robert] but also from the dialogue between Robert and Bertha" (*E* 158). In the gap between acts, the play attempts to produce a readerly wound of doubt, and makes not knowing the central event for interpretation. In the passage between decisions and events, in the ellipses or *aporia* created by this representational lapse, lies the possibility of our ethical response.

Joyce's audience is directed to Richard's moral dilemma concerning his relationship with Bertha and the ways in which it is either threatened or renewed by Robert's interest in his partner. In Richard's dilemma, Joyce anticipates the arguments of feminists such as Luce Irigaray and Gayle Rubin[32] who situate patriarchal marriage contracts in a market economy in which women are transformed into commodities for exchange and ownership. Richard, from within such a culture, defines his love for Bertha with recourse to the language and assumptions of commodification. But he resists the more traditional manifestations of that ownership in the forms of conventional legally or religiously sanctioned marriage or the explicit contractual agreement of fidelity.

Richard's moral imperative is elucidated in two scenes focused on the questions of love and ownership. When Bertha worries that Richard's love for her is a love of her simplicity and that this simplicity might allow him to abuse her emotionally, he reminds her (somewhat irrelevantly to her immediate concerns) that she joined him of her own choice and that he has never in any way bound her to him. She is, in effect, perpetually liberated. Richard claims "I have allowed you complete liberty – and allow you it still . . ." (*E* 65). Richard reiterates his use of the term "liberty" throughout their disagreements. And yet a reader might see a contradiction in his diction: can liberty be "allowed" or given?

The question of giving and of its implications for possession is explored in more detail when Richard discusses gifts and ownership with his son. Richard asks Archie,

> Do you understand what it is to give a thing?
>
> Archie
> To give? Yes.
>
> Richard
> While you have a thing it can be taken from you.
>
> Archie
> By robbers? No?
>
> Richard

But when you give it, you have given it. No robber can take it from you . . . It is yours then for ever when you have given it. It will be yours always. That is to give. (*E* 56)

Acting on the assumptions he shares with Archie, Richard is perhaps unwittingly trapped in a quite traditional marital framework when by "giving" Bertha freedom he insures that she cannot be "taken" from him (as Robert threatens) and that she will therefore always "belong" to him. Bertha herself is fully aware of this emotional possession and the costs to her in forming any other love relations, sexual or familial.

While Richard's discourse on liberty and possession implies his ownership of Bertha, he also attempts to create a more obviously generous version of their relations. In Act 2, confronted in his bachelor cottage while waiting with Richard for Bertha's arrival to their pre-arranged assignation, Robert threatens to "take" her from Richard. Richard replies that to possess a woman even if it were possible, would not be love. His alternative definition of love is to wish a woman well. Robert's approach, apparently more passionate and certainly more familiar, emerges in the language of possession and control, the sadism Joyce attributed to his character in the working notes for this play. "The play, a rough and tumble between the Marquis de Sade and Frieherr V. Sacher Masoch. Had not Robert better give Bertha a little bite when they kiss? Richard's Masochism needs no example" (*E* 157). Joyce's note indicates that neither sadism nor its self-effacing twin, masochism, is an ethical option. While Richard's language in this scene is generous, the masochism that motivates it will have effects on its object as cruel as those of Robert's sadism, in part because his masochism is self-involved to the extent that he boxes his corner rather than opening his subjectivity to another's partnership. Concerned only with his moral evaluation of himself, Richard's masochism inflicts pain on Bertha and, at the same time, excludes her.

Richard asserts a theory of love and the bond between lovers based on a new twist on the old theme of ownership: as in the traditional marriage, Richard owns and wants to continue owning his wife, but less traditionally, he owns her by insisting on her liberty such that she can never be taken from him. Richard justifies the apparent conflict in his logic by noting that Bertha has always owned herself because she gave herself to him (rather than being taken) when she accompanied him to the continent without being asked directly, giving herself outside the institution of marriage in which she would have been given. According to this logic, Bertha maintains her "virginity of soul," keeping her soul by giving it such that it can never be robbed from her. Her gift, preceding Richard's, absolutely precludes his ownership and insures her freedom.

However, Bertha's virginity of soul, her freedom within her marriage, is a fiction produced by Richard's moral narrative. James McMichael, in addressing fidelity and license in *Ulysses* confronts a similar question expressed in the language of authority. He argues that Bloom's conflict with Molly stems not from his lack of authority in the marriage but rather from an excess of authority. "He has been authoring for more than ten years since Rudy's death a story in which Molly agrees to his substituting domestic favors and small sums of cash for the unrestrained attentions he knows she craves from him. . . ."[33] Bloom authors a version of their marital history and based on that narrative authorizes a pattern of affectional and sexual neglect. According to McMichael, he fears his wife's desire because full intercourse might result in the birth of another, potentially endangered, child. Molly, conversely, is prevented from authoring "her own story of the marriage, a story within which she allows herself to call her husband for what she wants most, Molly has been conforming to the character that he has authored for her" (*ibid* 21). In her monologue, Molly authors a narrative of marital love reflecting that "a woman wants to be embraced 20 times a day almost..." (*U* 18.1407–1408); while her husband authorizes his own version of love in which his material attentions, substituted for more physical or verbal affection, sufficiently demonstrate his fidelity. By buying her sentimental novels, for example, he indirectly expresses his own sentimental attachment. Like Bloom, Richard, while trying to author an innovative marital structure is unable to recognize the pain induced by his refusal to recognize Bertha's contradictory narrative. His expressions of generosity take the place of her need for his openly expressed desire. Intending a partnership of equity, he creates an atmosphere of coldness and indifference. The framework he builds does not accommodate Bertha's love story.

Bertha understands that she and Richard live in a culture in which the claims of ownership have come to signify love. Richard's refusal to behave within this conventional model on the moral grounds of its gendered asymmetry, leaves Bertha with two dilemmas. First, she finds it difficult to feel that Richard loves her because he refuses to use the familiar language or take recourse to the structures that define love for everyone else in their culture; yet he has not successfully found another means of expressing that love. Second, Richard's decision cannot be experienced as loving from Bertha's position in which a version of their *shared* commitment is being defined and even imposed *singularly*, from his perspective and investments alone.[34]

Richard's unstated desire is to be generous. His desire arises out of a repetition compulsion, an attempt to compensate for the childhood deprivations caused by his mother's severe judgments with a generosity modeled on that of his father. But the unspoken desire to be generous, which he exhibits not only in encouraging Archie's adventure but also in licensing Bertha's possible infidelity, is at odds with his desire for absolute loyalty and affection, a desire he expresses inadvertently when he refers to Robert's illicit kisses as thievery.

This childhood need for generosity and its harmful effects on his present relations are revealed in Richard's conversation with Archie about ownership and giving, a context which Joyce emphasizes by returning to Archie's request at the close of Act 1. Archie has asked Richard if he may accompany a local dairy farmer in the morning as he goes on his rounds delivering milk; more specifically, he wants Richard to intervene and get permission from Bertha, whom the child perceives both as more stringent and, perhaps as a result, the greater parental authority. Archie's interest in this adventure comes from a sense of curiosity: he admires the cows and wonders how a cow can "give milk" (*E* 56). Richard's answer to his son's concrete question focuses abstractly and theoretically on giving and ownership, though Archie's interest is almost certainly more mechanical or biological: what is the process by which cows are able to produce milk? To answer that question completely Richard would be required to embark on the initiatory discussion of re-production and perhaps even sexuality. Joyce suggests Richard's, at least unconscious, understanding of this curiosity when he responds with a question about sexuality of his own: what constitutes my relationship with the woman with whom I live, is it based on giving? on ownership? When Richard tells his son that giving prevents a person from being robbed, Archie wonders:

How could a robber rob a cow? Everyone would see him. In the night perhaps.

Richard
In the night, yes.

Archie
Are there robbers here like in Rome?

Richard
There are poor people everywhere. (*E* 56)

The parental Richard is an idealist: generous with his son and presum-ably with material objects, empathic with the poor, thoughtful if a bit distracted. The Richard who turns to Bertha in the next moment is far less admirable. He forgets to ask for permission on Archie's behalf, return-ing instead to his obsessional questions about ownership, about Bertha's loyalty, fidelity, or sexual curiosity. When he discovers that Robert has kissed Bertha, he calls his old friend a thief, implying that Robert has taken something Richard owned and did not choose to give away. Robert may be poor in love but, according to Richard, that particular poverty does not excuse his theft. Bertha may deserve her liberty, and yet her affection is a commodity her partner would own.

Bertha, knowing that Richard will confront Robert about this "theft," feels that Richard owns her by making her less lovable for others. She curses Richard: "The work of a devil to turn him against me as you tried to turn my own child against me" (*E* 64). At the same time she understands that Richard's hurtful actions come directly from his own childhood ex-perience: "Because you never loved your own mother" (*E* 64). Bertha feels

that Richard has tried to turn their son against her by showing him only
an absent-minded affection and permissiveness, while she has had to take
the role of the stringent parent who, to paraphrase *Finnegans Wake*, must
in undivided reality draw the line somewhere (*FW* 292.31). She intuits
the extent to which Richard is reacting to his own family history in which
his mother defined their world through the limits imposed by the Roman
Catholic church and was harshly judgmental about any lapse or exile
beyond those limits. Richard describes his mother as having a "harshness
of heart" through which she judged him based on Catholic principles
and never forgave: "She died alone, not having forgiven me, and fortified
by the rites of the holy church" (*E* 23). The rites of the church fortify
her, both in her dying and in her hardness of heart. Richard, in asserting an unconventional familial relation to Bertha and Archie, is partly
engaged in reaction-formation, an attempt to differ from his mother
(rejecting Catholic moral principles and marital laws). At the same time
he echoes her harshness (he is unable to entertain Bertha's desires when
they contradict his own moral principles). Wanting to be a different kind
of parent than his own hurtful mother, he emulates his father's permissiveness, an example of which we are shown in the tickets his father gave
him for the performance of *Carmen*. His father's generosity has become
his ideal. Bertha, on the other hand, sees that generosity alone is insufficient in a parent and that Richard's obsessional relationship with his
work makes him absent to his son. Not wanting Archie to harbor the
kind of resentment and anger his father feels, she teaches her son to
love his father. In return, she becomes the parent who monitors rules,
while Richard is free to act out his obsessional generosity. Bertha and
Richard have managed to duplicate the roles in the earlier generation's
marriage; she imposes restrictions and he absentmindedly bestows gifts.
Bertha associates limits with caring and with love; she is creating a safe environment of piano lessons, regular meals, and clean hands within which
Archie can experiment with transgression and permission (for example,
she does not impose the full piano lesson on him at the beginning of the
play).

Playing this role, Bertha, like the sisters in *Dubliners*, adapts herself to
the figure of the gnomon. She presents herself to her son as an ethical
frame, providing the parameters in which he can assert his own subjectivity. Bertha is aware of the extent to which she is incomplete, open to the
partnering of a loved other, while Richard asserts his completion continuously, demanding that she adapt to the moral imperative he suggests

without clearly defining. Richard desires fusion, a perfect partnership attained without the need of specification or demand.

Levinas, writing about love in Proust's *A la recherche du temps perdu*, describes such a desire for fusion as inauthentic, a vestige of ontology that asserts being before knowing: "One sets out from the idea that duality should be transformed into unity – that the social relation should end in communion. This is the last vestige of a conception identifying being and knowing – that is, the event by which the multiplicity of the real ends up referring to one sole being, and by which, through the miracle of clarity, everything I encounter exists as having come out of myself."[35] Wanting to know Bertha, to be able to anticipate her choices without making his own desires apparent, Richard insists on an absolute knowledge that would destroy Bertha's difference. He cannot see that "the success of knowledge would in fact destroy the nearness, the proximity of the other. A proximity that far from meaning something less than identification, opens up horizons of social existence, brings out all the surplus of our experience of friendship and love, and brings to the definitiveness of our identical existence all the virtuality of the non-definitive" (*ibid* 104). At the same time that Richard asserts her liberty, he denies Bertha's difference.

But the moral and emotional dilemma dividing these characters is in many ways not the focus of the play but a red herring. When a fish woman, in one of very few intrusions of realism in this drama of manners, cries out "Fresh Dublin bay herrings!" (*E* 139) in counterpoint with Richard and Robert's confrontation in the cottage, the verbal juxtaposition indicates that something is fishy. The play is layered with deception; this particular conflict is a red herring, distracting the audience from the central issue. The central issue is not so much the conflict between Richard and Bertha or their alternately innovative and conventional definitions of love; rather the crucial focus is conflict itself, the failure of understanding, the impassable passage, the impossibility of knowing.

In pursuing his theory of liberation or generosity, Richard encounters something he had not anticipated: the failure of knowing. He had been owning Bertha by "knowing" her in the non-Biblical sense as much as the Biblical one, by asking her to report her every romantic or sexual interaction with Robert. But in the encounter in the cottage, Richard realizes that he will not ever really know. Even if Bertha were to report her choices, as she has up until that moment and as she is still willing to do, he will never know the intimate contours of her encounter with Robert. He confides in Bertha:

I have wounded my soul for you – a deep wound of doubt which can never be healed. I can never know, never in this world. I do not wish to know or to believe. I do not care. It is not in the darkness of belief that I desire you. But in restless living wounding doubt. To hold you by no bonds, even of love, to be united with you in body and soul in utter nakedness – for this I longed. (*E* 147)

Acknowledging the failure of knowing, he must also recognize Bertha's otherness, her essential difference from him and the privacies of her consciousness. The doubt resulting from his failure of knowledge inspires his desire. Desire requires not owning or knowing; it requires doubt and difference because, to use a spatial metaphor, desire is motion toward another. And for there to be motion toward, there must be distance, to use spatial terms again, or difference, in psychological terms. Or, as Kristeva and Oliver indicate, desire is made possible by difference.

I V

The doubt and difference that Richard experiences are echoed in the audience, in our failure of knowing instilled by the gap in information between Acts 2 and 3. And like Richard we experience desire for Bertha; we're more curious about her, attentive to her words, and the nuances of her expression because we don't know. Suspended between Richard's attempt to create a love based on symmetrical and reciprocal relations and Bertha's equally sincere effort to emphasize the need for an explicit and emotionally satisfying language of love, the audience of *Exiles* is poised to experience *aporia*. The "prohibited passage" in the text (to use Derrida's language), between Richard and Bertha's experiences and expectations, is vexed with disagreement and even incommensurability, but it does not call for intervention or for the forging of a compromised solution. This *aporia*, to quote Derrida, "is not necessarily a failure or a simple paralysis, the sterile negativity of the impasse. . . . (When someone suggests to you a solution for escaping an impasse, you can be almost sure that he is ceasing to understand, assuming that he had understood anything up to that point.)"[36] Similarly, a viewer's insistence on resolving the insoluble dilemma posed in this play is an act of misinterpretation.

The gap between Acts 2 and 3 and the doubt that it instills, is a reminder of the representational separation between narrative and audience that produces an *aporia* in the midst of our more determined interpretation of the play. In other words, not knowing crucial information about the melodramatic relations in this play is a reminder to the audience of the deceptions of representation itself, the idea that knowing what happened within the play will resolve moral dilemmas that are represented in the theater and that are also experienced by the audience. The gap in representation and the irresolvable impasse between Richard and Bertha's desires throws the audience back on its own resources of interpretation. At the moment that the audience is arrested by *aporia*, that audience has an opportunity for ethical reflection inspired by representational ellipses.

As Derrida addresses this concept, the *aporia* arrests us before a division or separation that is not inherently negative but may instead offer an opportunity, as before a liminal space such as a door, border, or threshold, "or simply the edge or the approach of the other as such" (*ibid* 12). That which appears to block progress (this incommensurability of the other or the unknown region beyond the threshold) "*would no longer be possible to constitute* [as] *a problem*" not because the solution is evident, but because the gap is seen as a promise rather than an obstacle (*ibid* 12, emphases original). The gap allows the viewer to see the extent to which he or she constituted that difference or threshold as a problem merely to avoid an encounter with otherness.

In the face of *Exiles*' ethical dilemma, with its multiple demands that cannot be brought into agreement, but in which each actor has a stake, an audience can see the equity of each claim and even empathize with each actor. But nonetheless, in the audience, each viewer is located on the other side of a divide, a border, or a threshold produced by the very process of representation. Positioned outside the object of contemplation, a viewer can empathize but never inhabit. And because no audience can inhabit Bertha and Richard's dilemma as such, there is no longer any problem; rather, the dilemma itself becomes a desired situation, the opportunity for an encounter with the other. Because a viewer can never cross the border, this viewer is allowed a perspectival distance that would be impossible on the other side of the representational border. Suspended between two positions which are incommensurable, and far from seeing them as mutually exclusive, as the characters might, the audience may experience sympathy, may identify with both sides. In the moment when a viewer can see all and at the same time realize the constraints on that vision, the limitations of this multiple perspective, in that moment, the viewer is interpolated as an ethical subject.

We become ethical subjects by interpreting in the hollow place between the acts, which is not to imply that we assume moral righteousness, but that we experience the wound of doubt in place of dangerous moral certainties. That wound carries us toward an other, as Richard is carried toward Bertha because of the doubt instilled in him by the failure of knowledge. The *aporia* created in us in the activity of interpretation emanates out of the gaps in Joyce's work, the places where we are asked to suspend decision, to entertain ambivalence, to inhabit the ethical space of interpretation.

v

The audience's ethical responsibility to the drama is figured by Beatrice Justice who plays the elusive role of muse, reader, and judge in the creative process envisioned by the play. She is not presented as a model to be emulated in producing moral behavior; rather, she presents the possibility of ethics in acts of creativity by modeling in her own behavior the responsibilities of author and audience in the production of art.

Beatrice's apparent role in the drama is minor; her presence in the first act furthers the couplings and betrayals between the three characters who make up the prominent French triangle that is the play's focus. In the second act she is physically absent from the stage, and her return in Act 3 does little to forward the action. Yet Joyce, in his notes written while composing the play, reveals her centrality to his conception and reminds himself (and perhaps future directors) to maintain her presence even when she is physically absent from the set. "During the second act as Beatrice is not on the stage, her figure must appear before the audience through the thoughts or speech of the others. This is by no means easy" (*E* 159). Beatrice's absence from the action is a physical reminder of her more metaphorical distance within the play (in other words, she is less enmeshed with the other characters than they seem to be with one another). Though she had promised herself in marriage to her cousin, Robert, and though her eight-year correspondence with Richard carries an erotic charge, she seems remote both from these men and from Bertha, even in their moments of confidence or confrontation. Richard expresses that remoteness in the first act when he claims she could never "give [herself] freely and wholly" (*E* 22). In Richard's complex philosophy of ownership, this statement indicates that she will never be possessed either by a man or by systematic beliefs. (He doesn't think, for example, she would succeed in a convent.) But it also means, according to Richard's exchange with Archie, that she will never completely own herself; not having been given, she is available for the taking.

Her ambiguous condition is reflected in the extent to which each of the other characters maps his or her desires onto Beatrice, assuming understanding of her experience, motivations, and desires without specific knowledge.[37] Bertha, for example, in the final act claims: "You hate me. You think I am happy. If you only knew how wrong you are!" To which Beatrice replies ambiguously "I do not" (*E* 126–127). Beatrice's emotions, as Bertha assumes them, reflect less on Beatrice's experience and more on Bertha's own conflict: her confusion about her love relations with Richard and Robert's impact on them, her failed attempts to share in her partner's work, her vexed mothering of Archie. Self-contained, Beatrice reveals little of herself, yet the others in the drama play to her witnessing, attempting to gauge themselves in her opaque responses.[38] She is akin to the audience in a darkened theater; the players on stage measure their success in the (perhaps ambiguous) reactions beyond the footlights.

Richard explicitly engages Beatrice as an audience, writing to her regularly during his family's nine-year exile from Ireland. While in Rome, Richard sends her chapters of his book-in-progress as he is writing it and corresponds with her about the work. As his audience, his first reader, Beatrice also serves as his muse and guide, a role indicated by her name, with its echoes of Dante's Beatrice. Richard, on their reunion in Ireland, acknowledges her role in a series of rhetorical questions through which he reveals himself and attempts unsuccessfully to force her self-revelation. "Tell me, Miss Justice, did you feel that what you read was written for your eyes? Or that you inspired me?" Beatrice refuses the trap set by this authoritative rhetorical gesture, responding only "I need not answer that question" (*E* 18–19). Since his return, Richard has been writing obsessively, working long hours in his study. He asks Beatrice if she'd like to read his new work claiming her as his model and comparing his activity to a painter producing sketches from a live model. Beatrice astutely refuses the comparison – "It is not quite the same case, is it?" (*E* 17) – knowing that she has in no way stood before him fully revealed for his representational imitation. Rather, her role as model is one in which the promise of her response, her willingness to read and react, inspires Richard's creativity. And it is precisely through her opacity, through her refusal to be reduced to a known (or owned) object, that Beatrice is so successful in her capacity as an ethical muse.

Joyce was alerted to the dangers inherent in transforming a woman into a model and a muse early in his career in his careful interpretation of Henrik Ibsen's late play *When We Dead Awaken*. In his review of that play for the *Fortnightly Review*, Joyce emphasized the conflict between artist and muse/model and quoted at length Irene's description of the spiritual result of having been transformed into Rubek's masterwork. "They came and bound me – lacing my arms together at my back. Then they lowered me into a grave-vault, with iron bars before the loophole. And with padded walls, so that no one on the earth above could hear the grave-shrieks." Joyce registers the deadening effect of the model's role in his comment on this passage in Ibsen's play: "In Irene's allusion to her position as model for the great picture, Ibsen gives further proof of his extraordinary knowledge of women" (*CW* 54). Implicit in Joyce's commentary is an awareness of the extent to which women commonly serve as the models taken for objects in a masculine world.

Luce Irigaray makes a similar argument in philosophical terms in *Speculum of the Other Woman*, in which she argues that masculine subjectivity has historically constructed itself on the materiality of the feminine, which it imagines to be inert and of the earth in order to be able to constitute itself as complete and to understand that completeness through the simple logic of opposition to feminine lack. Considering women as the material in and through which men create their subjectivity, Irigaray writes: "If there is no more 'earth' to press down/repress, to work, to represent, but also and always to desire (for one's own), no opaque matter which in theory does not know itself, then what pedestal [*socle*] remains for the ek-sistence of the 'subject'?"[39] Margaret Whitford in her study of Irigaray notes that the "underside of male creativity is the death-like immobilizing 'appropriation' of 'nature.'"[40] Ibsen suggests a similar dilemma concerning masculine creativity in relation to the feminine as material for inspiration in *When We Dead Awaken* when he poses the problem: what happens when the model speaks back to the artist, resists her status as inert substance upon which creation may take place? Joyce takes this question as one point of departure for his own play in which both women resist Richard's creativity when it depends on their quiescence and inertia. Bertha and Beatrice speak back to the process of creation, demanding roles as equal partners in the production of love and art.

While Richard may desire the ease and accessibility of an artist's paid model, as indicated in his failed comparison of himself as a painter producing sketches from Beatrice's live form, Joyce resists that role, critiques the injustice of reducing a woman to an object for mimesis or a servant to the poet's inspiration. He indicates that resistance in two ways. Firstly, Joyce refuses an audience's scopophilia, the possibly prurient interest that might be satisfied by witnessing the love scene or failed love scene between Bertha and Robert in the cottage. As in so many of his other works, Joyce draws a curtain before a woman's body and her love (readers never, for example, directly witness Molly Bloom's assignation with Blazes Boylan), granting women characters a privacy that resists the prurience of mimesis and its claims to full revelation. Secondly, Joyce indicates his difference from Dante in naming his muse Beatrice *Justice*. He both indicates her singularity with this name and suggests the contours of her role in the name's descriptive capacity.

Beatrice is just, an ethical muse, a role that each of the other characters recognizes. Robert, for example, tells the others that Beatrice has an admirable "conscience" merely because she partially prepared Archie's piano lesson on the train returning from Youghal. For the audience, Beatrice's conscience, her ethics, might lie in her merged desire and acceptance. It is clear in the opening scene that there has been an erotic element in the lengthy correspondence between Richard and Beatrice and that much of her motivation in the letter exchange derives from her desire for Richard. That desire pains Beatrice in the present in her clear understanding of this distant partner's obligations to and love for Bertha and Archie. At the same time, desire makes Beatrice a kindly reader. She wants to see Richard's new work though it may be "sometimes cruel" (*E* 17) because she accepts both the cruelty and generosity in her intellectual partner: "That is part of your mind, too" (*E* 17). Beatrice, in her combined privacy and desire, understands clearly what the others in Richard's life grapple with unsuccessfully: Richard's masochism, passivity, and even generosity are forms of cruelty, and yet that very cruelty is a part of the charismatic and seductive mind that draws the others to him inexorably, and that makes him, even in his desertion of his country, as Robert suggests, the perfect Irish patriot.

In her ambivalence and desire, Beatrice figures the ethics of interpretation. She stands between positions; her face turns equally to each of two opposing emotions. Her desire allows her to be responsive in justice without judgment; her perceptive and – to use Derek Attridge's word – innovative responsiveness fosters another's creativity.[41]

CHAPTER TWO

Ethical knowledge and errant pedagogy

What youthful mother, a shape upon her lap
Honey of generation had betrayed,
And that must sleep, shriek, struggle to escape
As recollection or the drug decide,
Would think her son, did she but see the shape
With sixty or more winters on its head,
A compensation for the pang of his birth,
Or the uncertainty of his going forth?

(Yeats, "Among School Children")

I

Describing Beatrice's ethical inspiration in *Exiles*, Joyce raises a question that is to preoccupy him and to recur in his works for the remainder of his career: how is it possible to convey knowledge ethically, without recourse to authoritarian imposition? In "The Sisters," he provides an example of unethical ways of teaching: the priest instructs the boy to memorize by rote a pre-ordained collection of information that is codified by the church as knowledge. Yet, Joyce indicates that this very form of knowledge in its elitism and pre-determination produces in the boy a failure of insight, an inability to face his others (the eponymous sisters) with an ethical awareness of their position or context and his responsibility to them. Stephen Dedalus has similar experiences as both a student and a teacher under the supervision of his authoritarian headmaster, Garrett Deasy.[1] In these two instances, among others, Joyce suggests that methods of conveying knowledge have ethical implications: to teach by rote in school may have a blinding effect on a student's ability to understand in other contexts; the knowledge gained by that means may be misused or used primarily to subjugate others. Resisting the authoritarian pedagogy exemplified in the educational system through which he himself was trained, Joyce suggests another method of knowing, which is also exemplified by Beatrice's ethical interpretation. This alternative method involves encountering an other in his or her context or habitat (drawing again on the literal meaning of ethics). Stephen practices this way of knowing in his own pedagogy in *Ulysses*. Facing his students and seeing their difference from him, he acknowledges both their context and the knowledge they have already acquired. He engages those of their responses that might be considered erroneous according to more conventional standards. Admitting the knowledge his students have accumulated, he finds ways, more or less successful, to provoke, expand, or increase both their intellectual capacities and their access to and retention of information. Joyce also indicates, representing an encounter with headmaster Deasy, that Stephen's errant pedagogy has the potential to address wider political issues.

As Joyce's fictions suggest and as ethical philosopher Lorraine Code argues explicitly, "knowing well is a matter of considerable moral significance."[2] One example Code provides in making this point is in the development of prescription drugs: a researcher should know the long-term effects of a medication before recommending it for general patient use; as its inventor, that researcher is ethically responsible for the long-term effects the drug will have. Ethical responsibility, according to this principle, requires both a theoretical disposition and a practical application. In *The Gift of Death*, Jacques Derrida emphasizes the interdependence of ethical practice and ethical knowledge. Drawing on Levinas's concept of responsibility as the crux of ethics, Derrida argues that the ethical subject must be able to answer the question: what does it mean to be responsible? Responsibility, with its inherent suggestion of response or the call to respond, implies activity, a practice that includes but also extends beyond "conscience" or "theoretical understanding." Concurrently, responsibility suggests a thoughtful form of response: ethical action is aware of what each response signifies, in both its initiation and its effects. Derrida argues that "one must always take into account this original and irreducible complexity that links theoretical consciousness (which must also be a thetic or thematic consciousness) to 'practical' conscience (ethical, legal, political), if only to avoid the arrogance of so many 'clean consciences.'"[3] To demand responsibility without knowing what a response might entail would itself be unethical. Knowing and responsibility are interdependent processes.

Drawing on this same Levinasian supposition of the essential responsibility of the subject to another, Margaret Whitford also emphasizes the link between epistemology and ethics in her work on Luce Irigaray. To know ethically, the subject must be conscious that his or her subjectivity is *constituted* in relation to others, whether that other is the unconscious, other people in a social relation, or the Lacanian Other. And concurrently, then, the subject's knowledge will have real effects on his or her others. In each of these cases, Whitford notes, "epistemology without ethics is deadly."[4]

For Joyce, ethical knowledge rests on *making change*. I use this phrase to indicate a constellation of concepts Joyce punningly associates with the metaphor of a coin and its relation to other forms of change in *Ulysses* and *Finnegans Wake*. This metaphor, like so many others in Joyce's oeuvre, links the micrological to the macrological, the ethical to the political. First, Joyce indicates that the current political situation (both in 1904 when *Ulysses* takes place and in the period leading up to its publication in 1922) and the education system it fostered relied on totalitarian forms of control. The colonial administration which referred ultimate authority back to the *crown* is represented in an economic system in which *crowns* are spent to acquire material goods and other benefits.[5] Joyce also recognizes that the period of Irish history on which he is reflecting was a time of considerable political *change*. Following the death of Charles Stewart Parnell (dubbed the *"uncrowned* king of Ireland") in 1891, Irish political life was characterized by remarkable flux and turmoil. The demand for Home Rule through parliamentary compromise, which Parnell had advocated, was no longer a clear political strategy. The vexed debate during the Christmas dinner in *Portrait* (*P* 30–39) registers Joyce's sense of the deep ethical and political divides that emerged in Parnell's wake.

Second, Joyce indicates a series of associations and divisions concentrating on ethical issues of *sovereigns* and *sovereignty*. An authoritarian model might suggest the moral importance of adherence to *sovereign* authority in the form of the *crown* or the church and enforce that adherence through an educational system that would promote obedience. Stephen's model in *Ulysses* (and perhaps Joyce's by implication) relates sovereignty to political and personal autonomy, an ethical responsibility to choose one's own path separate from the reassuring but potentially dangerous and stifling presence of an exterior *sovereign* authority and its attendant "truths." For Stephen, in his pedagogy if not in his personal and familial interactions, an ethical sovereignty means also a responsibility to one's context, immediate, domestic, or national.[6] His teaching technique reflects this ethical responsibility. In contrast to the moral absolutism in his environment, Stephen's pedagogical ethics become progressively more situational, particular, and responsive. Margaret Urban Walker's description of feminist ethics might apply equally to Stephen's developing approach. She notes that this alternative ethical theory "does not imagine our moral understandings congealed into a compact theoretical instrument of impersonal decision for each person, but as deployed in shared processes of discovery, expression, interpretation, and adjustment between persons."[7] Like Walker's moral epistemology, Stephen's educational ethic is a continuous process that relies on discovery and adjustment to new contexts, new information, and new agents.

II

Stephen's ethic is formed in a continuing act of resistance to authoritarian control which begins in his childhood, as represented in *Portrait*, and continues in his adult life as described in the pages of *Ulysses*. In the Catholic schools Stephen attends, pedagogical authority is presented as absolute. The priest's authority seems both natural and just because it is supported by all of the institutional structures that form the students' milieu. The priests who guide Stephen's Latin lessons could also potentially hear his confession and absolve his sins, change wine into blood, and bread into flesh. Their authority is understood to come directly and without mediation from God. The lessons that Stephen learns in school, even when apparently neutral, reinforce the authority of the institution and its representatives, his teachers. For example, in the hand-writing lesson depicted in the first chapter, Stephen is unable to participate because he has broken his eye glasses on the cinder path. Yet he is aware of the content of the lesson and has even memorized the phrases his fellow students copy out. The apparent object of the instruction is to learn the proper formation of letters; however, these letters also spell out a moral lesson that promotes behavior designed to support the authority of the school: "*Zeal without prudence is like a ship adrift*" (*P*46, italics original). Teaching the boys moderation in behavior promotes the school's objective of stifling rebellion and instilling obedience.

Louis Althusser has argued that a political system can only maintain its stability by "reproducing" itself and its ideologies in each of its subjects. While in some cases this indoctrination is produced in obvious ways through legal and penal systems, the "reproduction" is more effective when it is cloaked in institutions, such as a school, in which ideology can be presented as neutral information or knowledge.[8] However, institutional structures such as Stephen's school are riddled with ideological gaps, fissures, and contradictions which make it possible for agents like Stephen (and his more adventurous peers) to resist the moral authority of the institution.[9] Stephen notes two such gaps when, during the Latin class immediately following the writing instructions, he is brutally punished for his non-participation. First, he notes that the authority which is presented as both absolute and natural can also be contradictory: Father Arnell excuses him from his lesson; Father Dolan beats his hand with a pandy bat for being idle during the same class. If the priests' authority were absolute, it would be based on a transcendent truth and would therefore be consistent. When the rector sides with Stephen and allows that Dolan's punishment was in error, the rector indicates a further fissure in the authority that dictates Stephen's education. Second, the covert doctrine inculcated in the writing assignment is directly contradicted by the behavior of the school's prefect of studies. In accusing Stephen of being a "lazy little schemer" (*P* 50), neglecting the facts and punishing him based on this supposition, Dolan acts like a "*ship adrift*," displaying "*zeal without prudence*." Having so directly and brutally experienced the authority of the institution, Stephen is primed to note the extent to which that authority is illusory, constructed rather than natural.

As his schooling continues, he observes that this authority is exercised not in the service of some greater moral or intellectual good but in the service of its own survival and perpetuation: authority in this context serves the end of sustaining authority. Resisting the tautological structure of these institutions, Stephen finds his own path to knowledge, primarily through curiosity (initially sexual curiosity). To preserve his intellectual integrity, he develops a habit of resistance to empty institutional authorities which is again evident when, as an adult, he represents that authority as a teacher and undermines it at the same time (calling himself a "learner").

While Stephen recognizes and resists injustice in the inconsistent authority of the priests, he is not himself always capable of being just. His misogyny is often and cogently remarked upon;[10] he is almost equally arrogant in his treatment of men.[11] I do not wish to suggest a developmental model for understanding Stephen's ethics; he does not necessarily become more capable of ethical response as he matures. While he is often sympathetic and even just, he is as frequently blind to difference and its attendant responsibilities. When he responds to Bloom's hospitality in "Ithaca" with a particularly vicious, anti-Semitic song, his ethical failure is glaring. Yet the development of an ethical conscience for himself (and ultimately his nation) is of primary importance to Stephen. His nascent ethical sense derives from his ability readily to imagine, and it emerges when he imagines another in his or her own habitat or context. He realizes he has wronged Emma Cleary, for example, when he imagines what would happen if he sent her the romantic poetry she has inspired him to write. Initially, he anticipates the ridicule and incomprehension his work would be subjected to if she were to share these tributes with her family.[12]

> If he sent her the verses? They would be read out at breakfast amid the tapping of eggshells. Folly indeed! The brothers would laugh and try to wrest the page from each other with their strong hard fingers. The suave priest, her uncle, seated in his armchair, would hold the page at arm's length, read it smiling and approve of the literary form.
>
> No, no: that was folly. Even if he sent her the verses she would not show them to others. No, no: she could not.
>
> He began to feel that he had wronged her. (*P* 222)

Imagining his poetry read in the context of Emma's family life, Stephen is able to glimpse her isolation, the extent to which her private satisfaction in being loved or admired would be misunderstood and distorted by her seemingly jovial and appreciative family. When he sees her in this context, he recognizes that she would be kind and just to him, that she would protect his poetry and preserve it from possible ridicule.

But when Stephen thinks of her as an extension of his own being in the totality of his fears and shames, his version of her is less just:

> A sense of her innocence moved him almost to pity her, an innocence he had never understood till he had come to the knowledge of it through sin, an innocence which she too had not understood while she was innocent or before the strange humiliation of her nature had first come upon her. Then first her soul had begun to live as his soul had when he had first sinned: and a tender compassion filled his heart as he remembered her frail pallor and her eyes, humbled and saddened by the dark shame of womanhood. (*P* 222)

Stephen humbles Emma in his imagination by assuming both her "innocence" and "shame" only in the context of his own sexual experimentation and the guilt and humiliation he has experienced in connection with it. The fear of women resulting from the shame Stephen has been taught to experience in the place of desire, leads him to imagine that Emma herself would experience being a woman, and coming into self-awareness, as a "dark shame." For Stephen it is impossible to imagine that Emma might have a different, perhaps more positive, experience of her burgeoning sexuality (a positive experience suggested perhaps by her flirtation with the priest, a flirtation that sparks Stephen's jealousy and provokes him to imagine her as "shamed"). Unable to imagine Emma experiencing the same events in different terms, unable to see his responsibility to recognize her in her own context, he subsumes her experience as an extension of his own sexual shame. He submits her to the injustice of his totalizing conceptions.[13]

Joyce emphasizes that this kind of conceptual totality is a form of extreme injustice by drawing analogies between personal relations and political or national transactions. Imagining Emma only through the structures of his own experience to the exclusion of her particular context is a form of colonization equivalent to, though different in its effects from, national imperialism. Joyce offers a critique of imperialism through the particularities of personal ethics in the immediate encounter with the face of an other. Specifically, in Stephen's teaching at the Dalkey school Joyce presents an oscillating comparison between the pedagogical methods through which a teacher encounters his or her student and other forms of authority – national, institutional, or spiritual – which may be comparably ethical or totalizing.

III

In "Nestor," as one of his students haltingly recites John Milton's "Lycidas," Stephen contemplates this poem and other tributes paid to the Christian God. "Lycidas" is a pastoral elegy on the death of Milton's friend Edward King who drowned crossing the Chester Bay to Dublin; his death provoked Milton to contemplate in poetic form his own relations with God. "Lycidas" is also an explicitly imperial poem, as Lawrence Lipking has argued, written in part to support England's colonization of Ireland.[14] That the Dalkey School students are expected to recite this poem as a part of their curriculum is further indication of the ideological interpolation of these boys as imperial subjects. The name Edward King might also have reminded Stephen in 1904 of King Edward who was then on the throne as ruler of England and Ireland. His associations with that figure of authority could be considered one of the sources for his subsequent contemplation of Jesus's resistance to Caesar, the imperial sovereign during the Roman occupation of Israel. Listening to the poetic recitation, he draws an association between Milton's poem and the Biblical passage in which Jesus discusses monetary tributes as forms of adherence or resistance to imperial control. Stephen recognizes the extent to which his students' attitude toward his authority has parallels in the political and spiritual situation Jesus addresses. "It lies upon their eager faces who offered him a coin of the tribute. To Caesar what is Caesar's, to God what is God's" (*U* 2:85–86).

The Biblical incident to which Stephen refers here is narrated in the three synoptic Gospels (Matthew 22:15–22; Mark 12:17; Luke 25). In Matthew's version the story runs thus:

> Then went the Pharisees and took counsel how they might entangle him in his talk.
>
> And they sent out unto him their disciples with the Herodians, saying, Master, we know thou art true, and teachest the way of God in truth, neither carest thou for any man; for thou regardest not the person of men.
>
> Tell us, therefore, What thinkest thou? Is it lawful to give tribute unto Caesar, or not?
>
> But Jesus perceived their wickedness, and said, Why test me, ye hypocrites?
>
> Show me the tribute money. And they brought him a denarius.
>
> And he saith unto them, Whose is this image and superscription.
>
> They say unto him, Caesar's. Then saith he unto them, Render therefore unto Caesar the things which are Caesar's; and unto God, the things that are God's. (Matthew 22:15–21 [15])

Jesus's response exemplifies a resistant means of survival under two some-times conflicting and sometimes complicit masters: the Pharisees and the Herodians appear in the story as representatives of the Jewish Temple and the Roman Empire, respectively. Jesus's suggested payment of the coin collapses the system of signification between the coin and the political authority that mints it. To read the representation of authority in this literal way implodes the contract between Caesar and his subjects and folds the authority thus represented back upon itself. Returning the coin made by the sovereign to that sovereign renders this monetary system a kind of coined narcissism. The symbol of power returns to its source without having collected the allegiance of sovereign subjects.

Addressing Jesus's comment on paying tribute with Caesar's coin, Slavoj Zizek in *The Sublime Object of Ideology* argues that obedience to arbitrary social authority can become a method by which to question that authority. By accepting socially prescribed norms and roles, though they may lack justification, by accepting the idea of the law for its own sake, a subject may be freed from the constraints of those same rules and laws, in which case, "the way is open for free theoretical reflection. In other words, we render unto Caesar what is Caesar's, so that we can calmly reflect on everything."[16] Zizek understands the payment to Caesar in his own coin as a sort of short-circuiting of the system of total authority. But

and only the earth!
only their own
continued suffering!

he also considers the possibility that this short circuit may be an illusion. It is the distinctive form of authoritarian ideology, according to Zizek, to demand obedience to form for the sake of form alone rather than for any greater end that obedience will achieve: "Do it because I said so." Further support for Zizek's view may be found in Jesus's Sermon on the Mount in which he tells his followers that the meek will inherit the earth. This statement has too often been interpreted institutionally (and especially in colonial contexts) as justification for meek adherence to authoritarian rule among Christian followers who may expect some balancing of the books in the afterlife. In attempting to implode the system of authority by practicing empty obedience, the subject is sutured into that system in spite of his or her resistance.

Zizek's quandary is reflected in Stephen's attitude ("I will not serve" [*P* 239]) about paying his Easter duty according to his mother's request in *Portrait*. He believes that no form is empty and so he refuses to practice the conventions of Catholic devotion or obedience lest he be sutured into the ideology of an institutional authority. As he remarks to Cranly, "I fear . . . the chemical action which would be set up in my soul by a false homage to a symbol behind which are massed twenty centuries of authority and veneration" (*P* 243). However, Stephen also realizes the extent to which his insistent opposition to Catholic authority pained his mother in her last days when she wished to see him reconciled with God through the offices of the church. Cranly reminds Stephen of his callousness: "Your mother must have gone through a good deal of suffering. . . . Would you not try to save her from suffering more. . .?" (*P* 241). Cranly suggests an ethical response to Stephen's dilemma by reminding him of his initial habitat in the womb and his responsibility to his mother: "Whatever else is unsure in this stinking dunghill of a world a mother's love is not. Your mother brings you into the world, carries you first in her body" (*P* 241–242). Refusing his mother's wish in favor of adherence to his own principles, Stephen shows little responsibility to his context, to the love his mother felt for him, the sacrifices she made to give him life and sustain that life. In asserting his difference from her, Stephen fails to acknowledge the extent to which May Dedalus has always recognized and fostered the differences between herself and her son.[17]

Joyce demonstrates his continuing preoccupation with this quandary when he sets *Finnegans Wake* during Easter night and morning and returns repeatedly to considerations of guilt and confession. In the section on Shem the Penman (I.vii), who reminds many readers of Stephen, he follows a series of references to revisions of his earlier texts with a raucous send-up of Easter confession and its relations to childhood nurturing and motherly concern.

> Let us pry. We thought, would and did. *Cur, quicquid, ubi, quando, quomodo, quoties, quibus auxiliis?* [Language from the Latin confession prayers.] You were bred, fed, fostered and fattened from holy childhood up in this two easter island on the piejaw of hilarious heaven and roaring the other place (plunders to night of you, blunders what's left of you, flash as flash can!) and now, forsooth, . . . you have become of twosome twiminds forenenst gods, . . . you have reared your disunited kingdom on the vacuum of your own most intensely doubtful soul. Do you hold yourself then for some god in the manger, Shehohem, that you will neither serve nor let serve, pray nor let pray? (*FW* 188.8–19)

This reference to the doubtful soul recalls Stephen Dedalus and his refusal of confession and Easter obedience; his policy of "*non servium*" is also repeated when the narrator chides him for his religious hubris and filial neglect.

Though months have now passed since his mother's death, even in his classroom Stephen exhibits the outward signs of terrible grief, signs indicating the resonance of their last conflict in his present preoccupations. He still wears mourning clothes in spite of Buck Mulligan's ridicule; the riddle he tells to his students, whose enigmatic solution is the "fox burying his grandmother under a hollybush" (*U* 2:115), reflects a private grief that cannot readily be communicated, but that is, at the same time, always present to the mourner. In describing this conflicted relation between son and remembered mother, Joyce is in no way advocating the idealized version of the mother common in Ireland at the turn of the century, nor the primary narcissism that would buttress that idealization. Joyce figures in Stephen's grief the conflict that responsibility to one's context (embodied in the mother) instills. Through that conflict Joyce is able to emphasize that an ethical subject must be responsive to contradiction and ambiguity, that a fixed moral stand such as Stephen's anti-authoritarianism, is not always, by definition, an ethical position.

Stephen's investment in errancy is also in part his heretical investment in resisting the church. An alternative ethical position is exemplified by Julia Kristeva's term "*heréthique*" which punningly signifies both a woman's ethic, "her-ethic," and an errant or heretical ethic. However, Kristeva suggests that an ethical form of heresy may be exemplified in the mother's love of the other who is her child.[18] She suggests that this love of the other is as heretical as it is ethical. As Marilyn Edelstein notes: "Rather than being an abstract set of moral principles, ethics is, for Kristeva, a relational, dialogic *practice* in which one acknowledges both the otherness of the other and the otherness of the self to itself."[19] Stephen's continued mourning signals the failure of his resistance to authority as a guiding moral principle; Joyce's own letter describing his encounter with his dead mother and the sympathy that extreme otherness inspired in him exemplifies Kristeva's *heréthique* as ethical practice.

In *Ulysses*, Stephen is acutely aware of the authoritarian structures of which he is a subject. In conversation with his temporary roommate, Haines, an English tourist who both exemplifies and resists British imperialism, Stephen draws a connection between Jesus's colonial context and his own. However, his mode of resistance, relying on errancy and mistakes, differs from Jesus's absolute trust in and obedience to a transcendent and benevolent God.

– I am a servant of two masters, Stephen said, an English and an Italian.
– Italian? Haines said.
   A crazy queen, old and jealous. Kneel down before me.
– And a third, Stephen said, there is who wants me for odd jobs.[20]
– Italian? Haines said again. What do you mean?
– The imperial British state, Stephen answered, his colour rising, and the holy Roman catholic and apostolic church. (*U* 1:638–644)

The authority that sometimes calls on Stephen for odd jobs is Erin, the errant island nation whose emerging political identity was in 1904 often dependent on unexamined, romantic forms of nationalism. Stephen prefers to resist the nationalist call he is subjected to by such friends as the Fenian Davin who questions his political allegiances in *Portrait*. Echoing the imperial concerns explored in the Bible, Stephen recognizes the similarities between his situation and that of the Israelites under Roman rule.[21] But he adapts Jesus's rhetorical example to resist each of his masters. Following his particular Luciferian ethic, "*non serviam*," also borrowed from his interpretation of Milton (in this case, *Paradise Lost*), Stephen refuses to serve any of the three masters available to him; instead, he subverts the economy of imperial signification. Employing an errant politics, Stephen hears the nation *Eire* (the Irish word for Ireland) as err or error (just as Joyce heard both error and Erin in learn which he writes as "lerryn" in *Finnegans Wake* [*FW* 200.36]). He resists the errands and odd jobs to which Ireland calls him, and follows the paths of errancy and mistake that have so frequently marked and even marred Irish political life.[22]

Stephen's teaching method, reliant on just this kind of errancy, avoids empty forms of authority as a means for retaining order and conveying knowledge in his class.[23] At his best when he is teaching, though certainly not confident of his methods or his control, Stephen encourages learning through an ethics of response, thus cultivating creative thought processes and promoting the kind of curiosity that has furthered his own knowledge and education. Rather than relying on a codified distinction between fact and error, which he worries will promote a "dull ease of mind" (*U* 2:15), Stephen prefers to encourage knowledge by joining his students in their own preoccupations, by entertaining their associations as valid forms of knowledge. In his history lesson, for example, reviewing Pyrrhus's empty victory at Asculum in 279 BC, Stephen passes over Comyn, a student clearly well versed in facts and accustomed to the approbation those facts accord him (" – I know, sir. Ask me, sir, Comyn said"). Stephen calls instead on Armstrong, a student who, it seems, is often distracted. In posing his question to Armstrong, Stephen focuses (ethically) on the student's dwelling or context, on the place from which he comes to this encounter in the classroom:

– Wait. You, Armstrong. Do you know anything about Pyrrhus?

A bag of figrolls lay snugly in Armstrong's satchel. He curled them between his palms at whiles and swallowed them softly. Crumbs adhered to the tissue of his lips. A sweetened boy's breath. Welloff people, proud that their eldest son was in the navy. Vico road, Dalkey.

– Pyrrhus, sir? Pyrrhus a pier. (*U* 2:21–26[24])

Posing his question to Armstrong, Stephen imagines the boy's own experience sympathetically. He thinks of the child's preoccupation with food, of his parents, his brother, and his home. Stephen focuses not on the error of Armstrong's clearly unstudied answer, but on the effect of his answer. "All laughed. Mirthless high malicious laughter. Armstrong looked round at his classmates, silly glee in profile. In a moment they will laugh more loudly, aware of my lack of rule and of the fees their papas pay" (*U* 2:27–29). Acutely conscious of class dynamics, Stephen gauges with great sensitivity the relations among his students. He knows that Armstrong has lost face with his fumbling answer and that his own response to the student will determine both the extent of this power loss and also his own control in the classroom. But Stephen is unwilling to gain that control at the weaker student's expense by asserting facts and his own privileged access to them. Rather, he reasserts his position both by sympathy (his answer protects Armstrong by allowing him another chance to answer correctly), by pointing to the imaginative virtues of his answer, and by diverting the student's attention through word play. When Armstrong defines a pier as a "kind of bridge," Stephen replies, "a disappointed bridge" (*U* 2:32 and 39). His playful affirmation of Armstrong's groping answer diverts the mirthless, punitive laughter of students who would take the boy as their victim for his incompetence. His joking response indicates the areas in which the other boys might themselves be incompetent: they are puzzled by his humor, have difficulty following a path of association. Though he is aware that his form of control in the classroom is precarious given their habituation to the kind of authoritarian pedagogy he himself was schooled in, he regards his own position as secondary to the imperative to protect the weakened student. Temporarily, Stephen wins their attention and acquiescence by his combination of sympathy (a recognition of and response to their own condition) and desire (their awareness of their own confusion and the implicit demand for clarification in their troubled gazes). Rather than asserting control, Stephen teaches the students the extent to which control is temporary and provisional; at one moment they have it because they know more than Armstrong; at the next, it is lost because they are not sure they understand the lesson any longer: their expectations have been frustrated. Stephen diverts the direct link between arbitrary, factual knowledge and power or control, preferring instead the properties of verbal play and associative insight.[25]

IV

Stephen's ethical form of knowledge is most moving and effective in his exchange with Cyril Sargent after the class has ended. Against the backdrop of a hockey game played in the school yard, Stephen assists this clearly delicate and unattractive student whose weakness is underscored by an implied contrast with the strong boys playing hockey outside. Sargent has fallen below the mark in his math lesson and the schoolmaster, Deasy, has asked that he copy the assigned sums out again correctly and by rote from the master's example, and then have them checked by Stephen. But as Joyce points out in *Finnegans Wake* this method of teaching easily results in "the learned lacklearning, merciless as wonderful" (*FW* 252.6–7). Evaluating both the sums and the student, Stephen is initially repulsed by the child's feeble appearance and by his poor scholarly aptitude:

… His thick hair and scraggy neck gave witness of unreadiness and through his misty glasses weak eyes looked up pleading. On his cheek, dull and bloodless, a soft stain of ink lay, dateshaped, recent and damp as a snail's bed.

He held out his copybook. The word *Sums* was written on the headline. Beneath were sloping figures and at the foot a crooked signature with blind loops and a blot. Cyril Sargent: his name and seal. (*U* 2:124–130)

Presenting Sargent through his teacher's eyes, Joyce describes a person who is in many ways Stephen's other. Unlike Stephen, who excelled in school, Sargent is barely able to keep up. The child is ugly: both scraggy and thick, his dull cheek and the ink stain on it call to mind a snail's bed; his signature impression on the world seems to Stephen best described by the child's own blot in his copybook. That Sargent is compared to a snail may be an indirect reminder of both Stephen's and the reader's ethical responsibility to this student. The snail carries its habitat or dwelling with it. One cannot see a snail without seeing its context, cannot see its context without recognizing how weak the body is that it requires this hardened carapace that is dragged with it from place to place. In Stephen's encounter with Sargent, Joyce indicates that the other to whom we are called to respond ethically is not always obviously desirable. He may be the moist, snail-like child at the back of the class whose ineffectual work evokes irritation. Yet the ethical subject is called to a sympathetic encounter with that other in his or her nakedness. Joyce indicates through Stephen's associative processes the means through which repulsion can transform into ethical treatment based on sympathy and even desire:

Ugly and futile: lean neck and thick hair and a stain of ink, a snail's bed. Yet someone had loved him, borne him in her arms and in her heart. But for her the race of world would have trampled him underfoot, a squashed boneless snail. She had loved his weak watery blood drained from her own. Was that then real? The only true thing in life? His mother's prostrate body the fiery Columbanus in holy zeal bestrode. She was no more: the trembling skeleton of a twig burnt in the fire, an odour of rosewood and wet ashes. She had saved him from being trampled underfoot and had gone, scarcely having been. (*U* 2:139–147)

Stephen first sees in Sargent a face that only a mother could possibly love, a thought that leads to his recognition that a mother *had* loved him, had nurtured him and appreciated him, and without that love he would have been obliterated by a brutal world. If he responded brutally to the child, Stephen would align himself with an unethical world rather than with this true thing: a mother's love. Cranly had made Stephen aware of his cruelty and his responsibility to his own mother when in *Portrait* he evoked May Dedalus's difficult life, her numerous pregnancies, the early deaths of several of her children, the arduous care of the living ones, and the loss of domestic security that came with her husband's alcoholism.

In his preparatory notes for *Ulysses*, Joyce describes Stephen as an embryo. And in Cranly's words he evokes the indebtedness of the embryo to his or her mother and the consequent responsibility to anticipate what an other "feels." But like the revered, intellectual, Irish saint, Columbanus, whom he remembers during the arithmetic lesson, Stephen had deserted his mother, refused her troublesome emotions along with her request that he observe Easter conventions.[26] He returns to her from Paris only to attend her death bed, to see her body whittled away to the proportions of a twig, and to inhale the bodily scent of wet ashes caused by her disease. Having lost her love, Stephen has become more aware of its value. He realizes that the context from which he came, the context of knowing the world first by knowing his mother's love, leaves him with obligations to see each person as his mother saw him – though weak, deserving of protection, recognition, and response. Working beside Sargent, who is like his embryonic self in his snail's body protected by a snail's shell, Stephen draws on the vulnerable experience of the embryo protected by a mother's body to rethink knowledge and his methods of attaining it and to turn to sympathy as his ethical technique for instruction.

Instead of a Cartesian knowledge of his own existence being his Archimedes lever, the one known thing from which other things might be known, "*Amor matris*: subjective and objective genitive" (*U* 2:165–166) (or mother love, both given and received) is the one element of knowledge from which all others must proceed. Joyce implies (in a gesture one might understand through Susan Bordo's concept of sympathetic epistemology) that knowledge emerges from the first ethical relation with an other. In Levinasian terms, ethics is first philosophy.

Stephen, when he realizes this ethical responsibility, which relies on his acute and individual perception of Sargent's situation and condition, is able to be an extremely effective teacher.[27]

> Sitting at his side Stephen solved out the problem. . . .
> Across the page the symbols moved in grave morrice, in the mummery of their letters, wearing quaint caps of squares and cubes. Give hands, traverse, bow to partner: so: imps of fancy of the Moors. . . .
> – Do you understand now? Can you work the second for yourself?
> – Yes, sir. (*U* 2:151–162)

Remembering *Amor matris* and his own ethical responsibility to this stranger, Stephen sits beside Sargent and imagines his habitat, the snail carapace in which he resides, the thought patterns through which he approaches his work. And having taken on this ethical responsibility, Stephen is able to see clearly Sargent's view which Joyce reflects in the gorgeous language of dance: Sargent is dyslexic. When he tries to work the arithmetic problems the mathematical figures dance across the page exchanging places, reversing positions, emerging in unexpected places like the dancers in a complex mummery.[28] When Stephen realizes Sargent's condition, the habitat in which he thinks and from which he sees, he assists him successfully and Sargent is able to work the sums independently.

For Stephen, then, it is insufficient pedagogically to demonstrate or impose knowledge. Knowledge arises sympathetically, in a conversation between subjects. That sympathy, however, must also allow for a difference between self and other, between Stephen and Sargent. Stephen cannot assume that he *knows* Sargent's experience but he is responsible for *acknowledging* it. Acknowledging is sympathetic, feeling beside or along with, while knowing might be described as empathic, assuming the feeling of the other as one's own, a totalizing gesture (to use Levinas's language).[29] To underscore this distinction it may be helpful to refer to Stanley Cavell's allied distinction between knowing and acknowledging. Cavell indicates that it is impossible to *know* another's experience (of pain, for example) because it cannot be quantified "numerically or literally." My pain or understanding of pain can never be precisely the same as an other's experienced pain. "So the phenomenological pang in having to say that knowing another mind is a matter of inference . . . remains after we have granted what seemed to be lacking in our knowledge of the other."[30] However, that lack in knowledge, that specific phenomenological pang, calls upon the subject to respond ethically in a gesture of sympathy. "But why is sympathy expressed in this way? Because your suffering makes a claim upon me. It is not enough that I *know* (am certain) that you suffer – I must do or reveal something (whatever can be done). In a word, I must *acknowledge* it, otherwise I do not know what '(your or his) being in pain' means" (*ibid* 263). Pain enunciates the gap between self and other, between what can be known and what can only be acknowledged. The other's pain calls on each of us to respond without comprehension, both in the sense of knowing and in the sense of subsuming the other to the principles of the self.[31] For Levinas pain can also be posited as the experience of the other's excess or alterity which destabilizes one's own sense of consistent subjectivity. "There is the pain which confounds the ego or in vertigo draws it like an abyss, and prevents it from assuming the other that wounds it in an intentional movement when it posits itself in itself and for itself. Then there is produced in this vulnerability the reversal whereby the other inspires the same, pain an overflowing of meaning by nonsense."[32] Meaning as a form of knowledge is predicated on the closure of self; the other interrupts that closure and induces the vertigo of an incompletion and an allied responsibility that exceeds one's knowledge or sense, with nonsense. Simon Critchley makes a similar point in recognizing the incommensurable difference between self and other, "a dimension of separateness, interiority, secrecy or whatever, that escapes my comprehension. That which exceeds the bounds of my knowledge demands *acknowledgment*."[33]

Working the sums alongside his student, Stephen acknowledges Sargent's intellectual pain, his feeling of inadequacy, while also recognizing the incommensurable differences between himself and his student. It is that difference, the failure of comprehension, that allows Stephen's gesture of pedagogical and ethical sympathy. As Kelly Oliver points out, it is difference that allows sympathy and connection. That Stephen experiences in this encounter a failure of the kind of knowledge he had used to buttress his sense of self is indicated in the following chapter in which he performs a kind of experiment with Berkeley's theories of sensation. Closing his eyes and examining the knowledge he can gain from his other sensations, he recognizes the limits of cognition.[34]

V

Stephen's teaching method is heretical, or to use Kristeva's term, *heréthical*, in the sense that it deviates from the accepted or orthodox pedagogy exemplified by his schoolmaster. It is also heretical because he relies on error, his own and his students', as the source of discovery and ultimately knowledge. As he quips later in the novel to his friends in the National Library, "A man of genius makes no mistakes. His errors are volitional and are the portals of discovery" (*U* 9.228–229). While his students are almost certainly not geniuses and their errors may not be volitional, those errors are nonetheless portals of discovery, both for themselves and for their teacher.[35] According to Stephen's adage, heretical thought is the basis of intellectual discovery.

Heresy derives etymologically from Latin and Greek roots (*haeresis* and *hairesis*, respectively) meaning "taking for oneself" or "choice" and has come to be defined as erroneous religious belief or doctrinal error. According to Jacques Derrida in *The Gift of Death*, heresy is the "essential condition of responsibility."[36] Because, Derrida argues, heresy implies choice or decision as well as a difference from doctrine or institutional belief, it is tied to responsibility as a practice of responsiveness to the particular and the conditional demand of an other even when, paradoxically, that response necessitates a resistance to orthodoxy.[37] Following doctrine makes compassion (or feeling with) impossible because it precludes the flexibility that a careful response would demand. If responsibility, rather than an adherence to a pre-ordained set of moral codes, is the absolute condition of ethical behavior, then the ethical subject in exercising choice or preference for the other will be a dissident or heretic when measured in the terms of moral orthodoxy.[38] Stephen is an experienced heretic, in both senses of this word. When, in his childhood, he approaches the rector to report Father Dolan's abuse, he must choose between two orthodoxies: his father's admonition "never to peach on a fellow" (*P* 9) and Dolan's unjust application of school policies to his particular transgression. In visiting the rector, Stephen is acutely aware that though he has the, at least temporary, support of his schoolmates, his choice is ultimately taken for himself, in his own defense and as his own responsibility.

Stephen is also accused of heresy, in the sense of erroneous religious belief or doctrinal error. Mr. Tate, the English master in his second school, accuses him of heretical thought in his weekly essay. He points to a specific passage concerning the "Creator and the soul" in which Stephen writes "*without a possibility of ever approaching nearer*" (*P* 79). Stephen hastily corrects the heresy by saying he meant never "*reaching*" rather than never "*drawing nearer*." But his error is instructive, an indication of his increased alienation from the Catholic church and also an indication of a heretical and, according to Levinas's terms, deeply ethical belief. Though the context is unclear, Stephen seems to be arguing that there is an incommensurable and insurmountable difference between the Creator or God and the soul or self. In making this argument, Stephen indicates the indissoluble difference between self and other (both *autre* and *Autrui*, in this case). Respecting that division, at the same time that he admits responsibility in a process of partial identification, he is able, as an adult, to see differences in his immediate context and to face and respond to his others (to Armstrong and Sargent, on the one hand, and to Deasy, on the other) without subsuming their interests to his own.[39]

That Stephen's ethical pedagogy has political implications becomes apparent when he goes to the headmaster's office to receive his pay. In his meeting with Deasy, Stephen encounters another who is as much his opposite as is Sargent, though Deasy's contrary disposition has more sinister political implications. While Stephen is apparently less sympathetic to Deasy, he exhibits in his encounter with this authority a similar responsibility to that he employed with his student. He relies on Deasy's errors, as he relied on those of his students, to indicate ethical alternatives to the schoolmaster's moralizing pronouncements. In this encounter with his other, Stephen's concerns are largely political, as I will indicate. Deasy's institutional authority in the context of the school is aligned with other kinds of authority which have been irresponsible, which have insisted on subsuming the other under the totalizing impulses of the self. In this meeting with Deasy, the reader may see how the immediate ethical response has wider social and political implications, and that pedagogy may be practiced not only with students but also with peers.

Teaching according to his own ethical, errant methods, Stephen must actively resist the pedagogical expectations of the Dalkey school. The extent to which he must resist becomes apparent in his meeting with the school's headmaster, Garrett Deasy. Deasy is associated with nearly every form of authoritarian control: with educational authority, with the British empire, with the perceived rectitude of religion. It is through error that Stephen attempts to respond ethically to his schoolmaster and to the orthodox morality Deasy imposes on his subordinate. Noting the factual errors in Deasy's moralist rhetoric, Stephen attempts to indicate choice, or, more specifically, alternative ethical responses that might replace Deasy's totalizing orthodoxies. The headmaster believes that morality comprises a known set of universal formulae to be found in canonical sources and that the transmission and justification of those universal codes is the duty of the moral agent. Stephen wrests ethics from this normative morality by noting the fissures in Deasy's rhetoric.[40]

Joyce emphasizes the extent to which Deasy's moral philosophy is sustained more by rhetoric than by value when he pairs the headmaster's ideologically coined phrases with a collection of coins in his office and with the devalued Irish pounds with which he pays his subordinate. In pairing rhetoric and coining, Joyce draws on a long philosophical and literary history, from Heraclitus and Plato to Goethe and Shakespeare, through which this metaphor has been developed.[41] Ralph Waldo Emerson, in his 1837 essay, "Nature," contributes to the discussion concerning language and value with a comment on the loss of ethics that is signified by clichéd language: "The corruption of man is followed by the corruption of language. When simplicity of character and the sovereignty of ideas is broken up by the prevalence of secondary desires . . . and duplicity and falsehood take place of simplicity and truth, the power over nature as an interpreter of the will is in a degree lost; *new imagery ceases to be created, and old words are perverted to stand for things which are not; a paper currency is employed when there is no bullion in the vaults.*"[42] Emerson's devoted reader Friedrich Nietzsche, in his 1873 essay, "On Truth and Lying in an Extra-moral Sense," uses coins to describe worn-out "truths" impressed in emptied rhetorics that nonetheless still have currency.

What is truth? a mobile army of metaphor, metonyms, anthropomorphisms, in short, a sum of human relations which are poetically and rhetorically height- ened, transferred, and adorned, and after long use seem solid, canonical, and binding to a nation. Truths are illusions about which it has been forgotten that they *are* illusions, worn-out metaphors without sensory impact, coins which have lost their image and now can be used only as metal, and no longer as coins.[43]

Nietzsche notes the extent to which truths are mobilized into truisms, robbing us of the awareness of language as a symbolic system just as wear effaces the symbolic significance of the coin's exergue, leaving behind only a worn disc of metal. In "White Mythologies," Derrida, remark- ing on Nietzsche's coin, notes that "if we were to accept a Saussurean distinction, we would say that here the question of metaphor derives from a theory of *value* and not only from a theory of *signification*."[44] The coin mimics this illusory system of metaphorical truths. As part of an eco- nomy, the coin bears the illusion along with its exergue that it has the same value as the goods or labor it purchases, though, in fact, the metal with which it is made might be worthless according to other measures. The habits of language and of economy obscure value in favor of a catechetic signification. While Nietzsche reflects a suspicion of metaphor as poten- tially devious, able to efface the clear edges of truth through the detours of comparison and association, Joyce, like Emerson, relies on discursive innovation, and in Joyce's particular case on the errancy of metaphor, to rescue ethical complexities from worn-out moral assumptions.[45]

Waiting in Deasy's study for his weekly salary, Stephen observes the schoolmaster's case of Stuart coins. Deasy's allegiance as a "West Briton," or loyal British subject in Ireland (West of Britain), is exemplified by his collection of these artifacts of imperial control. "On the sideboard the tray of Stuart coins, base treasure of the bog . . ." (*U* 2:201–202). The Stuart coins on Deasy's sideboard were minted by James II who, after being deposed from his place on the English throne in 1688, retreated to Ireland.[46] James II was Catholic and this particular Christian allegiance was instrumental in gaining Irish support in his attempt to wrest the English throne from the Protestant contender, William.[47] Accepting Irish allegiance, James II used the country as a *base* for his attempt to reclaim the British throne. In 1689 he de*based* Irish currency by coining money out of inferior metals. The resulting Stuart coins were as useless as James's attempt to retake England from his base in Ireland. But by the early twentieth century, the rarity of the Stuart coins had given them value as collectors' items while the contemporary Irish economy suffered the continued effects of English economic exploitation. The coins in Deasy's case bear a motto that is particularly indicative of James II's aspirations: "Christ in victory and in triumph."[48] For Stephen, and perhaps for Joyce, the motto resonates with the Roman Catholic Church's imperious control over Ireland.

Stephen remembers James's exploitation of Ireland's soil and her subjects when he looks at the collection; and he thinks of those coins as "base treasure of the bog. . . ." The oxymoronic "base treasure" evokes the idea of the baser metals used to coin currency that could only become treasure by obsolescence. The phrase also draws out the baseness of James's action in creating worthless treasure. The bogs of Ireland, however, proved the opposite of a treasure in James's military effort, bogging him down, in effect: it was in Ireland, at the Battle of the Boyne, that William won military victory, and James, giving up his bid for England, was forced to flee to France. The bog also refers to parts of Ireland that were unpopular with colonial interests, land that was difficult to cultivate for agricultural purposes; its poverty guaranteed that it stayed mostly free of English control.[49]

Pairing the Stuart coin with Stephen's earlier association with the provenance of coins ("To Caesar what is Caesar's, to God what is God's") reveals the wider implications of Stephen's formulation. James's coins are inscribed with the desire to conquer, to be victorious and triumphant, referring back to the interests of the sovereign who coined them rather than to an economic system that might benefit by them. The coins are circulated primarily to authorize the sovereign they represent. The trick question to which Jesus replied with the rendering of Caesar's coin back to him was designed to catch the religious leader between allegiance to the Jewish temple (to which the coins might have been tithed) and the Roman Empire under whose authority they were minted. Jesus's seemingly naïve response bypasses the dilemma and promises allegiance to neither authority. To spend James's coins in the way Jesus spends Caesar's coin might subvert their relation to sovereign authority. But even the resistance to imperial rule provided by Jesus's model is made problematic when the church is suggested as the second master in the inscription on James's coin. The coins, by their referential system, authorized by both Christ and James II, must be rendered both to the King and to the Church. Ireland is caught in between, just as Stephen is a servant to both masters.

Stephen's resistance to serving these two masters is informed in part by another Biblical text. In the context of discussing money with the Pharisees, Jesus says: "No servant can serve two masters; for either he will hate the one, and love the other; or else he will hold to the one, and despise the other. You cannot serve God and money" (Luke 16:13). That money is allied with the imperial order Stephen is called upon to serve is made clear by the relation in language between the sovereign coin and the sovereign king or queen. Jesus suggests an alternative to serving Caesar or the Temple authorities when he advocates an unimpeded rendering unto God. But Stephen has not been able to formulate an unmediated relation to the Christian God, such as Jesus suggested, rather he finds the intervention of the Roman Catholic church precludes any unimpeded spiritual beliefs. When Cranly suggests that he might change religions in order to recoup his faith, Stephen replies cynically: "What kind of liberation would that be to forsake an absurdity which is logical and coherent and to embrace one which is illogical and incoherent?" (*P* 244). He envisions God as another imperial master and resists the idea of service to God and the particular privilege Jesus accords such service. Stephen's faith is mediated by an imperial order whose center is in Rome. The status of being a servant at all becomes a problem for Stephen as it has been for the Ireland that occasionally wants him "for odd jobs."

The ritual prayer that preoccupies Stephen's thoughts and the apostolic images that surround him in Deasy's study where he observes the Stuart coins further emphasize his understanding of Ireland's doubly servile situation:

As on the first day he bargained with me here. As it was in the beginning, is now. On the sideboard the tray of Stuart coins, base treasure of the bog: and ever shall be. And snug in their spooncase of purple plush, faded, the twelve apostles having preached to all the gentiles: world without end. (*U* 2:200–205)

The apostolic spoons emphasize the presence of Christian authority in the imperial equation, while the counterpoint quotation of the *Gloria Patri* recalls religious tribute. In full the prayer reads: "Glory be to the Father and to the Son and to the Holy Spirit, as it was in the beginning, is now, and ever shall be, world without end." While ritual prayer appears to provide an odd counterpoint to musings about money and various kinds of "financial settlement," if the passage is read according to the models for tribute provided by the Biblical precedent, the prayer can be seen as an ironic payment of tribute to the Roman Catholic church through ritual glorification. While Caesar coins the money that Jesus suggests be returned to him, the "holy Roman catholic and apostolic church" coined the phrases of ritual glorification that the servant Stephen returns to that imperial master. Stephen returns the phrases of the faith in the way that Jesus returns the coin to Caesar, without acknowledgment of the master's sovereignty. He resists the church by reducing the *Gloria Patri* to meaningless fragments at the same time that he observes the reduction of Christ's apostles to kitsch images on spoons.[50]

Stephen's English master is embodied when Deasy, the "West Briton," enters the study. In the ensuing conversation about paying Stephen's modest salary,[51] Deasy and Stephen exemplify differing approaches to sovereign authority. Stephen sees the coins with which he is paid as signs of the power that coins them; his response is an ironic resistance. Deasy, on the other hand, sees in the distribution of English coins a necessary adherence to the economic models provided by the empire. Giving Stephen a lecture on the importance of saving money, Deasy indicates that saving coins is an English virtue and invokes Shakespeare as an authoritative English source on money:

Money is power. When you have lived as long as I have. I know, I know. *If youth but knew.* But what does Shakespeare say? *Put but money in thy purse.*
– Iago, Stephen murmured. (*U* 2:237–240)

Stephen's correction is indicative. He notes Deasy's error in attributing this acquisitive sentiment to Shakespeare and identifies the statement as that of the arch-villain, Iago. His correction also creates a context for the passage within the play. "Purse" having been, in Elizabethan England, an idiomatic reference to female genitals, Iago in saying "Put but money in thy purse" refers not only to the possible seduction of Desdemona by Roderigo but to the means by which that seduction might be achieved. The idea of putting money in one's purse in this context, then, has everything to do with the brokerage of human beings through money (Stephen's reading) and very little to do with putting aside a little nest-egg (which is Deasy's claim). Stephen's reminder of Iago's swindle resonates with the brokering of human beings in Ireland under

English sovereignty.[52] Deasy's discourse works against the authority of his intentions. Stephen reads the meanings available in the school-master's error, indicating the ethical conflicts masked by Deasy's moral certainties.[53]

Joyce suggests the limits of this kind of moral certainty by noting the extent to which Deasy's epistemology is compatible with bigotry, with racism and misogyny. When Stephen places Deasy's reference in the context of Iago's ill-usage of Desdemona, he prepares a reader's resistant interpretation of the schoolmaster's misogynist habits of thought. Deasy attributes all worldly evil to women's influence, beginning with Adam's fall and continuing through the fall of Troy, Ireland's loss of sovereignty, and the ruin of Parnell:

A woman brought sin into the world. For a woman who was no better than she should be, Helen, the runaway wife of Menelaus, ten years the Greeks made war on Troy. A faithless wife first brought the strangers to our shore here, MacMurrough's wife and her leman, O'Rourke, prince of Breffni. A woman too brought Parnell low. (*U* 2:390–394)

This particular, misogynist version of myth and history is certainly not original to Deasy. The "citizen," expressing nearly opposite, nationalist sentiments, also blames Devorgilla (the "faithless wife" who "first brought the strangers to our shore") for Ireland's colonization.[54] At the same time that he blames women for the presence of strangers in Ireland, Deasy's sympathies throughout the episode clearly lie with those same strangers. His version of history is as clichéd as his rhetoric: when it is not women who are to blame for the corruption of modern life, it is Jews.[55]

Deasy is pictured at the end of the second episode, having pursued Stephen to recount an anti-Semitic joke, in the light of his clichéd coinage. "On his wise shoulders through the checkerwork of leaves the sun flung spangles, dancing coins" (*U* 2:448–449). The physical descrip-tion of Deasy spangled in coins of sunlight is twinned with his repugnant indictment of the Jews. The image recalls Deasy's theory that the Jews by denying Christ have "sinned against the light," to which Stephen replies "Who has not?" (*U* 2:361 & 373).[56] The opposition of light and dark at this culminating moment in the "Nestor" episode elucidates their conflicting moral views. The coins of sunlight on Deasy's body indicate his faith in British sovereign authority on which the sun never sets. The patches of darkness around them indicate, in conjunction with his com-ment on sinning against the light, his own sins of racial and gender hatred. But the mottling of his darkness with coins of light makes the image more ambiguous. It indicates the problems inherent in pairing qualities of light and darkness with their traditional metaphysical correlates of good and evil, introducing a more complex application of ethical thought.

In "Circe," Deasy is again portrayed covered in these changeable synechdochic coins:

GARRETT DEASY

(bolt upright, his nailscraped face plastered with postagestamps, brandishes his hockeystick, his blue eyes flashing in the prism of the chandelier as his mount lopes by at schooling gallop) *per vias rectas!*

> (A yoke of buckets leopards all over him and his rearing nag a torrent of mutton broth and dancing coins of carrots, barley, onions, turnips, potatoes.)
> (*U* 15:3986–3992)

In the fanciful language of the "Circe" episode, readers can see Deasy transformed into a physical representation of his various prejudices. Deasy rides a simultaneously submissive and truculent nag (she gallops at schooling pace and yet rears). He carries over his shoulders a yoke attached to buckets containing an agricultural stew comprised of the "coins" of Irish produce. In the disturbance, the produce comes to decorate his body like the coin-shaped spots on a leopard's coat, recalling the spangling of light and darkness at the end of "Nestor." The image draws on an association both to Deasy's faith in sovereign authority, and also to his position on foot-and-mouth disease and its relation to Irish agricultural economy. Deasy quotes his ancestor's, Sir John Blackwood's, motto, "*per vias rectas*" or "by straight roads," in another indication of the ways in which his moral rhetoric disguises more complex ethical dilemmas. Blackwood was offered a peerage in exchange for a pro-Union vote, which would transfer administration of Irish affairs to London. Blackwood refused and "died in the act of putting on his topboots in order to go to Dublin to vote against the Union."[57] His son, J. G. Blackwood, betrayed his father's intentions and was made Lord Dufferin for his Union vote. Deasy's imperial sympathies lead him on straight paths built on erroneous assumptions; Stephen's allegiances to Eire inspire his errant, detouring paths.

Deasy's object in meeting with Stephen extends beyond paying his salary and instructing him in virtue. He is also trying to use Stephen's connections to publish an article on foot-and-mouth disease. " – I don't mince words, do I?" he asks of the letter he would like Stephen to broker to the one of two Dublin newspapers, the *Evening Telegraph* or the *Irish Homestead*. "Foot and mouth disease," Stephen responds ironically by reading Deasy's prose out loud (*U* 2:331–332). The letter, or at least the parts of it Stephen skims, makes mincemeat of language; Deasy merely recirculates previously coined phrases: "Courteous offer a fair trial. Dictates of common sense. Allimportant question. In every sense of the word take the bull by the horns" (*U* 2:335–337). Deasy's empire-supportive rhetoric gains currency by justifying the kind of expansionism made emblematic in the Stuart coins. His interest in foot-and-mouth disease and the possibilities for preventing it are (though a bit anachronistic as there had been no outbreak of the disease in years) both economically privileged and imperial. He tells Stephen: "You will see at the next outbreak they will put an embargo on Irish cattle" (*U* 2:338–339). Preventing the disease would boost Ireland's agricultural industry but identifying the precise beneficiaries of that boost raises a more complex issue.

The Irish potato famines between 1841 and 1847 brought about two major changes in the country's agricultural economy. The first involved major reforms in the landlord-tenant relationship after the "Land War," whereby farmers would theoretically be able to buy the land they farmed as tenants. The second was the move from tillage or crop farming to cattle farming that brought larger net profits, required more land and less labor. The move to cattle farming created a new class of landowners, many of whom replaced old landlords broken by the Famine, and who had come in part at least from the indigenous Catholic and Gaelic families of Ireland. Some of these land "reforms" were created in 1860 by the Deasy Act, a law which regulated land tenancy in favor of large landholders.[58] The new agricultural economy created by these laws mirrored the old in that it maintained a gulf between land-owning farmer and landless laborer much like the former gap between landlord and tenant. The low demand for labor, additionally, forced landless families to emigrate to the cities or abroad.[59] Deasy's name indicates his allegiances with landed privilege. While it is somewhat simplistic to equate the struggle for land and cattle ownership with the traditional conflict between native and colonial settler, these are precisely the terms of the debate for many of the characters in *Ulysses*. Deasy's concern with foot-and-mouth disease gestures to his sympathies with the privileged classes, and also, in part, with colonial settlers of Irish land.[60]

Requesting that Stephen find a publisher for this letter, Deasy produces a "moral remainder"; his demand, the demand of an other to which Stephen is called to respond, is in direct conflict with Stephen's allegiances with those who would be wounded by Deasy's political views. Margaret Urban Walker notes that the term "moral remainder" indicates "some genuine moral demands that, because their fulfillment conflicted with other genuine moral demands, are 'left over' in episodes of moral choice, and yet are not nullified."[61] Stephen resolves this dilemma by producing another kind of remainder, tearing the remainder of Deasy's letter, the white space on which he has not written, to write a poem made up of a pastiche of Deasy's words (his rhetorical remainders) and Stephen's preoccupation with his obligation to and ambivalence about his mother (who in the poem appears as a vampire), provoked in part by his encounter with Sargent. He produces from Deasy's pages and his rhetoric a form of the gnomon discussed in chapter one. By tearing the rectangular page and writing on the remaining parallelogram, he indicates the incompleteness and insufficiency of the author's political rhetoric at the same time that he indicates his own dependence on and connection to that language. Neither subject is complete, neither in morality nor in rhetoric. In this critique, morality is envisioned as dangerously empty rhetoric, ethics is the revision of that language into the newly minted phrases of an intertextual poetry that questions the independence of the subject.

VI

While Stephen resists Deasy's imperialist propaganda in conversation, the headmaster's language emerges in his poem, composed in episode three. When Stephen leaves the Dalkey school he walks toward the center of the city along the shore of Dublin Bay. Gazing out to the sea initiates a series of multi-lingual connections, frequently repeated throughout the text, from the sea (*mer*) to the mother (*mère*): "Tides, myriadislanded, within her, blood not mine, *oinopa ponton*, a winedark sea. Behold the handmaid of the moon. In sleep the wet sign calls her hour, bids her rise. Bridebed, childbed, bed of death, ghostcandled. . . . He comes, pale vampire, through storm his eyes, his bat sails bloodying the sea, mouth to her mouth's kiss" (*U* 3:393–398). Joyce's prose follows Stephen's barely conscious association of the sea with his mother, the constrained course of her adult life, and his own haunted guilt about her death.

Evoking the mother in this context, Joyce provides another suggested explanation for Stephen's continued mourning. He experiences guilt over the conflict remaining between them at her death. But he is also unable to come into maturity as an ethical agent by recognizing his responsibility to others, not just to his weakened student and his bigoted boss but also to his peers and friends. That failure is predicated on his inability to recognize his first context, the ethical habitat provided by his mother. Rather, he feels compelled to reject her as Columbanus did, to turn away from her call. That rejection and its allied insistence on his sovereign autonomy, leave behind another moral remainder that expresses itself in mourning. Stephen feels obliged to or responsible for the conditions of his first habitat and at the same time worried that a return to that home in its dire conditions will drown him in familial alcoholism and poverty. This moral remainder is made most clear in his encounter with Dilly at the book seller in "Wandering Rocks."

– What are you doing here, Stephen?
  Dilly's high shoulders and shabby dress.
  Shut the book quick. Don't let see....
– What have you there? Stephen asked.
– I bought it from the other cart for a penny, Dilly said, laughing nervously. Is it any good?
  My eyes they say she has. Do others see me so? Quick, far and daring. Shadow of my mind.... She is drowning. Agenbite. Save her. Agenbite. All against us. She will drown me with her, eyes and hair. Lank coils of seaweed hair around me, my heart, my soul. Salt green death. (*U* 10:854–877)

Unable to recognize the degree of this ethical quandary, Stephen renders his mourning and his ambivalence in his poem, describing a vampire draining the blood from a woman's body in a violent kiss. The vampire image contains his recognition of May Dedalus's ethical responsibility in creating his first habitat, in the warm blood of her womb, and within their home recognizing his difference from her, fostering his intellectual and esthetic autonomy. The poem also registers his unkind response. The blood of her welcoming womb is transformed in his writing into the threat of blood drained from her body in the vampire's kiss.

Inspired to write his conflicted thoughts into poetry, Stephen searches his pockets for paper and finds his salary and Deasy's letter. "Paper. The banknotes, blast them. Old Deasy's letter. Here. Thanking you for the hospitality tear the blank end off" (*U* 3:404–405). Dismissing as useless the paper money in his pocket,[62] Stephen turns instead to Deasy's letter, repaying the schoolmaster in his own coin by parodoxically thanking him for the hospitality of this blank space as Deasy, in anticipation, thanks the newspaper for a spare column. However, Deasy's writing and the hospitality it affords affect Stephen's composition. His reflections on the sea and the mother, on the mouth, womb, and tomb, are filtered through his memory of Deasy's rhetoric: foot-and-mouth disease becomes "mouth to her mouth's kiss" (*U* 3:400) and then *"Mouth to my mouth"* (*U* 7:525).

A final version of the poem is recorded in the *Aeolus* episode when the newspaper editor notices the gnomon created on the page by Stephen's borrowing.

> *On swift sail flaming*
> *From storm and south*
> *He comes, pale vampire,*
> *Mouth to my mouth.*[63]
> (*U* 7:522–525)

Though the poem is conflicted and violent, it also may give voice to a victim, "mouth to *my* mouth." Unable to recognize his mother in life, Stephen begins to give her voice, albeit voicing his own preoccupations in relation to her, after her death. The poem does less to recognize May Dedalus's condition than did Joyce's letter to Nora Barnacle concerning his own mother's death. But it represents, perhaps, an emerging responsibility in this young poet.

Stephen's emerging ethic in *Portrait* and *Ulysses* is interpretive. It relies on locating the self in the space between subjectivities, on compassion, sympathy, and response. The figure for that compassion and sympathy in both texts is the figure of the mother, May Dedalus, who recognizes the difference of the child from her body and yet responds to and nurtures that child. Her love is described both as the only true thing and as the word known to all humans. In its universality, *amor matris* nonetheless conveys the provisional and interpretive facilities of ethical subjectivity which recognizes difference and is called to respond to that difference in its particular habitat or context.

CHAPTER THREE

Ethical opposition and fluid sensibility

> A river is not a woman.
>   Although the names it finds,
>   The history it makes
> And suffers –
>   The Viking blades beside it,
>   The muskets of Redcoats,
>   the flames of the Four Courts
> Blazing into it –
>   Are a sign. . . .
>
>   And in my late forties
> Past believing
>   Love will heal
>   What language fails to know
> And needs to say –
>   What the body means
>   I take this sign
> And I make this mark:
>   A woman in the doorway of her house.
>   A river in the city of her birth.
> The truth of a suffered life.
>   The mouth of it.
>   (Eavan Boland, "Anna Liffey")

In *Finnegans Wake,* Joyce amplifies the meditation on May Dedalus in *Ulysses*, presenting Anna Livia Plurabelle as an ethical agent, a figure (sometimes quite literally, as when she becomes a geometrical figure) through whom ethical relations might be understood and engaged. In suggesting this capacity, Joyce differs from a traditional and even patriarchal equation of maternity with moral rectitude, an equation exemplified in his time by the extremely conservative roles assigned to women as moral exemplars within the domestic sphere. ALP does not always act in accord with the standard moral codes of her culture or her

time. Rather, she presents in her own interactions and in the habitat she
provides for her children, an ethical understanding formed by her assumption that oppositional categories are interdependent though never
interchangeable.[1] ALP also figures the relations between the ethical and
the political, a relation that this chapter will particularly address.

I

As Julia Kristeva and Luce Irigaray have indicated (see my introduction),
and as Joyce also suggests in describing ALP's relations with her children,
subjectivity emerges in the relation of a child with the first context or habitat provided by the mother, the womb. That literal context and the relations of distinction, interaction, fecundity, dependence, and generosity
established there provide a model for ethical relations in broader contexts
that allow the subject to recognize both connection and differentiation
between self and others. Contrary to some versions of psychoanalytic
theory in which separation or individuation from the mother is requisite
for developing a mature subjectivity, Joyce's texts emphasize continuities
between subjects, imagined through the *metaphor* of the womb as a basis
for ethics.[2] ALP provides just such a habitat or ethical context for her
children, and in the *Wake* she is also the most prominent agent for engaging oppositions and presenting an ethical relation between self and
other.

ALP is often embodied as the river Liffey running through the city
of Dublin and out into the Irish Sea (though Joyce would agree with
what Boland asserts, that a "river is not a woman"). The city of Dublin
embodies a version of her husband, but as the banks of her river (flowing
through that city) are also a figure for her twin sons, Shem and Shaun,
who always represent oppositional categories: time and space, passion
and reason, fantasy and pragmatism, colonized and colonizer, and so
forth. ALP indicates, as I will suggest below, the extent to which the incommensurability of the twins' opposition is also an indication of their
interdependence; they form their identities by distinguishing self from
other and in doing so, become reliant on that other for a sense of self.[3]
Indicating the extent of their interdependence, ALP provides an ethical
model in which a recognition of difference is paired with an acknowledgment of responsibility.[4]

ALP embodies an ethical approach to interpretation both in the sense
that she finds meaning in texts, digging up the letter concerning her
husband's sin and interpreting its contents, and in the more literal sense
of placing between, mediating between her divisive sons, a role that Joyce

metaphorizes in the stream that flows between two opposing banks. With the metaphor of the stream, Joyce indicates the importance of fluidity in producing ethical interpretation. Her fluid rhetoric, as I will suggest below, upsets stable oppositions while at the same time preserving specific differences and indicating the contiguity of seemingly divisive positions. While the fluid properties of interpretation are presented as local and specific, concerning the relations between reader and text or between mother and sons, they also have wide implications in national and political spheres. The basic questions of opposition embodied in the river metaphor are also present in Joyce's exploration of Ireland's colonial history. Drawing connections from microcosm to macrocosm, Joyce indicates that the immediate ethical responsibility in an intimate act of interpretation may also constitute a public or political intervention.[5] Interpreting a text and governing a nation are not unrelated acts.

The artists of the Irish Revival made a similar case in the preceding generation.[6] To reclaim control of their nation they believed they had first to lay claim to its cultural productions.[7] In a context in which their culture was defined by British colonial influence as "other," as all that was deficient or reprehensible, they were determined to collect a cultural memory and produce a vital tradition that would redefine what it meant to be Irish. Joyce was able to see in this precedent the extent to which the Irish Revival was equally dependent on British colonial culture as another "other" against whom they could produce self-definition and a distinctive cultural identity. This dialectic of oscillating "othering" was as unavoidable as it was necessary. In his own work, Joyce indicates the necessity of having an other in conjunction with whom one becomes a self. As much as that other is necessary to one's sense of self, one is ethically responsible to that other.[8]

ALP's river language performs Joyce's ethics as it undoes the political and moral certainties upon which her sons base their identities. Her language is tidal, as is the river Liffey, ebbing and flowing, suggesting and contradicting, posing a possibility and entertaining equally its opposite. Behind this unsettling fluid prose is the suggestion of another intention in her language: to remind her sons of their ethical responsibility to one another, a responsibility that stems from their differences.

II

Emmanuel Levinas suggests an ethical potential in discourse at just this point in which language unsettles certainty with the alternative of responsibility. He describes this possibility in *Otherwise Than Being* in which he presents the idea of written or spoken language as the "Said" whose certainties are "knotted" by the ethical impulse of "Saying."[9] Levinas presents the *Saying* as the ethical impulse to respond to an other which can be manifested and at the same time undone in the specific thing *Said* which may reduce or "thematize" that ethical impulse. Saying is absorbed in the Said "to the extent of being forgotten in it" (*OTB* 37). He describes Saying as a "light" or "resonance" that can be identified in the Said. Saying exposes the subject to alterity and at the same time acknowledges responsibility to an other in a gesture that destabilizes the centrality of the self in deference to the other. In this sense, Saying is "Otherwise than Being." It is also the "'extraordinary everydayness' of my responsibility to and for others."[10] Levinas often said that his philosophy could be distilled into the simple utterance, "*Après vous, Monsieur,*" a banal statement that both reveals and conceals an ethical impulse to regard and respond to an other, to place that other before oneself (both in the sense of being *before* and *aware of* another and in the sense of giving precedence to the other).[11]

Levinas's example of the Saying implicit in the Said recalls for me another, perhaps more dramatic, example of this commonplace gesture of ethical responsibility and connection. In the Texas state prisons in Huntsville where many of the capital sentences handed down by the justice system are actually carried out, the guards have a practice described as the "tie down." Before a death-row prisoner is administered the lethal injection that will end his or her life, this prisoner is strapped to a medical gurney with bonds around the arms, legs, midsection, and head. Four volunteer guards are each assigned a set of bonds to secure; according to their own accounts the "tie down" has been refined to a virtual science, and the prisoner is secured within twenty or thirty seconds. But the guards remark that the most unsettling part of this entire disquieting procedure is that nearly every prisoner says "thank you" to the guards who have just tied the body down so this prisoner can be killed by the state. There is no irony in the commonplace politeness that may constitute this individual's last words. We might ascribe unbreakable habits of politeness to the prisoner unless we remember that these are often the most violent and uncivil of our country's citizens, men and women who have presumably committed more than one extremely violent crime, and spent many years in the unruly confines of the prison system. Perhaps they identify with the difficult assignment the guards take on in the "tie down," and signify their forgiveness with these last words. But it seems far more likely that Levinas's theory holds in this extreme example. It is the last gesture of the prisoner to make ethical contact, to meet the naked face of other in this final, banal utterance (Said) that contains the majestic Saying of ethical responsibility.

While the impulse may be to respond to an other, that response as manifested in language subordinates the ethical impulse to what Levinas theorizes as the totalizing tendency of language.[12] However, the skepticism of philosophical thought presents a constant interruption in the totalizing "Said" of language. In "Language and Proximity," Levinas ventures that not only philosophical language may interrupt the "thematizing" Said. He proposes that the first word in any interaction, the word in which one makes contact with or approaches a neighbor, is an act of Saying. Further, the ethical gesture involved in making such contact breaks up the tendency he locates in language to impose on or subsume the listener. Thus, "the saying in being said at every moment breaks the definition of what it says and breaks up the totality it includes" (*OTB* 126). Subsumed by the Said, the Saying at the same time interrupts these absolutes.

Levinas envisions that interruption through the metaphor of a knotted length of thread. The thread (Said) is interrupted by knots (Saying) which, though made by thread, are not solely comprised of that thread. Simon Critchley glosses the metaphor, commenting that Levinas's text puts into play the thread (ontological Said), a series of knots (the interruption of ethical Saying) and a hiatus (which falls outside the metaphor but which Critchley describes as the "interruption of interruption"). In that hiatus, the ethical, which is other to or outside of the ontological can nevertheless be "articulated through a certain repetition of ontological or logocentric language, a repetition that interrupts that language."[13] Levinas envisions text through a metaphor of "binding and unbinding which preserves the absolute priority of ethical obligation." (*ibid* 178). Critchley also observes that the "Saying reside[s] as a residue, or interruption, within the Said."[14]

Joyce's readers may understand Levinas's image of the knot by remembering Molly Bloom's monologue at the end of *Ulysses* in which Joyce echoes Penelope's weaving and unweaving of her shroud (to delay choosing a suitor to wed) with the knotting and unknotting of Molly's language.[15] ALP performs a more fluid version of this knotting of the ethical impulse of Saying into language or the Said.[16] More particularly, Joyce's punning rhetoric interrupts the Said, knotting each word with another word, interrupting the stability of logos with the impulse of ethics. As Stephen Heath observes, in *Finnegans Wake* the "writing ceaselessly violates . . . the principles of identity and non-contradiction"[17] setting aside "writing as a space of inscription of differences" (*ibid* 52). In its punning rhetoric, its resistance to the totality of *logos*, the *Wake* writes toward the other, an invitation to difference from the space of the subject.

Levinas denies that it is possible for art to interrupt the Said with Saying. "The cello *is* a cello in the sonority that vibrates in its strings and its wood, even if it is already reverting into notes, into identities that settle into their natural places. . . . Thus the essence of the cello, a modality of *essence*, is temporalized in the work" (*OTB* 41). Art cannot, then, access the Saying in the Said, it can only reflect back on the Said, illuminate the essence of the Said in each performance or reading. Eaglestone explains Levinas's criticism with reference to *Finnegans Wake* writing that "Joyce's use of language in *Finnegans Wake* serves to highlight its nature as language: words show themselves off. . . . These do not go beyond essence, but rather, they bring out or make clear essence."[18] Only *philosophical* or *scriptural* language can perform the interruption of the Said to reveal Saying.[19] However, as Eaglestone notes, literature like philosophy and scripture employs language as its medium. Why then would literary language not be capable of this interruption especially in that it is, often explicitly, addressed to and responsible to an other, the reader.

While denying the possibility of Saying in literature, many of Levinas's examples of Saying draw on the idea of poetry or from specific literary texts. For example, he writes: "That this signification of saying without the said would be the very signifyingness of signification, the one-for-the-other, is not a poverty of the saying received in exchange for the infinite richness of the said . . . in our books and our traditions, our sciences and our *poetry*, our religions and our conversations; it is not a barter of the duped. The caress of love, always the same, in the last accounting . . . is always different and overflows with exorbitance the songs, *poems* and admissions in which it is said in so many different ways and through so many themes, in which it apparently is forgotten" (*OTB* 184, emphasis added). If Saying can emerge as overflow and exorbitance in poetry, it must then be *of* that poetry, the interruption designed within the Said in which Saying may exceed *logos*. Levinas also cites as an example of ethical responsibility a passage from Dostoyevsky's *Brothers Karamazov*: "Each of us is guilty before everyone for everyone, and I more than the others . . ." (qtd in *OTB*, 146).

Joyce's texts perform the ethical exorbitance of the Saying in the Said in his punning, knotty, woven, and unwoven language. Undoing each certainty with the language of extended possibilities, Joyce gestures to his reader indicating both his dependence on our interpretation and his attendant responsibility to us and to his subjects.[20] Nowhere is this more eloquently presented than in ALP's river language in which she emphasizes ethical responsibility in the context of political, social, and philosophical differences.

III

ALP and her children are figured in the geography of the city of Dublin, bisected by the river Liffey which is imagined as a version of Anna Livia (the traditional, local name for the river). The river's flow is bounded on both sides by the warring riverbank brothers, Shem and Shaun, who enact the movements of opposition and strife not only in the schoolroom but in the various historical, philosophical, and even geographical roles they temporarily embody. The river who is their mother and who flows between them, cannot bring their opposition into unity, nor does she erase their differences. Rather, difference is placed under erasure: it is scored through in its present condition only to underscore, to highlight and embrace, another logic of dissimilarity.[21]

To explore the relationship between doubles and oppositions, Joyce returned to his early interest in the heretic Bruno of Nola's theory of the coincidence of opposites.[22] While in his 1903 essay, "The Bruno Philosophy," he refutes Coleridge's version of Bruno, as a dualist who professes that: "Every power in nature or in spirit must evolve an opposite as the sole condition and means of its manifestation; and every opposition is, therefore, a tendency to reunion" (*CW* 134), by 1925 he seems to have abandoned that differentiation.[23] Bruno's philosophy, as Joyce was using it during the later stages of his career, unsettles a metaphysics of difference that depends on a preordained, hierarchical arrangement of oppositions such as body and spirit, passion and reason, feminine and masculine, colony and imperial center by pointing out the way differences coincide, and collapse into "indifference."[24] Joyce sets this version of Bruno's theory at the center of his text and illustrates it in multiple contexts that emerge from the central metaphor of the warring and yet mutually dependent brothers. Following Bruno, he notes a collapse of the double entities into an interdependence by embodying difference as a coincidence of opposites.

This version of Bruno's theory marks a radical shift from Joyce's earlier position, recorded in his essay on Bruno in which he criticizes Coleridge's interpretation. In 1903, he emphasized Bruno's mystical belief in the presence of divinity in the ordinary, the identity of the inconsequential and the infinitely great, an "enthusiasm for indifference." By the time he was composing *Finnegans Wake*, he had either accepted Coleridge's Bruno or employed this version as a helpful structuring device. He wrote to Harriet Shaw Weaver in 1925 presenting Bruno's theory as resting on the coincidence of opposites, a philosophy of reconciled differences. As Jean-Michel Rabaté indicates, at this later date Bruno's "monism can be seen as inverted dualism, as long as the preeminence of 'indifference' in the identity of contraries is asserted."[25]

At the beginning of her monologue, ALP explores difference and the coincidence of opposition when she describes her warring sons: "The sehm asnuh. Two bredder as doffered as nors in soun. When one of him sighs or one of him cries 'tis you all over" (*FW* 620.16–17). ALP describes two brothers as different as north and south, locked in opposition. This difference is placed under erasure by her correction in the next sentence; when one of them sighs or cries they remind her of HCE, of "you"; they are him "all over," unified in their shared similarity to another. She also expresses distinction between as the subtle difference between noise and sound ("nors in soun"). In this case, the difference depends upon the position of the perceiver, on the language an interpreter speaks. If that language is not Norse ("nors"), then the "soun" will be more likely to effect an interpreter as mere noise (nors) than as meaningful sound (soun).

The first sentence contains an anagram of the names ("sehm"-Shem, "asnuh"-Shaun) of the oppositional brothers. Phonetically, the first sentence also reads "the same as new." The brothers mark both oppositional positions and repetitions of the same position with the slight change of the new. In her next sentence, ALP illuminates the idea of the brothers as different sides of the riverbank; "bredder," which sounds like the English "brother," is spelled like the Norwegian word for riverbanks. The Norwegian element is confirmed at the end of the sentence with the emphasis on "nors" (Norse) elements. Similarly, in her phrase, "[w]hen one of him sighs or one of him cries," each brother has both a singular identity, "him," and a share in the combined entity formed by a reader's tendency to read "him" as "them" in this sentence ("When one of them sighs . . .").

The difference between the brothers is not only directional, north and south, but also qualitative. In Dutch, "nors" means surly while "soun" (written *zoen* in Dutch but pronounced "soun") means peace, reconciliation, and the kiss. But it is the same anew. It's not only "and" that is written between "nors" and "soun," the sound of the written "in" merges into the sound "and," allowing readers to interpret the word as a conjunction. The written word "in," however, also suggests that the elements of each can be located within the other. ALP describes two brothers: the surly in the peaceful, difference within the same anew. The rivalry of opposition is placed under erasure by ALP's ethical language in which difference converges on identity.[26] While opposition requires a well-defended subject position that can be encapsulated and transmitted in language, *Finnegans Wake* undermines the permanence of opposition by means of the rhetorical processes through which the two brothers are described.

Walking along the edge of the Irish Sea on Sandymount Strand, Stephen Dedalus reflects on the relation between the water's movements and language: "These heavy sands are language tide and wind have silted here" (*U*3:288–289). In "Proteus," Stephen envisions language as a heavy sediment whose surface is disturbed by the implacable and constantly changing influences of water and wind. While in this episode of *Ulysses*, Joyce suggests that language is a solid though alterable element, in *Finnegans Wake* language emerges in a constant, liquid state of flux. Joyce's last book records the tracings of water on land, the interaction of ALP and HCE, in a protean language aptly represented by the babbling flow of the river Liffey's fluidities as they wash against the weighty sediments of two changeable shores. While Stephen thinks of writing as sand itself, *Finnegans Wake* is presented as the writing of water on sand. If this prose is not fluent, in the usual sense of the term, it is turbulently fluid with the currents of varied languages and idioms.

The fluidity of language in *Finnegans Wake* demands of its readers (and at the same time demonstrates the methods of) a fluidity of perception, interpretation, and understanding.[27] Fluidity is also Joyce's sign for the ethical negotiation of difference between nations in a colonial situation, between siblings in a family, and between genders in a marriage. The necessary adoption of fluid perception trains Joyce's readers in an alternative, ethical mode of understanding opposition.

The river's physical appearance touches on opposition in order to destabilize it. Moving against opposite banks, the river enacts the principles of Bruno's theory as it draws by erosion the properties of the one into the other and makes one possible only by the existence of the other. Building on that first step, the river's currents pick up speed in the middle, altering the inflexibilities of binary forces with the playful complexities of currents in the stream. The river is the image through which Joyce critiques a history of dualist philosophy and begins to perform at its limit another approach that flows from the properties of fluid mechanics. Joyce's critique addresses dualism as a philosophy that made possible, by a metaphysics of separation and a preordained, hierarchical arrangement of difference, the dominant ideology of colonialism. Joyce's intervention into this philosophy, with his emphasis on the river's movement, responds not only to the thinking of Bruno, but also to a lengthy history of global imperial transactions.

Responding to the agonistic legacy of dualist theory, Joyce's introduction of fluid mechanics integrates the oscillating movement of fluids as a strategic model for negotiating the obstacles of opposition. In "Nightlessons" Joyce refers to Bruno's theory in which that oscillation is described through the metaphor of the river.

totum tute fluvii modo mundo fluere, eadem quae ex aggere fututa fuere iterum inter alveum fore futura, quodlibet sese ipsum per aliudpiam agnoscere contrarium, omnem demun amnem ripis rivalibus amplecti.[28] (*FW* 287.8–14)

Recognizing that, as Ferdinand de Saussure suggested, language arises out of an integrated system of differences, the dynamics of opposition in the model of the river erode both agonism and identity to introduce possibilities of integration. The rival banks are shown locked in a mutual dependence that wears away the positions both of rivals and of twins, of opposition and identity.

IV

Deleuze and Guattari also pursue the philosophical implications of the river metaphor, and develop their theory of "between-ness" by locating the negotiation of difference in the rapid currents *between* opposite river banks. They note that the middle, the location between oppositional properties or positions, need not be understood as a compromise or an average. Rather, it might represent a heightening of intensity, or to draw on the river metaphor, a place where currents increase their speed. "*Between* things does not designate a localizable relation going from one thing to the other and back again, but a perpendicular direction, a transversal movement that sweeps one *and* the other away, a stream without beginning or end that undermines its banks and picks up speed in the middle."[29] Instead of locating opposition on the permanent river banks, Deleuze and Guattari locate difference within the impermanent movements of the stream. The differential movement of currents within the water represents a theoretical conception of opposition as a transient interaction of current differences.

Writing about the mechanics of flow, which she associates with women's writing, Luce Irigaray in *This Sex Which Is Not One* describes a writing whose process, she asserts, is at its crucial level metonymic. The metonym, which relies upon contiguity, enables a language of "touching upon," and creates writing enabled by a logic of relation and connection or contact: what lies next to or is a part of the whole. Irigaray's idea of metonymy suggests a revolutionary resolution of the conflicts between identity and difference.

In an essay on fluid mechanics, Irigaray lists the shared properties of metonymy and fluidity, suggesting the role those properties might play in the negotiation of difference. She notes that metonymy and fluid mechanics are both characterized by the "dynamics of the near" and by the connections or friction between entities that are proximate to each other. Comparing metonymic thinking to the mechanics of fluids she notes that both are "hardly definable as such" because they are "easily traversed by flow by virtue of its conductivity to currents coming from other fluids or exerting pressure through the walls of a solid . . ." In each case, there is difficulty in making a "distinction between the one and the other."[30] The physical properties of fluids provide Irigaray with a model for the possibilities of cohesion between the "one and the other." The conductivity of fluid undermines the solid distinctions between "unities." By flowing between, for example, the river mingles the solid materials of the banks and the stream and makes problematic the idea of their distinct and separate identities. In a fluid system, as in metonymy, differences are associated through proximity rather than separated by their distinctive properties, as is the case in metaphor. That proximity and association provide the context for ethical response.

Irigaray argues that interpreting the flow of women's writing has been perceived as difficult because most readers have been accustomed to "solid" models for interpretation. If a reader falls back on habitual methods and congeals fluid language or paralyzes it, crucial information is lost. *Finnegans Wake*, like the women's writing she discusses, makes this habitual interpretive process impossible; this writing demands a constant movement of perception between fluid and solid in order to achieve any recognition or understanding of the text.

The mechanics of the fluidity informing *Finnegans Wake*, like the mechanics of the river moving between its two banks, are in a constant process of negotiating opposites. The movement does not produce homogeneity, nor does it prefer one side of the opposition to the other. Rather, the river allows for internal frictions between its two banks of contradiction. At points the language, like a river, can bring pressure to bear on one side while leaving behind a residue at the other. Sometimes the flooding of water over the bank is later replaced by the resistance and containment of the shore. There is constant renegotiation between the fluidity of the stream and the solidity of the land that alters the banks by either erosion or accretion. This model for language becomes a conceptualization of the colonial politics of cultural difference that emerges in *Finnegans Wake*. This image of the river interacting between and flowing through opposite concepts suggests another model for political history. In the context of the *Wake*'s exploration of Irish colonial history, the colonizer and colonist, England and Ireland, are figured as opposite sides of the river and the river's movement in between the two constantly destabilizes that opposition.

In contrast to the combined fluid and solid mechanics defined here, traditional methods of composing and reading text might be said to obey only the laws of solid mechanics. Based on a model of extraction, solid mechanics depend on orthodox and utilitarian connections between code and significance which narrow the gap in perception between expectation and gratification. The fluid associations in *Finnegans Wake* erode solid interpretive connections and disrupt a reader's habitual procedures for deriving significance.

The interaction of fluid and solid mechanics is evident in ALP's "languo of flows," (*FW* 621.22), the *Wake*'s version of the "language of flowers." This phrase describes the fluid writing style in ALP's letter in which she defends her husband, Humphrey Chimpden Earwicker (or HCE) against vague charges that he has been a sexual miscreant. The "languo of flows" recalls the codified language of flowers in which each bloom carries a burden of traditional meanings. ALP's language is an ethical version of the language of flowers. Rather than engaging in a codified language of courtship in which one partner tries to obtain the other, she writes in the language of defense in which she tries to describe her own experience of someone who has injured her, while at the same time defending him and reflecting on his position as viable and deserving of understanding. The important distinction and simultaneous comparison between ALP's language and the language of flowers can be better understood in conjunction with the latter as it is described in *Ulysses*. In this earlier text, Leopold Bloom receives a pressed yellow flower enclosed in his correspondence from Martha Clifford. He remarks on the heavy stylization both in her letter and in the language of flowers which relies on the stable or solid connection between bloom and sentiment:

He tore the flower gravely from its pinhold smelt its almost no smell and placed it in his heart pocket. Language of flowers. . . . Angry tulips with you darling manflower punish your cactus if you don't please poor forgetmenot how I long violets to dear roses when we soon anemone meet all naughty nightstalk wife Martha's perfume. (*U* 5:260–266)

Bloom's mischievous interpretation of Martha Clifford's words plays on the language of flowers, indicating the solid interpretative connection between each bloom and its corresponding sentiment. And also indicating the clichéd and prescriptive roles implied by that language for the relations between men and women. Martha attempts to entice Bloom by othering him; she emphasizes the differences between them and grants herself added moral virtue in contrast to his sexual lapses. By punishing him for transgressions of virtue, she can covertly experience the sexuality she both desires and fears. ALP's ethical language of response admits the proximity of her desires to those of her husband, even when he has betrayed and hurt her, even when his actions make him seem as different from her as it is possible to be. Writing fluidly, she acknowledges the proximity between the one and its other, rather than relying on distinctions to solidify and license her own, manufactured identity. The languor of flows in ALP's monologue responds to the language of flowers to enact its own, different method of engaging perception. The "languo of flows" disrupts received codes with the "undecidable" gesture of water's language. It is a writing in a constant state of flux that cannot be held in one stable signifying position before it flows into another.

ALP's "languo" or languid and woeful language of the river bed re-calls Molly Bloom's languid language of the marital bed, which moves with fluidity from the flows of the body outward into flows of associative thought. Molly makes explicit the relations between the body and her language: in the narrative events that inspire thoughts, her associations move from the flows of her body, micturation and menstruation, through various admirers, her children, her husband, and so forth. ALP's writing works similarly, reminding readers of Molly's flows in her river language. Despite this association, however, ALP's language is in a certain sense non-representational. Her language moves out into the landscape, her body becomes the river itself and the "languo of flows" becomes less abstract, more immediate to the body of the river and the babbling, flowing sounds it makes. ALP embodies the principle of the "languo of flows" in herself, in her fluid body.

Fluidity, as I have already noted, takes up the space between the dual elements figured as the brother river banks and conditions the multiplicity of their interactions. Fluidity invites a more flexible and responsive perceptual system through which we can read Joyce's extraordinary language. Joyce's writing in *Finnegans Wake* demands an altered process of interpretation that is compatible with the workings of fluidity: interpretation that allows for selective intrusions of understanding without collapsing into solidified habits of extraction. The fluid disorganization of the text redefines signification as that which generates possibilities of meaning as it touches upon and interacts with a reader's boundaries of knowledge and experience. A reader, following the interaction between fluid and solid in the river, resists the flow at certain passages, jutting into the stream attention to her own questions; at other times, a reader gives in to the flow and allows for erosion that language enacts upon the reader's expectations and prior understanding.

Joyce's composition relied not only on fluidity of perception but also on practices of exchange. He composed by adding on to early drafts the connections arrived at both from outside sources (in history or geography, for instance) and from internal ones in his own unconscious, which constantly exposed submerged patterns of association (see chapter four for a more detailed discussion of Joyce's compositional practices). To interpret this permeable text thus demands not just comprehension but exchange, not consumption but response, in other words, an ethical interpretation.

V

At the end of the "Ricorso," adulterated marriage is engaged on a number of different levels. ALP reflects in her monologue upon her marriage to HCE in a language that is constantly fluctuating; each of her conclusions about that relationship is grafted onto its own contradiction or exception. At the same time (and there has been much discussion of this issue) there is a marriage of voices, of ALP's meditation as mediated by the dreamer's imagination (if such a dreamer exists in the text) and reflecting back on himself.[31] The mingling of elements and voices in this concluding section makes it difficult to assign singular authorship within the text to any of its characters. There has been much argument, for instance, about whether this monologue is spoken by ALP or merely projected onto her by the dreamer's imagination. This complication in voice and attribute makes it easier for me to make the following point: because ALP is figured as the fluid river Liffey throughout the text and HCE as the solid land of Dublin, the monologue has as one of its major foci the effect of fluid elements on a solid landscape and the implications of that effect.

The idea of the river Liffey winds through ALP's inscription of herself as she signs her letter in defense of HCE: "Alma Luvia, Pollabella." (*FW* 619.16). The names she chooses for herself and which Shem transcribes for her mark her connection to the river. The "Polla" embedded in her surname refers in Italian to a spring of water; the source of both the river and author is represented as the spring from which water emerges. The source of fluidity is the fall of tears. Polla is written over her family name, Plurabelle, written over *pleur*, the fall of tears, or crying, the wail that will form her final monologue. The "Luvia" in "Alma Luvia" approximates the Latin *diluvium*, a deluge of water.

Describing both the composition of her letter in defense of her husband and the life she has chosen for herself with him, ALP defines the production of her writing and the production of her life in accordance with the flow of her river water: "On limpidy marge I've made me hoom" (*FW* 624.15). Or to express this condensed sentence more protractedly, the monologue is extracted from the lipid fats that float in the stream between limpid margins. ALP's discourse stands outside the "mainstream" to express the thoughts both of excess and of the excluded. The imagination of the margin is in excess of habitual assumptions and marks the limit space of thought and language. The margins of the river are its banks, and the stream of discourse as it passes along its own margins brings with it the erosion of other influences.

"Limpidy" recalls the limpid quality of ALP's prose. The word, associated with lymph, with the clear fluids of the body, in this case pertains to the clarity of ALP's stream. Joyce connects the image of the clear water with our understanding of limpid as a descriptive term for a clear and fluid literary or oratorical style. There is, however, a warning embedded in this limpid language. For the Liffey, as we know, is not such a clear stream; even outside of the city of Dublin the water is muddied or soiled by its margins, and within the city its filthy waters are far from limpid. Assumptions about ALP's limpid prose are complicated by the physical metaphor through which she transmits her ideas.

The "limpidy marge" also suggests (when paired with "marge" or margarine) the lipids in the human body. Lipids are a kind of fat, generally insoluble in water, which float in the bloodstream. The image of the lipid locates ALP's prose at the juncture between fluid and solid where they interact and yet are incommensurate with each other. The lipid also accentuates ALP's emphasis on marginal or excessive elements; lipids can become excessive in a corpulent body, and indicate at the same time an excessive element within the bloodstream. The lipids are paired with marge, suggestive of fatty margarine, excess or abundance. This fat metaphor engages ALP's body in her elderly years but it also indicates excess, a flowing over of the text into the margin as well as an erosion of the marginal into the text; lipid elements flow into the stream but cannot be dissolved by it; they maintain their autonomy. The emphasis in this limpid, lipid, marginal, margarine prose will be on the superfluous, on the fat that seems to cry out for trimming, but in this case makes up the corpulent and beautiful body of the text.

Suzette Henke has suggested that ALP is concerned about the growing corpulence of her limpid body and interprets ALP's complaint: "*I badly want a brandnew bankside, bedamp and I do, and a plumper at that!*" (*FW* 201.5–6) as a plea of insecurity about her body. "Characteristically projecting HCE's lack of sexual interest onto her own fading charms, Anna feels the need of a corset or girdle to contain her overflowing riverrun."[32] The language of the passage might also indicate ALP's own desire for growing abundance, excess, and corpulence. There are several cues to the reader that the river at this point is near or in the city of Dublin: ALP's age has increased, the city-dwelling washerwomen clean their laundry in this part of the river. But more clearly ALP tells us this herself as she feels "*the gay aire of my salt troublin bay and the race of the saywint up me ambushure*" (*FW* 201.19–20). Her water becomes salty as she moves toward Dublin Bay and feels the movement of the sea wind against the shores of her river mouth or embouchure. As the river Liffey moves into the city of Dublin it is hemmed in by concrete embankments which girdle and corset the flow of the stream, uncompromisingly shaping the water's physical design. Here ALP cries out for a "*a brandnew bankside*," one that can be "*bedamped*" by her influence, one that is "*plumper*," allowing for her limpid, lipid, liminal flow. When her wish is fulfilled, it is by the emergence of the river into the unbounded salt waters of the Irish Sea. ALP's recognition of excess, her engagement with her own margins, also recognizes her proximity to and even interdependence with others, her husband and son who are embodied as her riverbanks. The figure of excess, then, also models an ethics of proximity and response.

The geography of the river Liffey is a constant presence in Joyce's narrative. Like most other rivers that flow through major cities, the Liffey is hemmed in by concrete embankments on either side. The immobility of the river's banks in the city of Dublin seems to provide a physical refutation of any argument concerning the revolutionary action of fluids upon solids; the erosion or accretion that can occur in the interaction between concrete and water is minimal. In fact, the purpose of the concrete embankments within the city is to prevent this mutable interaction between fluid and solid. If this is the river that ran through the author's imagination when he wrote ALP's words and designed her interactions with her sons (the banks of that river), how are we to understand the relations between fluid and solid explicated by the geographical image provided in the city of Dublin?

Stephen Conlin and John de Courcey, indicate, in *Anna Liffey: The River of Dublin*, that from 1600 "the Liffey has been progressively confined within quay walls, land reclamations and the great walls in the bay."[33] The year 1600 also marks an era of increasingly organized English control in Ireland. Roy F. Foster begins his indispensable history, *Modern Ireland*, with the year 1600, which he marks as a pivotal point in colonial rule. In that year, "[t]he last great Gaelic counter-attack under Hugh O'Neill, Earl of Tyrone, was challenging the imposition of Englishness."[34] By 1607, however, the defeated O'Neill was living in exile. The concrete embankments of the Liffey with their attendant dissolution of interaction, emphasis on conformity, and distortion of fluid lines provide a particularly potent image of the results of colonization.

The city of Dublin was the center of colonial power in Ireland under both the Vikings and the English. The river's straitened shores within the city illustrate the constraints of colonial rule, a rule that ossifies the line of difference between cultures making ethical response more difficult.[35] Under colonial influence, the oppositional organization of perception hardens difference into immutability. The traffic of thought is deployed between solidified, binary borders, like the river's dirty waters between their concrete shores.

But it is also at the colonial center, where the embankments are most concrete, that the river moves out into the Irish Sea and to a decrease in the influence and importance of its containing banks, to a concentration on flow and movement. It is precisely at the point at which the contrary structure of thought is organized most inflexibly and authoritatively that differentiating potentials begin to erode completely. The river flowing between its cement embankments through Dublin and out into the Irish Sea is a visual reminder that structures of rigid authority carry within them the potential for resistance and the means of self-destruction.

Elsewhere along the course of the river, however, the banks are more flexible; there are points outside the city of Dublin where the interaction between fluid and solid is more supple. While this interaction in thought is more obvious outside the boundaries of authoritative thinking, before ideas become concrete, the interaction continues even within authoritarian structures. Relying on a visual or geographical analogy, the river still erodes its banks even if they are made of stone; it is only that the pace slows to imperceptibility. Similarly, the relationship between the structure of contraries and the fluidity of Joyce's thought proceeds at different paces and with varying results. Recourse to solid or to fluid models of perception fluctuates, as does the geography of the river.

The geography of the river, like the body of the mother, is a sign of fluctuation, of mutation and variation; the Liffey provides a physical embodiment of the fundamental concept of change. Certainly the image of the river has traditionally provided the metaphor for a discussion of change in time conceived both as linear progress and as a cyclical recurrence of events. And, as is frequently the case, Joyce makes use of traditional associations while altering their significance. His use of the river as a metaphor for change or flexibility does not emphasize primarily the usual idea of a sequence of events. Rather, the river represents a theory of change as ethical, as a negotiation between immovable and oppositional extremes that works by alteration from within or between.

VI

The genre of rumor permeates the text with its concerns about the nature of HCE's original transgression and the contents of ALP's "mamafesta" in his defense. In the eighth chapter, known as "Anna Livia Plurabelle," two women stand on opposite banks of the river Liffey and wash out their dirty linens in public. This physical enactment of the cliché for gossip motivates the language of rumor that accompanies their work. Inspired by the babble of the river, the women gossip about the river, about Anna Livia Plurabelle. "O / tell me all about / Anna Livia! I want to hear all / about Anna Livia" (*FW* 196.1–4). The form of their discussion is influenced by the river's movement, not just because they are babbling, but also because, as rumor, their talk moves in a fluid relationship with ALP's history. Though we generally assume when hearing a rumor that it has some legitimate originating source, in some ways rumor has its source at each utterance; it circulates and is distorted with each iteration. Gossip moves in the fluid space between truth and lying and, collapsing the space between the two, nonetheless opens up a new region for language which assumes simultaneously the negligibility and importance of truth and of solid understanding. Rumor moves in flux, traversing and yet escaping the claims of legitimacy and authority.[36] The babble of the laundresses makes particularly lucid the fluid mechanics which engineer the writing of this chapter. Their situation on the banks of the river signifies fluidity; their conversation is larded by constant references to rivers (in the passage that follows, to the rivers Bann, Duck, Drake Creek, Line and May).

Early in the chapter, one of the women asks the other about the propriety of the marriage between HCE and ALP. Her question, which in its phrasing indicates a previous source of rumored knowledge, is responded to by the other washerwoman from the liquid space between information and fantasy.

Was her banns never loosened in Adam and Eve's or were him and her but captain spliced? For mine duck I thee drake. And by my wildgaze I thee gander. Flowey and Mount on the brink of time makes wishes and fears for a happy isthmass. She can show all her lines, with love, license to play. And if they don't remarry that hook and eye may. (*FW* 197.11–17)

The first question solicits information concerning whether HCE and ALP's banns were ever licensed (or sanctioned) by the Catholic church (Adam and Eve's being a church in Dublin) or if their coupling is illicit, a sin like the original coupling between Adam and Eve. But the interlocutor also seems to ask whether their matrimonial bonds were loosened or disengaged.

This doubleness of attachment and sundering is condensed even in the idea of the bann. The bann is a public announcement of engagement which permits the legal marriage of a couple in the Catholic church. The word derives, however, from "ban," a prohibition or interdict. The gossip's question suggests the possibility that the couple were spliced (slang for marriage) aboard ship, by a captain, in an Anglican or secular ceremony (the lines that follow sound like the Anglican marriage ceremony). But this splicing indicates an adulterous opening in the marriage. A ship-board marriage would not constitute a proper Catholic bond in the washerwomen's eyes and would not then carry with it the idea of banning, of a prohibition on other attachments. Rather, the marriage is a splicing, an activity which literally involves the necessity of unraveling in order to bring together.[37]

The flow-er and the mountain (whose juxtaposition recalls the engagement between Molly and Leopold Bloom contracted amidst the rhododendron on Howth Hill) are pictured on the brink, at a transition place. The word brink is of Scandinavian origin and in Danish means an edge. The edge where the couple meets is in the reproduction of Issie on Christmas, a feast celebrating birth. But they are also pictured as an isthmus, perhaps the isthmus at Sutton (near Howth), where a narrow neck of land joins two bodies of land and separates two bodies of water. The description of their marriage, like the isthmus, is one of simultaneous separation and union.

This marriage in language is also one that subverts received meanings, coined phrases. The brink of eternity becomes the brink of time. The stock ending of Irish folk tales, an ending indicative of resolution, "And if they don't live happy that you and I may," is altered to indicate simultaneous rupture and congress, "And if they don't remarry that hook and eye may!" The laundress's answer replaces the initial issue of the legality of marriage with a question of its durability and places herself in a contingent relation to the coupling. She suggests herself as a possible replacement for ALP, if the original couple does not fit together perfectly, like a hook and eye. The adulteration and changeability in this marriage of opposites increases the couple's opportunities for flexibility and responsiveness. While their union may not be moral, according to the washwomen's orthodox standards, it is ethical in the terms Joyce establishes.

VII

Joyce explores colonial ideology through his metaphor of the differential interaction of the river with the land that borders it, and through the marriage of ALP and HCE. The reconfiguration of the issue of difference within the marital situation gives his readers complex access to understanding systems of difference and their ethical implications. Looking at the strategies for maintaining separation within the union of marriage, we find patterns of compromise and cohesion as well as betrayal and subversion of control. Joyce's treatment of the marriage between his central characters also incorporates much of the violence and coercion characteristic of a colonial system.

It is through the marriage of contrasts in the union of ALP and HCE that Joyce allows readers to see difference as not merely structurally oppositional and irresolvable. Marriage in *Finnegans Wake* is a fearsome, violent, colonizing exchange; but it is also a transition into interdependence; it is presented both as pitched battle and as passionate love. ALP describes the ways in which invader and invaded exchange places; the masculine and the feminine become dependent on each other, and fear and joy are parts of the same emotional cues:

I was the pet of everyone then. A princeable girl. And you were the panty-mammy's Vulking Corsergoth. The invision of Indelond. And, by Thorror, you looked it! My lips went livid for from the joy of fear. Like almost now. (*FW* 626.26–30)

The structure of personal history is written over by Irish history and re-peated once again in her memory. She recounts the story of her seduction by HCE and his invasion of her body; at the same time, she illuminates a history of the seduction and colonization of Ireland by, successively, the Vikings and English.[38]

HCE, to whom she addresses herself, is both "pantymammy," a ver-sion of himself dressed in women's clothes, and "Vulking Corsergoth," the invading or penetrating hypermasculine "hero." But HCE only pantomimes these stereotyped roles; he is the "pantymammy's Vulking Corsergoth." Pantomime engages the dynamic of mimicry, approaching the object without actually taking up the place of the original.[39] Thus HCE's pantomime imitates both the ultra-masculine conqueror and the "feminized," conquered.[40] By touching on these oscillating possibilities, ALP's language recognizes each in the other. HCE is both a colonized Irishman and Thor ("by Thorror, you looked it!"), the god of the con-quering Norwegians.

The livid horror with which ALP contemplates her conquering hero beautifully encapsulates the conjunction through which the incommen-surable positions of different cultures are joined in colonization, just as different genders are joined in the act of seduction that she describes.[41] Dread is experienced on both sides and is a reaction engendered by the uncanny experience of absolute difference and absolute familiarity appearing simultaneously. In ALP's evocation, horror is double and interchangeable, for while we can imagine HCE, in his coarse Viking Visigoth guise, experiencing a horror of her native Irish difference, the words here define first ALP's horror at the violence of her conqueror, the assumption of his difference from her perhaps more peaceful ways. But the next sentence – "My lips went livid for from the joy of fear" – describes a simultaneity of horror and pleasure in her mutual recognition and abhorrence of HCE's colonizing strength. "By Thorror," says ALP, pantomiming the colonizing portrayal of such as herself and turning it back on the process of colonization itself. The projection of colonization doubles in her discourse as each member of the opposition is confronted with itself in the mirror of that opposition: "everything recognizes itself through something opposite."

The ambiguous negotiation of contradictions in this passage does not move in any singular direction – with the influence of English colonization on Ireland, for instance. Influences also move centripetally from the marginal colonized subject into the central power. "The invision of Indelond" refers, then, not only to the invasions of Ireland and India but also to the invasion of England by Irish and Indian visions. The "lond" in "Indelond" evokes both London and the entire country of England, the land east of Ireland. Invasion in this discourse is matched to envisioning, vision inward or imagination.

ALP describes not only opposites recognizing themselves in each other – invader and invaded, for example – but also colonial histories moving across seemingly huge differences to have similar visions. Ireland and India are woven together in the "invision of Indelond." ALP's "invision" arranges a palimpsest, inscribing a series of echoing subversions, betrayals, uprisings and suppressions over the received codes of colonial history.

"Like almost now," as ALP ends this particular memory. That "like" encapsulates her pantomime method throughout the passage. She creates through simile, a trope that carves out a certain distance or space between its objects, allowing one to touch upon the other like a river upon its banks without removing the identity of one in order to appropriate it into the image of the other. In each of her moments of simile, one object of discourse touches upon, approximates, or recognizes itself in the other ideas or images. But this overlapping does not allow for complete replacement.

The amalgamation of marital remembrances and political history superimposed together in ALP's words unleashes an association to a strong current in Joyce's theory of the colonization of Ireland. It is through the immediate domestic circumstance, and through the differential of gender within marriage, that Joyce is able to imagine and transmit a theory of colonization that clearly encounters and contemplates the mutuality and ambivalence of this experience. Joyce complicates our understanding of the lines of colonial history by restaging the terms of conquest in the situation of seduction, by understanding political power in the terms of marital negotiation.[42]

It is important to remember, however, that the particular marriage Joyce uses to make this suggestion, that of ALP and HCE, is an adulterous bond, a bond that is always changing, always other to itself.[43] We must not presume that these spousal positions will remain constant. ALP will not always represent a colonized and subjected Ireland, domesticated and domineered in her marriage. Nor will HCE always play the role of conquering invader and brutal husband. The roles that this adulterous couple enacts alter and change course.

Joyce recognizes that ossified, stereotypical readings of history become less true as they become more stable. If we are tempted to pair ALP with mother Ireland and HCE with the Viking Dane, if we position ALP always as the subject to HCE's violent colonization, we need only remember one of their first manifestations in the text. In the first chapter, the fable of the Prankqueen and Jarl Van Hoother changes the valences in the equation of colonization. ALP as a figure much like the pirate Grace O'Malley, "grace o'malice" (*FW* 21.21), and invades the land at Howth on the outskirts of Dublin, terrorizing the local lord and stealing his children. The fable concludes with the domestic scene in which the Prankquean settles into the Lord's home with his children and "they all drank free. For one man in his armour was a fat match always for any girls under shurts. And that was the first peace of illiterative porthery in all the flamend floody flatuous world" (*FW* 23.7–10). The relations of power are ambiguous in this concluding scene of the Prankquean episode. Though the pirate woman has been domesticated and "matched" by her mate, she is also a powerful ("fat" or fair) match for him though he wears "armour" (both armor and love) and she is only a girl "under shurts."[44]

The metaphors Joyce engages to render his theory of difference in gender and nation and the marriage of that difference are present also at the level of a single word, or rather in each single word in the text which embodies a coincidence of differences (national, linguistic, or conceptual). One of the most compelling examples of this conjoining of opposites in language occurs during an interruption in the children's guessing game in II.i. in a passage describing, among other things, the marriage of HCE to ALP, their bond is described as enduring "foriverever" (*FW* 242.30).[45] The sound of the word, babbling nonsense or the sound of water flowing over stones, draws attention to the disruptive potential of the river on the surrounding land, the flowing of the river ALP through the land of HCE. And the word "river" which glides through the middle of the word performs this disruption. "River" separates "forever" just as ALP's water flows between the two banks formed by her sons, Shem and Shaun, whose spatial configuration models the literal placement of "for" and "ever." But, just as the banks of the stream form one entity, the land, the father or HCE, so do these words recombine into one, "forever," which surrounds and contains the river like the more permanent land surrounding and containing the "impermanent waves" of water. "Foriverever" begins to signify a simultaneous marriage and divorce, disruption and connection between two differentiated elements, between "river" and "forever," between fluid and solid, water and land, ALP and HCE. The elements of the word merge and coalesce; at the sight of the overlapping "R" where the left bank and the stream meet to form "foriverever," there is an inextricable interdependence; the elements lean together in the muddy region where they share this "R."

The simultaneity of disruption and connection, divorce and marriage informs the passage which contains "foriverever" and describes ALP's flow:

Helpmeat too, contrasta toga, his fiery goosemother [fairy goodmother, mother goose, wild geese], laotsey taotsey [loa tze and the tao], woman who did, he tell princes of the age about. You sound on me, judges! Suppose we brisken up. Kings! Meet the Mem, Avenlith, all viviparous [vapor and birthing living young] out of couple of lizards. She just as fenny [funny, fanny, fen or marsh] as he is fulgar [vulgar]. How laat soever her latest still her sawlogs come up all standing. Psing a psalm of psexpeans, apocryphul of rhyme! His cheekmole of allaph *foriverever* her allinall and his Kuran never teachit her the be the owner of thyself. So she not swop her eckcot hjem [Danish: own home] for Howarden's Castle, Englandwales [HCE and Forster's *Howard's End*]. But be the alleance of iern [Latin: Ireland] on his flamen vestacoat, the fibule of broochbronze to his wintermantle of pointefox [chief priest, point of fact]. Who not knows she, the Madame Cooley-Couley, spawife to laird of manna, when first come into the pictures more as hundreads elskerelks' yahrds of annams call away, factory fresh and fiuming at the mouth, . . . he harboured her when feme sole, her zoravarn lhorde and givnergenral, and led her in antient consort ruhm and bound her durant coverture [law] so as she could not steal from him, oz her or damman, so as if ever she's beleaved by checkenbrooth death since both was parties to the feed it's Hetman MacCumhal foots the funeral. (*FW* 242.25–243.14, emphasis added)

Like Eve, companion to Adam, ALP is awarded here to HCE as a "help meet for him" (Genesis 2:18). "Helpmeat too" is the river Liffey, joined to England in the Charter of Prince John under the name "Avenlith." In the context of Eve's creation, "Avenlith," the name under which ALP is married, suggests a conglomeration of female stereotypes which will be associated with her: betraying and dangerous Eve, rebellious Lilith who refused to lie beneath Adam, and the virgin mother of God, whom the faithful hail as "Ave Maria." In any of her guises ALP is bound in marriage "foriverever" because "his Kuran never teachit her the be the owner of thyself." The laws of holy scripture have not taught ALP the principles of divorce and she does not, therefore, know how to be the owner of herself. (At the time of Joyce's writing, as we know, divorce was not legal in Ireland.) The river is also unable to be the owner of itself as its waters have been trained into subservience by a history of colonial invasion, represented here by Aulaf Cuarn, the Scandinavian king of Dublin. Under Scandinavian rule and with the development of Dublin, the waters of the river were straightened from their crooked course with stone embankments that remain today. ALP is contained by HCE; she becomes "Madame Cooley-Couley" or the wife of Earwicker in the guise of Finn MacCool. She is also "spawife to laird of manna." HCE is lord of the manor, property owner, perhaps of the castle at Howth, in his guise as Jarl Van Hoother. He is also lord of Anna, of her Irish soul and name. She can no longer appear under her own identity; a colony of England, she goes by her married name, no longer Anna Liffey she is merely the "spawife." The justification for this loss is that HCE harbored her when she was alone giving him the right to be her English sovereign lord and governor general. But when HCE harbored her, ALP was also Eve, the only woman on earth; his generosity carries with it the heavy suggestion of opportunism. If ALP was a harbor, a woman who had left her husband, she remains also a harbor, a woman with separate property rights from her husband.

Perceiving the married and divorced word "foriverever" teaches us to understand Joyce's comment on the marriage of two cultures in colonization. We know already that marriage is never complete; in spite of the inextricability of the union, we perceive, and perform in our act of perception, the incommensurable positions of two words, two bodies, two genders, and two cultures.

ALP may be subsumed as wife to the lord of the manor; yet, she emerges in her fluid form as Madame Cooley-Couley named with the French word that indicates her flow, "*couler*." She is spawife, a spa or mineral spring, marking the transformation of solid material into a fluid matrix. Her "fiuming at the mouth" invokes the Italian word for river; the fuming waters of the Liffey move away from solid land, past the harbor and out into the Irish sea.

The detachment within marriage is further demonstrated by the rise of the Avenlith "all viviparous out of couple of lizards"; her waters emerge vaporous on their crooked path from Chapel Izod through the city of Dublin, reasserting the habits of her pre-colonial flow. While her fluids move away from the land, separating from solid bodies, they also transform into a gaseous state, into vapor. The river transforms into fumes or steam where she is seen "fiuming at the mouth." The gaseous state is precarious, capable of explosion; the transformation of fluid elements into gaseous form in the fumes at the mouth of the river is associated with ALP's anger, her fuming, her foaming at the mouth.

In *Finnegans Wake* Joyce explores the complex interactions of difference and opposition as they are revealed in philosophical texts, in historical conflicts, and in sexual and familial dynamics. And he traces the relations between those systems of difference to indicate the causal connections between micrological and macrological processes. Exploring opposition, Joyce suggests the ethical responsibility of each subject to an other; he models the processes of ethical response through the figure of the mother and the properties of fluid perception and interaction she embodies. He suggests a variety of ethical reponses to political inequity based on a destabilization of both opposition and identity based on a recognition of the proximity or even interdependence of self and other.

CHAPTER FOUR

Ethical representation and Lucia's letters

He stopped. So did they all – hand glasses, tin cans, scraps of scullery glass, harness room glass, and heavily embossed silver mirrors – all stopped. And the audience saw themselves, not whole by any means, but at any rate sitting still. (Virginia Woolf[1])

I

On Monday, September 4, 1939, the day after England and France declared war on Germany, James Joyce wrote a letter to Lucie Noël Léon, who was his friend and the wife of his professional assistant, Paul Léon, asking her to visit his daughter, Lucia Joyce, a diagnosed schizophrenic who was isolated in a sanatorium at Ivry.[2] Joyce was extremely worried about the well-being of his beloved child. Concerned that the rapidly expanding war would soon overtake Lucia, he wrote to Mrs. Léon from La Baule in the French countryside, where he had retreated from Paris; and he expressed his fears that his troubled daughter was alone, in danger, and perhaps desperately afraid.

She is caught in a trap at Ivry. I was assured by Dr. Delmas at the Maison de Santé I could leave without the least anxiety, that he had made all the preparations here, that he had the big hotel edelweiss (70 rooms) to put his patients in, a fleet of cars to transport their staff and furnitures and the promised aid of government (who were requisitioning his Ivry establishment) to leave at once . . . He has made, I found out on Saturday, no arrangements whatsoever and has no means of transport available and cannot say what he will do or when. This after all my long planning that we should be near Lucia. We have been sent down here by Dr. Delmas on a wild goose chase while Lucia is alone and in danger and probably in terror in a city practically evacuated about to be if not already bombarded. And there is no place within hundreds of miles fit to receive her if I could even bring her here.[3]

The following Monday, he wrote again to Paris, this time to Paul Léon to tell him that Lucia had arrived in La Baule. His relief is palpable as he writes that she has arrived safely, that he has been able to see her for a short visit, and that her condition is good. He is preoccupied with finding a new *maison de santé* that would know how to respond to what Joyce describes as Lucia's impulsivity, where he could visit her often, and be with her should trouble from the political situation or from her own condition arise.[4]

Joyce's efforts to find Lucia a safe place to live where her condition could be treated were not completely satisfied, however; and in July of the following year he wrote to a former student and friend, Edmund Brauchbar,[5] "Ma Fille se trouve avec sa maison de santé près de S. Nazaire, donc en plein zone occupée sur la côte dangereuse – et cela malgré tout ce que j'avais essayé de faire d'avance pur assurer sa tranquillité."[6] The German occupation of France was rapidly advancing and Joyce was desperate to find a safe place for himself and his family to live. Given the cruelty of Nazi policies toward the mentally ill, finding a *maison de santé* for Lucia in neutral Switzerland was especially imperative. It was not until December 1940 that the Joyces were finally able to arrange entry into Switzerland for the rest of the family, but safe passage had not yet been obtained for Lucia. Joyce was never to see his daughter again. In January 1941 he died painfully of a perforated ulcer, still worried about Lucia, who was trapped in Nazi-occupied France, mentally ill, and holding an enemy passport.[7]

These letters from Joyce to the Léon family and Brauchbar present only the culmination of Joyce's difficulties surrounding Lucia's advancing schizophrenia.[8] During the 1930s, he first denied her increasingly severe mental disturbance and then worked tirelessly, and largely without success, to find a treatment for her condition. Joyce's letters to Paul Léon, placed under seal for fifty years following his death, illustrate in agonizing detail his daughter's declining mental health and his own emotional anguish over her condition. The letters vary in tone: some allow him to share confidences with his friend, to express his concerns; many are primarily strategic, to pay her hospital bills, to consult another expert. Carol Shloss points out a consistent pattern in the correspondence of his friends with each other and with him: Lucia "was considered a management problem."[9]

Joyce's extensive correspondence in the 1930s during the composition of his *Work in Progress*, as he called *Finnegans Wake* until shortly before its publication as a book, is reflected in the text's preoccupation with the exchange, interpretation, disposal, and rediscovery of letters. The *Wake* is littered with fragments in which characters write or dictate letters, or find the remains of discarded letters, piecing them together into new ideas. In the *Wake*, letters function to reveal a sin: their rediscovery discloses the trace of guilt and culpability. For example, as Shari Benstock notes, when "Issy learns to write letters . . . she retraces the father's sin, remembers an act in which she was a complicit witness; her writing is the return of the repressed, it is the 'trace' of desire. The sin is incest, the desire to make contact with the object of desire to bridge the gap between Self and Other."[10] The sin might also be described as emotional incest, the failure to recognize the difference between self and other in an over-identification that reduces the other to a version of the self. This habit of mind may result in appropriation within a relationship, rather than a willingness to face the other's difference in an act of sympathy.

Joyce's own letters during the same period serve a similar purpose, by revealing his culpable over-identification with his daughter. Though their apparent function is strategic, they also present another story, a story repeated in *Finnegans Wake.* Joyce's letters reveal a strong identification with his daughter (his attempt "to bridge the gap between Self and Other"), a preoccupation bordering on obsession with her disorder, and, most tragically, a fear of his own culpability in producing her schizophrenia.[11] Examining his conscience in the fear of revealing a sin, he worries that their family history of wandering (moving and changing homes frequently, changing languages and cultures) throughout Lucia's youth produced the wandering of her mind.[12] He also worries that her unusual thought processes might be a displaced and damaged version of his own artistry.

In his final work, Joyce records a vexed version of his identification with Lucia by presenting the complex and disturbing sexual dimension of Humphrey Chimpden Earwicker or HCE's relations with his daughter and her resultant dissociation and feelings of guilt and culpability. At the same time, he writes the story of the artistry he shared with his daughter, a commonality that was in many ways his salvation. Like Issy, whose letters serve to defend her father against shameful charges, Lucia was sympathetic with her father and expressed her identification both directly and in her imaginative creativity; her creativity helped Joyce to defend his own artistic project.

Perhaps, as Finn Fordham argues, Lucia's dance becomes a "metaphor for the book itself."[13] The dynamics of dance as modeled in the book both engage the reader to join in and then mock and sympathize with the reader's inadequacy, his or her difficulty in following the text's intricate steps (*ibid* 15). Fordham's description of the book as a kind of dance is comparable to my own understanding of the text's ethical engagement with readers which underscores difference and separation at the same time that it engages sympathy.

This chapter will trace the creation and composition of Issy in *Finnegans Wake* through Joyce's identification with Lucia, an identification he presents in figures of mirroring such as narcissism and inversion, and whose potentially damaging results he suggests in metaphors of incest. For Joyce, in relation to Lucia, identification can mean, on the one hand, a tendency to subsume the other person as a version of the self, to assume absolute similarity at the expense of individual difference. On the other hand, identification can also occur in the positive sense attributed to the term in psychoanalysis in which, for example, it indicates the process by which an infant recognizes his or her self as separate, with an *identity*, in relation to the mother. The infant understands the idea of a separate self and begins to define what that self is by a process of identification, by seeing his or her connection with the mother. Representing Lucia in his final work raised ethical questions for Joyce concerning the potential of characterization to usurp another, actual person's voice or self-definition, and also concerning the possible failure of that representation to acknowledge the gap or difference between the writer's concerns and desires and those of his subject.[14] Joyce's representational concerns were ethical in the sense in which I've defined ethics in the introduction to this book. In this sense, ethics defines one's responsibility to an other without what Levinas calls the "totalizing" impulse to subsume that other under the assumptions of the self. Levinas typifies representation as a form of violence that denies the alterity of the other. Rather the other exceeds any attempt to narrate, thematize, or describe. Joyce's own ethical practice is an attempt to acknowledge that excess within the work of representation.[15] Ethical representation cannot unambiguously endeavor to mirror or shadow one's own consciousness; rather, an ethical representation carefully delineates a sense of one's difference from an other while at the same time registering sympathy and responsiveness to the other, in other words, *partial* identification.

II

In *Finnegans Wake* Joyce innovates what Stephen Heath has called a "nonrepresentative representation," honoring the "propriety of difference" and its "difficulties."[16] Joyce resists the common, appropriative forms of representation that assume the truth of an other funneled through the assumptions of the self.[17]

Joyce's readers commonly presume that the writer drew on his own life experiences as the source material for his literature. Ellmann, for example, writes, "Joyce worried that he had no imagination, that his works were merely autobiographical."[18] Since Adaline Glasheen uncovered a connection in the *Wake* to Morton Prince's seminal study of multiple personality disorder in his *Dissociation of Personality*, a central emphasis in scholarship on Issy has been on her tendency to separate into double or multiple images, her multiple personalities, in effect.[19] But, while Issy is clearly based on Lucia, Issy's multiplicity should not be erroneously conflated with Lucia's schizophrenia, which is a distinct and separate disorder. Schizophrenia does not describe a splitting out into separate and discrete identities, as multiple personality does; rather, it describes a split between commonly perceived realities and the schizophrenic's emotional and intellectual responses. The association between Issy and Lucia might be located more accurately in questions of identification as a form of doubling, and in Lucia's strabismus, or slightly crossed eyes. Given his own eye troubles, Joyce was strongly sympathetic to Lucia's ocular disorder. In *Finnegans Wake* strabismus is imaginatively reconstructed as doubling in vision (double vision is one of the possible results of strabismus), both in the literal sense, in that Issy sees herself in doubles and multiples, and in the metaphoric sense, in which Joyce presents the artistic imagination as one capable of seeing in multiples.

Issy exhibits the splitting or dissociation of thought characteristic of schizophrenics but recuperated in *Finnegans Wake* as a privileged form of insight or understanding. Issy's footnotes in "Nightlessons," for example, often bear an odd or negligible relation to the textual fragments they appear to gloss. A more careful examination of many footnotes reveals the kind of loosely associative connection Joyce valued in artistic expression and credited as a particularly valuable form of knowledge. At the inception of the lessons, for example, the central text, which each of the three children glosses marginally, lists the nature of their school lessons as if they were points to be followed on a map or in a city: "Long Livius Lane [Livius: historian], mid Mezzofanti Mall [Mezzofanti: linguist], diagonising Lavatery Square [Laveter: physiognomist], up Tycho Brache Crescent, [Tycho Brahe: astronomer]" (*FW* 260.9–11).[20] Issy's gloss on Tycho Brahe seems unrelated and childishly or schizophrenically inappropriate: "Mater Mary Mercerycordial of the Dripping Nipples, milk's a queer arrangement." However, the astronomer Tycho Brahe triggers an association with the Milky Way which she filters through her own worries and curiosity about sexuality and childbirth, and transforms into mother's milk – the nursery cordial (the *Mater Misericordiae* or "Mater Mary Mercerycordial" was at one time the largest hospital in Dublin and is referred to also in the *Ulysses* episode devoted to childbirth, "Oxen of the Sun"). Issy is not alone in making such a connection, for each of the children associates intellectual with sexual forms of knowledge or curiosity throughout the aptly named "Nightlessons." Issy designates "Mater Mary" the patron saint of breastfeeding or nursing and also thinks about giving birth in a hospital attended by nurses (Mary Mercer founded both the Mercer Hospital and the Mater Misericordiae Hospital in Dublin). Issy displays childlike surprise and wonder at how the process of giving birth is a "queer arrangement" as is the milk-feeding of infants through the breast. Her unexpected association in this footnote, while initially dissociative, presents precisely the kind of reinvigoration of habitual connections that Joyce valued both in artistic expression and in his daughter's company.

Rather than emphasizing mental disability in his portrait of Issy, then, Joyce highlights her creativity, and reflects his own experience as a father in the relationship between HCE and Issy. The family representation in the *Wake* carries Joyce's paternal experiences of joy in his daughter's imagination and creativity,[21] his love for her, his concern that the strength of this love might border on emotional incest, and his guilt concerning her declining mental health. Joyce's presentation of Issy in this final text may be read as an attempt to memorialize or immortalize his own daughter (just as he commemorated his courtship with Nora Barnacle by setting *Ulysses*, his novel of marital love and its discontents, on the day his love affair with her began). But Issy's portrayal also carries Joyce's worry over the act of representation itself. Representing Issy, he explores ethical concerns about transforming a person, through representation, into a text. At the same time, he presents sympathy within the art of representation as a model for ethical relations. Writing about Issy, he attempts not to speak for another but to imagine the perspective of that other. To maintain this balance, Joyce must alternately retain and dissolve distance between his personal and his narrative perspective in order ethically to allow for multiple perspectives (or double vision) and multiple understanding within representation.

Joyce puns on the representational process (from the real or experiential into the fictional or narrative) throughout *Finnegans Wake* in the associative conversions of letters and litter into "littérature."[22] Joyce demands of his readers, in their turn, a self-conscious interpretive process, the analogous conversion of the fictional or representational into understanding, which raises questions about the ethics of interpretation, about how we piece together textual elements into patterns of meaning.

Interpreting Joyce's reflections on family relations in this final text, a genetic approach is particularly illuminating because of its "Joycean" insistence on texts as dynamic and because of the way it interweaves art and life; in a sense genetic criticism is textual biography. This critical approach follows the composition process from letters through drafts, manuscripts and page proofs; it is an interpretive process that requires, in this case, "prying into the family life of a great man" (*U* 9.181), an endeavor Joyce simultaneously promotes and criticizes in *Ulysses* (Russell offers this objection to Stephen's theories about *Hamlet*). *Finnegans Wake*'s provisional title, *Work in Progress*, suggests Joyce's interest in the process of writing, the composition and progression of a text. Following that interest, my method in this chapter will be to retrace the varying preoccupations revealed in the compositional process particularly as they circulate around the relationship between Lucia and Issy, investigating the artistry and the schizophrenia of the former, and the doubling and incest experienced by the latter.

David Hayman describes genetic criticism as the "profile of a creative moment,"[23] a scholarly practice that, by following the drafting process through notes and revisions, allows readers closer access to the procedures of textual creation.[24] In an essay co-authored with Michael Groden concerning the genetic method, Daniel Ferrar notes that this interpretive approach is consistent with the philosophical preoccupations of modernism itself, its resistance to teleology: "to postpone the closure inherent in the *written* text is representative of the Modern predilection for potentialities and processes over the finished work of art. The current practice of genetic criticism certainly develops from the same modernist or postmodern tendency. . . ."[25] Drawing on Umberto Eco's concept of the ideal reader, Jean-Michel Rabaté has described an "ideal genetic reader" as one who approaches the text with a "radical historicization of all possible interpretive strategies doubled with a no less historical material history of textual production."[26] There are many advantages to be gained by adopting this method for a study of the *Wake*. First, genetic criticism treats a literary work as inherently unstable, shifting and evolving. Rather than relying solely on the final printed version of a text and treating it as an inflexible, authoritative object, genetic criticism follows the process of manuscript production and reflects changes in approach, perception and understanding as the text evolves. Second, this method of interpretation or reception allows the reader to be responsive to the historical moment of the text's conception (by noting the time during which a word enters into the text, or the context in which another idea is deleted). This approach is especially well suited to the study of *Finnegans Wake* because Joyce's unusually lengthy compositional process means that the historical events, social circumstances, and family conditions to which he might have been responding in his fiction changed radically from the first draft to the final publication. Third, Joyce's particular, and perhaps obsessive, dedication to extensive revision allows the genetic critic to observe the evolution of an idea from first suggestion through alterations that increase nuance and contour in the final version.

The genetic method provides the tools through which a reader might attempt an ethical interpretation that would mirror Joyce's ethical representation. By following the shifts, adjustments, and reconsiderations recorded in his multiple revisions, a genetic reader might trace the difficult narrative of a father's love for his schizophrenic daughter and the painful opportunity that trouble presented Joyce, the author, in developing his narrative. The genetic method treats with respect Lucia's part in the creation of *Finnegans Wake*, while at the same time recognizing Issy's essential differences from Lucia; dissociating Issy in the split girl facing her mirror, Joyce was able to investigate the more vexed contours of relations between fathers and daughters and the ethical dilemmas those relations present.

Examining the text genetically and in relation to the context of its composition draws on the conventions of biographical criticism and can at its worst border on claims of intentionality. Though I am interested in the relation between Joyce's lived experience, his figuring of experience in the text, and the editorial or revision process the text undergoes, I hope to avoid the pitfalls of Wimsatt and Beardsley's "intentional fallacy." In examining the revision process, I am not arguing that these drafts give the reader privileged access to Joyce's aims. Rather, Joyce's process of continuous revision relies on a balance of chance and design. While he was invested in refinement (many of the changes he incorporates are certainly designed to achieve specific effects) he also took pleasure in the rough ideas that emerged from the chance assemblage of signs, as his continued emphasis on the discoveries made possible by error indicates.[27] The strongest example of Joyce's pleasure in the meaning derived from chance occurrences, and of the ways in which he incorporated those chances into his design, is provided in an anecdote Samuel Beckett shared with Richard Ellmann for his biography. Occasionally, Joyce dictated sections of his *Work in Progress* to Beckett, "though dictation did not work very well for him."[28] During one of these working sessions, there was a knock on the door which Beckett did not hear. Joyce called to the visitor, "Come in," and Beckett, misunderstanding, introduced the phrase into his dictation. When he read back the section Joyce queried this phrase and Beckett insisted that he had dictated it. Almost immediately, Joyce recalled the knock at the door and his own words; he asked Beckett to retain the error in the draft. "He was quite willing to accept coincidence as his collaborator" (*ibid* 649). A reader's interpretation of some changes Joyce made may align with his intentions, conscious or unconscious. Other effects achieved by revision arise by chance. A reader can hardly discern between the two, but might rather note patterns that emerge through the competing structures of chance and design.

I do not intend to give primary emphasis to the manuscripts through which Joyce composed his books, but rather to the creative process those manuscripts reveal. While Joyce reveals his interest in manuscript itself in his thematic emphasis on illuminated manuscripts such as the Book of Kells, and in the collaborative project of Lucia's Chaucer lettrines, which are a modern revision of illuminated manuscript, manuscript was not his ultimate interest.[29] Unlike Emily Dickinson's poetry, for example, which Jerome McGann,[30] convincingly argues was composed for manuscript rather than for print, Joyce composed his works with the explicit goal of publication in print form. As unhappy as he often was with the error-ridden books that resulted, manuscript was for him primarily a tool toward print publication. My concentration on manuscript in this chapter is intended to emphasize the evolving compositional process and its relation to Joyce's historical or biographical situation in order to recover developing ideas that might be lost by examining the text only in its final form and in the context of the single year in which it came into print.

III

The instability inherent in the genetic method is compatible with Joyce's thematic emphasis on the schizoid as a literary figure that personifies mutability. When using the term "schizoid," I distinguish between a literary metaphor and the psychological condition, schizophrenia, while at the same time drawing on the example provided by mental illness. Gilles Deleuze and Felix Guattari present the idea of a schizo in *Anti-Oedipus* as an alternative to some of the more rigid and predictable psychological conditions (such as neurosis) and textual modes promoted, as they argue, by capitalism. Glossing the relationship between the schizo and language, literary critic Philip Kuberski describes a tendency, prevalent in schizophrenics but also characteristic of creativity, to unsettle or destabilize the commonly accepted "intersection of time and space, cause and effect, subject and object, signifier and signified." The schizophrenic's discourse disrupts or suspends "the categories of genius, madness, nonsense..."[31] For Kuberski as for Deleuze and Guattari, the play in language common to schizophrenics is also a marker of revolutionary tendencies in literary creativity.

The schizo is perhaps the most controversial of Deleuze and Guattari's various and overlapping models (which include nomads, smooth spaces, becoming-woman, rhizomes, and the body without organs) because it relies heavily on a debilitating emotional illness at the same time that it distinguishes textual or social schizophrenia from the clinical diagnosis. In an explicit diagram in *Anti-Oedipus*, the authors distinguish between the "Schizophrenic process of deterritorialization" and the "Schizophrenic as a clinical entity."[32] Confirming this distinction, Guattari, a practicing psychoanalyst who worked with schizophrenics in his clinical practice, admits to never having met a schizophrenic of the kind that he and Deleuze describe in their utopian text. Unlike the clinical schizophrenic whose choices are limited by the disorder, a revolutionary schizo explores a range of possibilities beyond the limits prescribed by the social world of which he or she is a subject.[33] While these schizos are revolutionary, they have qualities similar to those of the clinical schizophrenic, such as unusually associative thought processes and the creative adaptation of language (seen in the word salads created by clinical schizophrenics). In clinical schizophrenia, however, unusual associations tend to ossify into repetitious ticks. The revolutionary schizoid, conversely, embraces multiplicity and change, contingency and the unexpected.

Although Lucia Joyce was diagnosed with clinical schizophrenia, Joyce's representation of Issy in *Finnegans Wake* suggests that he understood her illness, at least in its early stages, in a way that more closely resembles Deleuze and Guattari's understanding of the revolutionary schizo. Her unusual thought patterns might have allowed her a broader range of imaginative or creative options as a painter, writer, dancer, and choreographer. Joyce viewed the oddities in her writing that preceded the deterioration in her behavior as versions of his own creative play in the language of *Ulysses* and *Finnegans Wake*. On September 3, 1933, for example, she wrote a letter to Frank Budgen that is primarily concerned with the literary business between Budgen and her father, specifically concerning Budgen's memoir. Her style in this letter might be read as playfully punning or as riddled with odd errors in spelling indicative of a problematic halt in intellectual development.

Keep a close hold on your american wrights. The Continental wrights he [James Joyce] believes he can arrange for you with the Albatross Press who have published him. . . . The frase of the latin mass which you could not read is on Ulysses page I. The old catholics Augustiner Kirche are a good example of a Mooks gone Gripes.[34]

In the remainder of this letter, Lucia writes very knowledgeably and in great detail about doctrinal splits between the Roman Catholic and Eastern Orthodox Churches and also between Catholicism and Protestantism. Her adept comments to Budgen indicate an unusually strong understanding of her father's book: she sees the doctrinal conflict between the Mookse and the Gripes and the ways in which their perceived differences can also be manifested in merged characteristics. The oddities in her spelling ("wrights," "frase") can be read, in the context of writing about *Finnegans Wake*, as punning commentary: "wright" carries within it the merging ideas of writing and legal rights, of holding onto the rights for something that Budgen had written. Lucia's fluency in a number of languages – part of this letter is written in German – might provide another explanation for her original spelling choices.

Joyce's representation of Issy as schizo has been interpreted as his narrative exploitation of Lucia's schizophrenia; the portmanteau language of the *Wake* has been read as influenced by the word salads and phantasmagoria common among schizophrenics.[35] Yet Joyce himself resisted this label for his daughter; he resisted even recognizing her trouble. When Carl Jung, who was consulting with her, indicated elements in her poetry that were common in schizophrenic writing, Joyce remembered Jung's earlier comment on *Ulysses*, and proposed that, like his writing, Lucia's was an anticipatory, innovative literature not yet commonly understood. Jung agreed that some of her language was like the portmanteau words in her father's work, but he noted that they lacked the intention of the punning language in *Ulysses*. Jung worried that "she and her father . . . were like two people going to the bottom of a river, one falling and the other diving."[36] In a letter to his patron Harriet Shaw Weaver as late in Lucia's illness as 1935, Joyce wrote, "I am in the minority of one in my opinion as everybody else apparently thinks she is crazy. She behaves like a fool very often but her mind is as clear and as unsparing as the lightning. She is a fantastic being speaking a curious abbreviated language of her own. I understand it or most of it" (*ibid* 376). The language of Joyce's letter reveals a slight weakening in his position. He notes for the first time her odd behavior (acting like a "fool") and the gaps in his understanding of her (he only comprehends "most" of her "curious abbreviated language").

While Joyce's representation of Issy does draw on his observation of Lucia's patterns of thought and understanding, that representation encompasses several facets of his relationship with his daughter, not only the mental illness she developed relatively late in her life. Perhaps most importantly it reflects Joyce's belief in Lucia's thought as a form of artistic creativity or vision. The representation also allows him to explore his strong sense of identification with Lucia and his concern that this identification between parent and child might be an unethical, appropriating form of narcissism.

In the period leading up to World War Two (the period in which Lucia's self-sufficiency began to deteriorate), understanding of schizophrenia was shifting from Emil Kraeplin's theory that schizophrenia was a disease of the frontal lobes of the brain, to a more psychoanalytic model in which schizophrenia was related to faulty child-rearing practices or a disturbed family situation.[37] Lucia was treated by Carl Jung among other psychiatric experts, and it is likely that Joyce was more often presented with the latter explanation, which may explain, in part, his resistance to the diagnosis.[38] Today, understanding of schizophrenia has shifted again largely as a result of successful pharmaceutical treatment; many current clinicians approach schizophrenia as a physiological illness rather than a response to trauma.[39] This contemporary model may, however, be slightly reductive. Despite many attempts to find exact organic or bodily sources for schizophrenia, it is still defined today, as it was at the beginning of the century, as a "syndrome or symptom and sign cluster, without associated organic lesion, defined by its clinical phenomenology and detected by mental status examination and anamnesis" (*ibid* 11). In other words, there are no specific physical or physiological signs (such as the damaged frontal lobes Kraeplin described) that reliably indicate schizophrenia in subjects under study. Indications of this disorder are generally clinical: observed as behavioral, emotional, or social disturbances. The fourth Diagnostic and Statistical Manual (or DSMIV) used by psychologists and psychiatrists in diagnosing mental illness confirms the loose association between psychical and physical abnormality in this condition. "No laboratory findings have been identified that are diagnostic of Schizophrenia. However, a variety of laboratory findings have been noted to be abnormal in groups of individuals with Schizophrenia relative to control subjects. . . . .Abnormal laboratory findings may also be noted as either a complication of Schizophrenia or of its treatment."[40] While some physical abnormalities have been detected among schizophrenics, then, those findings cannot be reliably linked to the disorder itself as opposed to complications arising from either the disorder or its treatment.

The shared clinical (as opposed to physiological) signs of schizophrenia cluster around dissociation or splitting. In 1911, Eugene Bleuler, who first named this syndrome schizophrenia or "split mind," wrote, "I have chosen the name schizophrenia because the 'splitting' of the different psychic functions is one of its most important characteristics."[41] Examples of this splitting of psychic functions include the dissociation of emotion from thought (so that a thought or understanding more habitually associated in non-schizophrenics with grief or sadness might be paired with indifference or hilarity by a schizophrenic),[42] disruption in trains of association, the simultaneous presence of contradictory emotions or thoughts, autism, and disturbance of activity or volition. Schizophrenia is an intensely verbal malady: its symptoms are often manifested in language. Bleuler describes the word salad of the schizophrenic as "entirely unintelligible even though it may be built up, in the main, of ordinary words. The utterly inconceivable combination, both as to grammar and content creates the impression of an unknown language."[43] The hallucinations associated with this condition in popular culture are only a secondary symptom of the wider condition.[44]

Schizophrenia typically manifests itself in late adolescence or early adult years though it may go unrecognized until an acute outbreak or crisis.[45] Successful drug treatments such as chlorpromazine have centered neuroscience research on dopamine transmission. Resulting hypotheses tend to confirm Bleuler's emphasis on splitting or non-integration in schizophrenia and have focused on disrupted intercommunication between parts of the mind.[46] The success of these drug treatments paired with the genetic hypothesis, which arises out of increased risk of getting the disease if a close relation has it, would tend to point toward a biological explanation for schizophrenia.[47] However, those biological factors are often paired with the experiential; schizophrenics "do not usually form adaptations to the traumatic infantile world."[48]

This schizoid shifting in language and the dissociation between event and emotional response are characteristic of the *Wake* in general and most specifically of Issy, who is represented as a cloud in part to indicate her changeability. The text's mutability reflects or mimics the changeability of Lucia's thinking and may express Joyce's artistic allegiance with her shifting thoughts. At the same time, the psychoanalytic explanation for Lucia's disorder as a sign of family disturbance is manifested in Joyce's anxious exploration of the love between father and daughter as a sin.

IV

Joyce dramatizes the power of a father's guilt by putting HCE on trial throughout the book. This thematic preoccupation is manifested on several occasions by four old men who examine and question HCE/Shaun. In *Finnegan's Wake*, section III.iii, as their interrogation progresses, the jury's questions increasingly coalesce around the culpable sexual desire felt by an older man for younger women. This theme is signaled in references to Swift's Stella and Vanessa ("Stilla Underwood and Moth [Vanessa is a genus of moth] MacGarry [*FW* 526.23–24]), whom Swift/Shaun/HCE prefers to older women (described unflatteringly as "rawkneepudsfrowse").[49] That this form of desire is a sin or error is indicated by the jurors' associations with the punishment God ordained for original sin, that humans wander the world banished from paradise.

– Naif Cruachan! Woe on woe, says Wardeb Daly. Woman will water [or wander] the wild world over. And the maid of folley will go where glory. Sure I thought it was larking in the trefoll of the furry glans with two stripping baremaids, Stilla Underwood and Moth MacGarry, he was, hand to dagger, that time and their mother a rawkneepudsfrowse, I was given to understand, with super-flowvius heirs, begum. There was that one that was always mad gone on him . . . (*FW* 526.20–27)

"Wardeb Daly"[50] discusses HCE's crime in the park: ignoring women his own age ("rawkneedpudsfrowse," or women reduced to a frowsy role of a house cleaner ["putzfrau" in German] with raw knees from kneeling and scrubbing) in favor of her young daughters. One of these daughters is "mad gone on him" (has gone mad on him). An initial interpretation of this phrase might suggest that the young woman is mad about this older man or father figure and that love between an older man and younger woman is associated with Lucia's madness. The punning allusion to Maud Gonne in "mad gone," however, presents other possibilities. Maud Gonne was notorious for her romantic indifference to W. B. Yeats in spite of his years of devotion, and their situation might echo that of the pair in this passage. HCE's love for the young women who are versions of Issy may not be returned in kind; she may not be mad for him, but rather as indifferent as Maud Gonne. As early as the composition of "No Second Troy," Yeats also expressed some misgivings about Gonne, whose violent nationalism began to seem a bit "mad" to him. Joyce's reference to Maud Gonne troubles the associations between romantic desire and madness with the possibilities of ambivalence and indifference.

The words "mad gone" are introduced in the first draft of this section (the third draft of the subsection as a whole . . . Archive 47482-b-89.53), probably composed in November or December 1924.[51] In this draft, the phrase reads: "I was given to understand there was a peck (?) of them mad gone on him." Two months later, the numbers are reduced to only one admirer; a fair copy of the manuscript reads "I was given to understand there was one that was mad gone on him." (47484-23-p.124); the singular is then retained in each revision and incorporated in the published form of the passage. The confusion of number between multiple and singular in the drafting process and in the movement from two barmaids to one "mad gone" is exemplary of Joyce's presentation of Issy as a figure of double or multiple entities in one. When the passage was drafted in 1924 before the onset of Lucia's illness, the confusion between singular and multiple may have referred to her visual problems rather than to her madness, or the splitting in her consciousness. Lucia's strabismus, apparent in photographs in which her eyes look slightly crossed, may have resulted in double vision, seeing overlapping double or multiple images of an object that is actually singular. Double vision is also one of Joyce's metaphors for the perspective of the artist. In *Ulysses* it is presented alternately as parallax and as metempsychosis; parallax is an alternative to the limitations of having only one eye or one idea, as the Cyclops does, metempsychosis or reincarnation allows for this doubling in time. The Janus-faced ambivalence of "static" or "proper" art in Stephen's esthetic theory (discussed in the introduction to this book) presents another example of the double vision that allows an artist or visionary to see multiple possibilities in each singular situation.

Lucia's double vision is often presented in *Finnegans Wake* in Issy's mirror reflection, which she contemplates repeatedly in the text. As the juror's testimony in III.iii continues, he describes Issy gazing at her reflection in the mirror. In this case, two-in-oneness is not equated with madness as multiple personality or dissociation. Rather the mirrored image suggests a complex combination of double vision, narcissism, incest, and inversion or homosexuality. Issy contemplates her reflection in the mirror, the combination between herself and her reflection suggesting double vision. Her appreciation of that image evokes Narcissus's love of his own reflection in a pool of water.[52] Issy's image in the mirror is inverted, as all reflections are, and offers Joyce the opportunity to explore inversion or homosexual love, which was, and sometimes still is, associated with narcissism.

> Sure she was near drowned in pondest coldstreams of admiration forherself, as bad as my Tarpeyan cousin, Vesta Tully, making faces at her bachspilled likeness in the brook after and cooling herself in the element. . . .
>   – O, add sheilsome bridelittle! All of her own! Nircississies are as the doaters of inversion. [Necessity is the mother of invention.] Secilas through their laughing classes becoming poolermates in laker life.
>   – It seems to same with Iscappellas? Ys? Gotellus! A tickey for tie taughts!
>   – Listenest, meme mearest! (*FW* 526.28–527.3)

Following the testimony in which Issy is implicated for her narcissism, Issy herself enters the text and begins a lengthy monologue or testimonial by asking the court (and her own reflection in the mirror) to "Listenest." Lost in admiration for her own beauty, Issy speaks to her image saying: "Listenest, meme mearest!" She speaks of herself (*meme* in French) or a double of herself (me/me) which is both diminished (mere, in the sense of only)[53] and dearest to her ("mearest"). Issy is depicted as a narcissist in this passage both through her love of her own image (her investment in beauty and her association with the reflective qualities of water are signaled in a reference to *Pond's* cold cream) and also because of her difficulty in distinguishing between self and other, a quality of thought seen in infant narcissism.

It was not until the period between 1933 and 1936, when Joyce revised the version of this episode published in *transition* 15, that he added the reference to Narcissus. The period of this revision coincides with the deepening of Lucia's difficulties and therefore narcissism might be associated not just with a young woman's appreciation of her beauty but with the psychoanalytic theory which describes an increasing inwardness and inability to define distinct borders between self and environment characteristic of schizophrenia.[54] Beginning his revisions between 1933 and 1934 and finally completing them in 1936, Joyce puns on the cliché, "necessity is the mother of invention," by adding in the margin: "Nircess/issies are the doaters of intension [struck through to replace with inversion]. Secilas through her laughing classes becoming poolermates in laker life" (archive 47486a-112). In the typescript that followed he alters the passage once more to emphasize the idea of Issy's doubling within the word for Narcissus: "Nir*cississ*ies are the doaters of inversion,

Secilas through their laughing classes becoming poolermates in laker life" (archive 47486a 174; emphasis added).

Perhaps the invention Issy necessarily produces is the persona she develops in adapting to her father's peculiar love: inverted, narcissistic, and detached. Gazing into a mirror, pond, lake, or stream, Issy is associated with the mythic figure Narcissus, lost in admiration of an image of herself. The idea of narcissism in this passage allows Joyce to examine the relationship between self and other. In its most positive manifestation, narcissism is a self-love that fosters both insight and empathy.[55] In less positive manifestations it becomes a hermetic self-absorption that seals the subject off from any contact with others or with a world outside the self. Drawing on Ovid's example, Joyce emphasizes an ethical reading of the Narcissus myth. He suggests that a certain amount of self-appreciation is healthy but to be ethical that appreciation must be paired with self-interrogation in relation to others. Adoration of one's image (whether the beauty is physical, as in the case of Narcissus, or familial, in the case of the Joyce family) can prompt the narcissist to question whether this appreciation is what others have felt, which in turn fosters the beginning of ethical sympathy. In the case of *Finnegans Wake* and its narcissistic representation of the Joyce family, the literary image worked in the same way as the reflection in Narcissus's pool; it inspired love and an ethical realization of both sympathy and differentiation from another.

V

In the Ovidian myth of Narcissus and Echo on which Joyce bases his observations, Echo has been condemned for her artistry in story-telling. Her patter distracts Juno on one of her periodic missions to discover the object of Jupiter's philandering. Angry with the distraction, Juno punishes the nymph by making her unable to speak unless it is to repeat another's words. (Repetition is a problem Issy and HCE share; his repetition takes the form of stuttering). Thus Echo is robbed of her narrative gift and of her eloquence. This punishment is particularly painful when Echo falls in love with Narcissus but cannot communicate her love; she can only repeat the end of the cruel phrases with which he dismisses her, often with ironic effect:

> He bolted, shouting "Keep your arms from me!
> Be off! I'll die before I yield to you."
> And all she answered was "I yield to you."[56]

Having her love shunned, Echo succumbs to grief; her body withers away and only her echoing voice remains. It is not only Echo but also many "Hill-nymphs and water-nymphs and many a man" (Ovid III.403) who are subjected to Narcissus's negligence, mockery, and scorn. In his pride, Narcissus neither needs nor wants another, he is sufficient to himself. But his rejection causes sufficient pain that one of the rejected youths curses him: "So may *he* love – and never win his love!" (Ovid III.406). Nemesis answers the curse with unusual originality by condemning Narcissus to love only his own reflected image which he comes across while drinking in a pool. He is tantalized by the image, desiring the reflection in the pond and yet unable to reach it:

> Himself he longs for, longs unwittingly,
> Praising is praised, desiring is desired,
> And love he kindles while with love he burns.
> How often in vain he kissed the cheating pool
> And in the water sank his arms to clasp
> The neck he saw, but could not clasp himself.
>   (Ovid III.425–450)

On one level, Narcissus's infatuation with the image in the pool, which eventually causes his death, indicates the danger of self-absorption, being unable to see outside the self to recognize another. However, the encounter in the pool might also be understood as the first occasion of recognizing the other. In Echo, Narcissus could enjoy another repetition of himself; her words reflected back an aural image of himself as complete and self-sufficient. Maurice Blanchot notes that Echo's language is "not the language when the Other would have approached him. . . ."[57] In condemning him, Nemesis exaggerates Narcissus's solitude: because he is unable to recognize himself, he does not have a basis for recognition of an other. It is not until he recognizes the image as a mirror reflection that he also recognizes the need for otherness; wishing his "love were not so near!" (Ovid III.469), he expresses desire for an other having recognized the other in and as himself. As Derrida notes in *Prégnances*, Narcissus suffers paradoxically from separation and from nonseparation; "the possibility of the experience of the other" is inaccessible to him.[58] Recognizing that the image he loves is himself (nonseparation), Narcissus expresses a desire for separation, for the possibility of loving an other as he himself has been loved by others. Seeing himself clearly and recognizing his own beauty allows Narcissus to understand better the pain he has inflicted on others and particularly on Echo.

The Greek myth serves as a backdrop against which Issy's self love is presented: she gazes with admiration at her reflection and refers to herself as "Nircississies." The myth also serves as a device through which Joyce explores his own complex ideas about representing Lucia as Issy in the text. As early as 1924 when he began to compose this section, Joyce evinces some concern that his love for his daughter is only a manifestation of narcissistic identification with her, an identification that threatens to usurp her independence and even her identity. This love might be a version of narcissism that reduces his daughter to an echo of his thought, just as Echo is reduced to repeating the thoughts of a self-involved Narcissus. Issy speaks her author's thoughts and her speech is often presented as an echo, a series of repetitions ("*meme me*arest", Narc*ississies*"). However, like Echo's, Issy's repetitions are selective. When Narcissus asks "Is anyone here?", Echo answers "here," establishing herself and her demand for recognition though condemned to use another's words. Ovid underscores her responsive capability in using the word "*responderat*" to name her reply: the nymph does not merely repeat, she responds. Echo is an ethical figure, and a particularly tragic one, because though condemned to repeat an other's words, she is nonetheless capable of response to that other, and her response is one that insists on her own presence as other. Drawing on Ovid's choice of the word "*responderat*," Anne-Emmanuelle Berger notes of Echo, "she who by herself can say nothing other, nevertheless 'says' *what she wants* to Narcissus, something like: *here* (adest): someone is here; this affirmation of presence, or more precisely of a 'being-beside,' refers undecidably to the one or the other, to one therefore to the other."[59] According to Berger, the inauguration of speech for both Narcissus and Echo is in their desire. "At the beginning of language is the desire of the other: the story of Narcissus and Echo is in this sense a tale of the constitution of the living-speaking subject as desiring subject. To speak is to hear the call of the other" (*ibid* 633). To speak, then, is to initiate desire as an ethical impulse toward the claims of the other.

Representing Issy, Joyce attempts to create an opportunity for Lucia's voice to resonate through the text, if only as a responsive echo of her father's consciousness. Joyce also contemplates the ethical opportunity inherent in his narcissistic identification with his daughter by this implicit comparison with the myth of Echo and Narcissus. In Issy's repetitions, Joyce uses the occasion of representation to find within narcissism the possibility of recognizing an other in an act that, like sympathy or identification, demands responsibility to an other. Narcissism, in the Ovidian sense, becomes the ethical position from which to write of and to an other. Just as Narcissus experienced the desire of the other first by falling in love with himself as an inaccessible image in the pool, Joyce presents sympathy as the understanding of an other through a dissociation from self. In Joyce's conception, narcissism is the moment in which one loves an otherness within and is able to transfer that love of otherness in an ethically empathic relation.

The mapping of mythical figures onto historic ones might also be inverted in this fun-house mirror of the schizophrenic relation. Echo's story may also be understood as an illustration of trauma, of grief so extreme that the subject is separated from her body in an attempt to disavow the memory of pain.[60] Like Echo whose body disintegrates in grief while her voice calls out Narcissus's neglect, Issy separates from her body, speaking to her image in the mirror as if to an other whose pain she witnesses but does not experience. Joyce is implicitly inscribed in the text as a second person whose grief is produced by the dissociation of a narcissist. Like Echo, Joyce was a storyteller, and also like her he felt increasingly powerless and increasingly distressed by his loved one's descent into self-absorption. Extreme narcissism – not so much an exceedingly high opinion of oneself but an inability to see outside the borders of one's own subjectivity – is one of the difficult manifestations of schizophrenia.

Inversion is the figure for this tale of mirrors, reflections, and repetitions. Issy herself is inverted not only by the reversal of her reflection as she stares in the mirror but also in her sexuality. The rainbow girls are versions of herself, but they are also her partners in sexual play. Joyce engages the popular myth of homosexuality that is inscribed even in the current word for this love (homo-sexuality), that it is a form of self-love, love of the same, or narcissism. Issy, as an invert, is partner to the other rainbow girls ("doaters," lovers or daughters) who are versions of her; she loves her reflections, the inversions of her image in the mirror.

While his nineteenth-century predecessors such as Richard von Krafft-Ebing viewed homosexuality as a degenerative disorder, Sigmund Freud followed more recent theorists such as John Addington Symonds and Henry Havelock Ellis in describing homosexual love within the range of normative sexualities. However, in "On Narcissism," Freud describes homosexuality as a form of self-love or love of sameness in another, in which the lovers "are plainly seeing themselves as a love object, and are exhibiting a type of object-choice which must be termed 'narcissistic.'"[61] Psychological theorists following Freud greatly exaggerated this description in order to justify a reading of homosexuality as a mental illness. In fact, it was not until 1973 that the American Psychiatric Association removed homosexuality from the mental illnesses listed in the *DSM*. In classifying homosexuality as a mental disorder, practitioners ignored Freud's own emphatic refusal to regard gays and lesbians as mentally disabled. In his "Letter to an American Mother," Freud wrote that while homosexuality was often far from an advantage in a world that persecutes gays and lesbians, "it is nothing to be ashamed of, no vice, no degradation, it cannot be classified as an illness . . ."; he goes on to label homosexuality as a "variation of the sexual function" and to list a series of admired homosexual men, including Plato, Michelangelo, and Leonardo da Vinci. He emphasizes that while, were her son to receive treatment from Freud, the process might "bring him harmony, peace of mind, full efficiency," it would not be the goal of the analysis to "abolish" his sexuality.[62] Placing homosexuality within the continuum of expected resolutions to the Oedipal conflict, Freud nonetheless notes that homosexual "object-choice originally lies closer to narcissism than does the heterosexual kind."[63]

Difference in sexuality is thus defined solely as the difference of gender between male and female partners; loving a version of oneself by loving a person of one's own sex is understood as narcissism. In this model, other measures of difference – disposition, interests, beliefs – are seen as insufficient markers of "hetero"-sexuality. According to Michael Warner, "the allegory of gender protects against a recognition of the role of the imaginary in the formation of the erotic."[64] In the first love relation in an infant's experience during the Lacanian "Imaginary" stage of development, a child's sensory experience is characterized by "primary narcissism," an inability to perceive a border between the body of the self and the body of the mother. That initial love relation which has a certain pre-sexual erotic dimension, may be understood to pattern the adult erotics that follow. While we may prefer to believe that the failure of individuation that characterized child love does not apply to adult erotics, an element of that "imaginary" connection remains. As Michael Warner notes, "[t]o the extent that our culture relies on allegorization of gender to disguise from itself its own ego erotics, it will recognize those ego erotics only in the person of the homosexual, apparently bereft of the master trope of difference" (*ibid* 202). By adopting heterosexual practices, the individual can imagine he or she is engaged in a relationship with an other rather than in a narcissistic or (Lacanian) imaginary relationship in which boundaries between self and other are permeable. Heterosexuality as an allegory of difference assures the subject of his or her individuation and veils the possibility that this subject is in danger of narcissistically coopting the other into a version of the self. In homosexual love the reassurance of difference and separation must be developed through an allegory other than gender.

Joyce's ethics in representing Issy depend on a balancing between similarity and difference, between narcissism and responsibility. The self-absorption of extreme narcissism prevents the subject from recognizing others and thus presents the opportunity for abuse. (When Narcissus is defended against any input from outside his consciousness *before* he loves his image in the water, he is cruel to the nymphs. In his early self-absorption he cannot understand desire for another.) Self-love, however, also allows the subject to desire a version of the self that is slightly at a distance, effectively inaccessible (like the image of himself in the water that Narcissus comes to love). Unfulfilled narcissistic desire allows the subject to experience sympathy, to act ethically. Homosexual love was seen as a form of narcissism during Joyce's life (see, for example, Oscar Wilde's references to the myth in his portrayal of Dorian Gray). However, Joyce chose to emphasize the sympathy enabled by narcissism, in which by recognizing a version of one's own desire in another, a narcissist is capable both of desire and of kindness. Joyce emphasized the sympathy present in homosexual desire, in one instance among many, in his portrayal of Cranly's desire for Stephen Dedalus at the close of *Portrait*.

Jacques Lacan's "mirror stage" in child development treats the confusion around issues of identity and difference experienced by infants as they move from the narcissistic thought processes of the Imaginary to a recognition of otherness necessary to the Symbolic order.[65] Lacan describes the recognition of self in the mirror as the inauguration of subjectivity. Initially a child plays joyfully before a mirror, not recognizing the image that moves before her either as a reflection of herself or as an object outside her; the image is bound up in the narcissism that disregards boundaries. When, however, a child recognizes her own image in a mirror and recognizes that image as "empty" (in other words, the child is not fooled into thinking there is another child behind the glass; believing rather that the image is a flattened or "empty" version of the child herself), she will gesture before the mirror and experience through this play the relation between her body, which in this virtual reflection has definite limits, and its environment. The mirror stage is an *identification* in the psychoanalytic sense of the term in that the infant recognizes herself as separate, with an identity, in *relation* to the mother.[66] Playing before the mirror the child undergoes an intellectual transformation in which she develops a sense of herself as an *I*, as a subject that endures through the changes of experience. The image in the mirror, while it changes and gestures, is nonetheless always a representation of the same child, *I*.

In this "mirror stage," Lacan describes a doubled form of subjectivity. First, the child's narcissistic contemplation of the mirror image allows her to realize a world outside her body and to relinquish an infantile sense of omnipotence or self-absorption: she understands the concepts of self and interiority through her burgeoning understanding of the exterior and other. Second, in recognizing her image in the mirror and *identifying* with it, the child develops an understanding both of stability and of mutability: she sees that there is an *I*, or subject, who is reflected in the mirror, and also that this subject is in a constant process of flux and change.

This complex interchange of interiority and exteriority, stability and change, alienation and identification, through which the subject comes into being in the mirror stage prefigures the complexities with which that subject will enter into relations with others. Those relations follow the pattern of recognition through which the child first recognized an outside world in the movement in the mirror and then came to understand that world as a reflection of herself, her movements, her emotions. Relations with others in the exterior world follow the relation with self developed before the mirror in which the child moves between recognition of the image as "other" and absorption of the same image as "self." These mutable relations between self and other are apparent in Issy's immersion in and conversation with her others before her own mirror.

VI

Complicating the idea of the girl in love with her reflection, in his 1933–1936 revisions Joyce introduces Lewis Carroll's Alice, who moved through her image in the looking glass to a mirror-image, inverted world on the other side. "Secilas [containing the name "Alice" spelled backward, or inverted, as Alice is inverted in the mirror] through their laughing classes [looking glass] become poolermates in laker life" (*FW* 526.35–36). "Poolermates" may be read as a reference to the beloved narcissistic reflection in the pool where one sees one's mate. Alice's journey through the looking glass is paired with female inversion, or lesbian desire, both through the stereotype of narcissism "poolermates in laker life" and through the idea of unmarried working women (parlormaids) or women sharing living spaces (parlormates). By 1936 when he completed this revision, Joyce knew of Lucia's homosexual desires and relationships. Both he and Nora seem to have supported Lucia's sexual explorations, in part, perhaps, hoping that finding contentment or even happiness in love would mitigate her distressing symptoms.[67]

In the phrase, "Secilas through their laughing classes," Joyce refers both to Lewis Carroll's Alice and to Saint Cecilia, and in these references he condenses his oscillating responses to the sexuality of young girls, the possibility of childhood erotic desire, and the equal possibility of sexual abuse. Alice in her looking glass ("laughing classes") evokes the multiple Alices upon whom "Lewd's carol" (*FW* 501.34) bestowed his often sexualized affections. Like HCE, his fondness for girls was rendered both as innocent and as sexual. This conjoining is most evident in Carroll's 1858 photograph of Alice Liddell, to whom the Alice stories were originally told, and for whom Carroll committed them to writing.[68] In the 1858 portrait Alice is posed as a begging child. Her youthful, nearly androgynous body and her frank gaze suggest the innocence of childhood. But her pose is also erotic: her gaze is fully directed toward the viewer but her face is partially averted, a flirtatious combination of invitation and withdrawal. Her fist rests on one hip in a seductress's confident pose. Her tattered clothes are artfully arranged to conceal her nakedness but to reveal by suggestion an erotic body: her shirt falls open at her childish chest and rounded shoulders; her skirt is tucked above a bare knee and soft calf. The Alice of Carroll's photo is constructed by the eye of the camera as the photographer's erotic object.

That Carroll's Alice may not have been expressing her own eroticism or desire is emphasized by Joyce's pairing of Alice with Saint Cecelia ("Secilas"), one of Catholicism's many martyred virgins. According to the hagiography, Cecelia devoted her youth to the veneration of God; but in adolescence her father chose to cement social bonds by marrying her to a young patrician. Cecelia's devotion was great and during her wedding she sang to God "in her heart" (thus her service as patron saint of music and musicians) and received guidance to remain a virgin and dedicate herself to her Christian mission. Her faith was so strong that she was able to convince her husband, who also martyred himself to the cause.[69] Evoking Cecelia at this juncture, Joyce indicates the child's possible resistance to sexual exchange.

Joyce's inverted image of the girl in the mirror is a figure for the difference of female sexuality from male expectations. Responding in part to Lacan's description of the mirror stage and his claim that women never successfully complete the transition from Imaginary to Symbolic thought, Luce Irigaray in "The Looking Glass, from the Other Side" also evokes the metaphors provided by Alice's adventures. In making this comparison Irigaray emphasizes Lacan's version of female identity as multiple, permeable, and shifting but also indicates the extent to which a woman can be subject to masculine control and exploitation.[70] Irigaray's mirror figures not only the inauguration of subjectivity (as it does for Lacan) but also the projection of identity from men onto women as their "others."

Irigaray suggests, through Alice's adventures, that female subjectivity develops in resistance to the categorical approach enforced by the Lacanian "Law of the Father" and in relation to others in processes such as empathy in which a girl sees versions of herself in another. Irigaray writes: "*Representation by the other of the projects of the one. Which he/she brings to light by displacing them. Irreducible expropriation of desire occasioned by its impression in/on the other. Matrix and support of the possibility of its repetition and reproduction. Same, and other.*" In other words, understanding in this Imaginary, empathic mode presents specific difficulties for representation; empathy can present as self-evident fact ideas that are projections from within and which might border on usurpation and appropriation. At the same time, however, the empathic mode of representation presents an opportunity for understanding the merged worlds of self and other initially experienced in the mirror stage. Presenting the girl in the mirror, Joyce explores the difficult issues of representing in this imaginary world by negotiating between empathy, appropriation, and projection, in a dynamic gesture of ethical sympathy.

For Irigaray, the journey through the looking glass is also a metaphor for childhood molestation or incest. She refers to Alice's "violet, violated eyes"[71] in narrating the story of her sexual betrayal on the other side of the looking glass. Incest, in Irigaray's reading of Alice's adventures, is an experience that turns inside out a child's understanding of the world and of the authority or power of adults in it. Alice's adults are tyrannical: the girls upon whom Alice was modeled (Isa Bowman and Alice Liddell among others) had experiences with Charles Dodgson that at least bordered on the sexual, as Dodgson's photographs of Alice Liddell suggest.

While Joyce does not suggest that childhood trauma is the *cause* of inversion, he notes the coincidence between the experience of incestuous acts in childhood and later sexual inversion, a coincidence that is often assiduously avoided in late twentieth-century discourse. The taboo against linking homosexuality and incest arises in part in reaction to nineteenth-century discourses in which homosexuality was labeled a perversion or deviance from sexual norms, a condition to be cured. The idea that a lesbian chooses a woman partner as a response to the trauma of childhood sexual abuse would seem to support the notion of homosexuality as a form of perversion. In "Sexual Trauma/Queer Memory," Ann Cvetkovich notes that "the primary connection made between lesbianism and incest consists in *disavowing* the connection."[72] Laura Davis, author (with Ellen Bass) of an extremely influential self-help book on sexual-abuse survival, *The Courage to Heal*, has argued that if child molestation resulted in lesbian sexuality, the population of lesbian women would be far larger than it is. The experience of sexual abuse will factor in any sexuality, but inferring that "sexual abuse causes homosexuality is making an assumption that there's something wrong with being lesbian or gay" (62–63).[73] Rather than making this kind of reductive causal connection, Cvetkovich complicates the binarism that would define sexuality through the gender of a person's object of desire. Like many contemporary theorists, Cvetkovich prefers to use the word "queer" in order to indicate the "unpredictable connections between sexual abuse and its effects, to name a connection while refusing determination or causality." The idea of being queer, as such, resists the binary arrangement of sexuality commonly assumed in the words "heterosexual" or "homosexual." Queer identity also resists the overly simplistic idea that the choice of a lover of one sex or another could in itself heal the traumatic results of child abuse. However, although she rejects a causal connection between the experience of sexual abuse and queer desire, Cvetkovich does not dismiss "the value of exploring the productive and dense relations among these terms."[74] Joyce also traces connections between childhood sexual abuse and lesbian sexual identity without resorting either to binary distinctions between sexual desires or to causal relations. In his pun on inversion, he links Issy's sexuality and her looking-glass experience of violation: "Secilas through their laughing classes becoming poolermates in laker life."

Issy's testimony both conceals and reveals HCE's incestuous sin in language that indicates a child's feeling of culpability in her own violation: as if her normal and healthy dawning awareness of sexual desire were the cause of her father's arousal. Speaking to a dissociated, double version of herself, the mirror in which she sees her image serves as a metaphor for dissociation. Issy experiences a splitting within herself that protects her from remembered trauma. The traumatized child is projected outward into that other child in the looking glass and she chastises her double for inciting HCE's desire.

Of course I know you are a viry vikid girl to go in the dreemplace and at that time of the draym and it was a very wrong thing to do, even under the dark flush of night, dare all grandpassia! He's gone on his bombashaw. Through geesing and so pleasing at Strip Teasy up the stairs. The boys on the corner were talking too. And your soreful miseries [menses] first come on you. (*FW* 527.5–10)

This scene may be read in at least two ways. It may describe a literal molestation at the hands of the father. It may as well record either a child seeing her father's nude body or the so-called primal scene. Seeing her parents in a moment of grand passion, she might feel an Oedipal attachment to her father that disturbs her sense of familial propriety. While Joyce's concern about Lucia was focused on the violation of emotional and identity boundaries, he dramatizes that concern with images that may also be read as incest. For the purposes of clarity, I read the scene as one of sexual molestation, while I think it is equally important to hold in mind an alternative reading of the Oedipal family drama.[75]

In this monologue, Issy worries that she is complicit, that her love for and trust in her father invited the breach of boundaries from which she suffers. Accused of enticement by her molester, she internalizes a version of herself as a culpable seducer. Writing from the perspective of a young girl speaking to herself in the mirror, Joyce addresses these troublesome thoughts. "Of course I know you are a very vikid [wicked or viking – in which case she was the intruder or aggressor] girl to go in the dreemplace [bedroom] and at that time of the draym [at night] and it was a very wrong thing to do, even under the dark flush [shame] of night, dear old grandpassia." The girl shifts between self-accusation and accusation of her assailant, the "dear old grandpassia" (grand father or man with a grand passion). She oscillates between a drive to accuse her father by naming his sin and testifying to her abuse and a wish to protect her loved father by accusing herself.[76] Standing before the mirror, Issy rehearses the words through which she was threatened and enticed. "Still me with you, you poor chilled! Will make it up with Mother Concepcion and a glorious lie between us, sweetness, so as not a novene in all the convent loretos, not my littlest one of all, for mercy's sake need ever know, what passed our lips or" (*FW* 527–28.35–36, 1–3). The images and language of religion (Immaculate Conception, the glorious mysteries of the rosary, a novena, and the Loreto convents of Dublin) serve to reinforce the secrecy of the interaction.

The first draft of this encounter is perhaps more explicit and more frightening in its presentation of seduction and threat in child molestation: "Listen meme dearest, Of course I know you are a wicked girl. Still you look so lovely. You do. Listen, meme sweety [sweety marked through to leave sweet but altered again to sweety in the next draft]. It's only the two of us [struck through to replace with "us two"]. Of course it was very [replaced with downright] wicked of him, now really it was. Still, listen, me and you will make it up so as nobody [inserted: of course] will ever know. So [inserted: meme mearest,] be free to me and listen, you you beauty, we'll be true to you." Rehearsing the lines of threat before her mirror, the child converts the couple formed by her assailant and herself with a coupling of herself and her double in the mirror. The mirror allows Issy to enact the strategy of a survivor who detaches from physical experience. She is her own double, "meme . . . you you," the experienced self and the body split off and projected as both whole and other in the image in the mirror. The dream world that young Issy enters is the world through the looking glass, a place that inverts and disturbs safe expectations, but also a place of fantasy where she can detach from the world of physical experience which has become threatening and painful.

Presenting incest as a theme in *Finnegans Wake*, Joyce addresses not only physical child abuse in the form of sexual molestation but also parental anxiety about the boundaries between sexual love and familial love, and the places where that line can been crossed. While Issy, as a character within the text, presents the profile and speaks the words of an exploited child, Joyce's production of this character presents the occasion for considering ethics. As a parent to a deeply disturbed daughter, Joyce sees in Issy the textual locus where he is able to investigate the family dynamics that might produce childhood disturbance and to indict himself for an emotional version of the physical violation of boundaries Issy has experienced. Exploring this uncomfortable territory, Joyce follows Sigmund Freud, who in theorizing family history sought a way to understand the intense bond between fathers and daughters, a bond that often crosses into sexual desire or even abusive behavior. Though Freud made some quite serious errors in disbelieving the frequent incestuous abuse of his women patients and theorizing instead a daughter's desire for her father, he was also probably right to see the way in which the affection shared between a girl and her father might have a disturbing sexual dimension.[77] Writing and revising Issy's testimony before the mirror as his own daughter descended into increasing narcissism and dissociation, Joyce records his parental worry about responsibility for Lucia Joyce's illness through the exaggerated mirror of HCE's sin. Joyce also displays some concern that the encompassing identification he feels with his daughter might be intrusive, a violation of boundaries that is the psychological equivalent of physical incest.[78]

Kuberski argues that *Finnegans Wake* inscribes the father's uncomfortable and dangerous desire for his daughter as the desire for an "other," in the Lacanian sense. He notes that this daughter is understood narcissistically as a version of the father's self. Joyce is aware of these two possibilities and the first is readily presented at the inception of the novel in the sexual response of Willingdone (HCE) to the urinating jinnies (Issy and her multiples). A healthy resolution to this disturbing exchange of desires within the family could be the daughter's patterning of desire onto another object, a lover outside the family. This possibility seems impossible for Issy who is always trapped within the incestuous family, coupling with her father, brothers, and versions of herself. And it was, sadly, also impossible for Lucia whose various heterosexual and homosexual courtships (including her persistent affection for Samuel Beckett) were never to come to a satisfying conclusion. A diagnosis of schizophrenia arrested her in the place of the daughter and the child. *Finnegans Wake* imitates the horrors of incest in that it records the strong identification Joyce felt with Lucia in the exaggerated form inspired by the author's grief and guilt over her condition. But noting this focus on incest I do not in any way wish to imply that Joyce himself would have molested or mistreated his daughter. Though Lucia's case may for some point toward childhood trauma, there is no specific evidence either in the copious records that document the life of the Joyce family (except in the most rudimentary translations between fiction and the life of its author) or in Lucia's condition itself to suggest the specific trauma of incest.

Cheryl Herr argues in "Fathers, Daughters, Anxiety, and Fiction" that Joyce subordinated Lucia's independence to his own concerns as a writer and that he encouraged her to end her dancing career not so much because it taxed her strength, as because it rendered her too separate from him. Describing Lucia's catatonic state after her engagement to Ponisovsky, Herr argues: "It would seem that the efforts of the family to project Lucia out of their conflicted embrace into a world in which she would have to take on a separate self produced a sign . . . that there was no true self there to be called upon."[79] Lucia, according to Herr, experienced her primary sense of identity in the "aesthetic-emotional" bond she shared with her father where she was "forced to feed from [his] trough and to enact his own ambivalence and compulsions" (*ibid* 196). She manifested this shared identification by choreographing her break-downs in time with Joyce's ocular crises and surgeries. In this way, as Herr argues, Joyce was able to register his own fear and ambivalence about his writing and to claim love and loyalty from his friends without himself having to break down. Herr argues, in effect, that Joyce did not merely identify with Lucia, nor only represent a version of her in his final text. Rather, she contends, Joyce made Lucia act as his text: by voicing his thoughts and concerns she became a version of his consciousness; however, "articulating his anxieties about being understood and valued apart from his work, she ultimately forfeited the ability to speak for her-self and passed most of her life in a mental institution" (*ibid* 192). While the identification between this father and daughter was strong and their concerns often overlapping, it seems equally possible that rather than co-opting his daughter's perspective and voice, he instead attempted to suspend his own position and to speak through her perspective when presenting Issy in *Finnegans Wake*.

In *James Joyce and the Problem of Justice*, Joseph Valente proposes the latter interpretation when he notes that Joyce's narcissism or identifica-tion took the form, not of subsuming his daughter, but rather of under-standing himself in reference to her. He notes that Joyce was able readily to identify with her mental conditions because he had long felt a sense of "mystic participation" with her, a participation rendered first through the relationship of Leopold and Milly Bloom in *Ulysses*. Valente also notes the narcissism inherent in Joyce's love for Lucia but notes "it is not *just* the narcissism of endless self-elaboration and self engrossment, which seeks to aggrandize the psychic enclosure by colonizing the other, it is also a primary or mirror-stage narcissism in which the ego models itself *after* the other in order to get its bearings *from* the other, to reinforce or reestablish the psychic enclosure itself."[80] This mirror-stage narcissism is also the condition through which Joyce describes Issy, indicating his sense of the mutuality of his and his daughter's conditions. This mutual-ity formed the ground against which Joyce depicted the schizo Issy in an attempt to give voice to his own daughter. Rather than rendering Lucia as insane throughout the text, Joyce imagined Lucia as a splitting off of his own imagination, a double of his creativity. He presents his intense identification with her, his experience of two-in-oneness, as doubling and multiplicity within Issy's characterization.

In the final, published version of a series of questions posed by Shaun/ HCE (*FW* I.6), Joyce registers questions about the nature of filial love implied more broadly in the relationship between HCE and Issy. "What bitter's love but yurning, what' sour lovemutch but a bref burning till shee that drawes dothe smoake retourne?" (*FW* 143.29–30)[81] Through a metaphor of burning and smoke, this passage takes up the question of the relations between sexual love and familial love. If it is Shaun who poses this question, a courtship may be implied by his youth and by his frequent appearance as a Don Juan or Cassanova. On the other hand, as a family member, and even as a version of HCE, Shaun's presence evokes issues of family love and its darker relative, incest. The phrase "what' sour lovemutch but a bref burning" indicates the brevity of sexual desire in courtship or a love match which is intense like a burning but possibly brief as a result; this love may be characterized more by yearning than by satisfaction. The match that is struck by desire burns rapidly into "smoake." (I characterize love in this way in relation to Issy only and not as generalization about passionate love: Issy's love affairs in the text are the infatuations of a child; they change rapidly and burn out quickly, much like Lucia's adult love affairs.)

That the love shared between father and daughter is a more lasting love, is suggested by the phrase "smoake returns" in which the smoke of a fire returns to its source, just as a daughter might return to one of her sources, her father. Issy, who is often rendered as a vaporous cloud – an image readily associated with smoke – sometimes turns into rain thus transforming into her other source, her mother. Issy is associated with Lucia both through her shifting affections and also through the phrase "she that draws," which refers both to the flame that draws on air to burn and Lucia's ability to draw illustrations. This "smoake" that contains the oak from which it was burned evokes the relationship between artist daughter and author father; her creativity is a continuation of his own, both his bequest to her and the gift she returns to him. As Joyce noted, "[w]hatever spark of gift I possess has been transmitted to Lucia and has kindled a fire in her brain."[82] The metaphors of burning, the spark, smoke and fire suggest not only the varieties of love shared between father and daughter but also Joyce's image for their shared creativity.

The response to this question (number ten) is sometimes referred to as Issy's monologue and elsewhere as a dialogue with Shaun in which

Issy does most of the talking.[83] One particularly rich fragment from this exchange addresses love and desire, schizoid experience, and the ethics of representation. This moment might be described as metanarrative (in a loose sense of the term), in that it conveys the impression of a character breaking the frame of representation to speak directly to the author about the way in which she is being represented.[84]

That I chid you, sweet sir? You know I'm tender by my eye. Can't you read by dazzling ones through me true? Bite my laughters, drink my tears. Pore into me, volumes, spell me stark and spill me swooning. I just don't care what my thwarters think. Transname me loveliness, now and here me for all times! (*FW* 145.17–21)

The section of questions and answers that contains this passage was composed quite hurriedly under deadline and for publication as an installment of *Work in Progress* for *transition*. According to the *Archive*, the entire initial composition of the episode took place in the spring and summer of 1927. During that time (and during the longer period between 1926 and 1929) Lucia was embarking on a serious career as a dancer and choreographer; and she spent approximately six hours in the studio each day, her activity and creativity comparable to her father's dedication.[85] In 1927 Lucia showed no concrete sign of the mental collapse that would preoccupy her family in the 1930s. Composing this section of twelve questions, Joyce's idea of his daughter was as a split version of himself, a companion artist capable of the quick associative word play he himself engaged, yet talented and disciplined in her own art. He was also aware of her as an attractive woman who had been courted and would continue to be courted but with whom he shared a different, perhaps more enduring love. This version of the daughter figure is rendered in the 1927 composition.

Each of the first five drafts written that year emphasizes Lucia's dancing and her burgeoning sexuality as: "Count all your quick of my rhythmic ticks . . .". Lucia's "rhythmic dance," as her modern dance technique was labeled,[86] is layered through the idea of arithmetic which, especially in "Nightlessons," is associated with a woman's genitals and with the changes (addition and subtraction or menstruation, pregnancy, and childbirth) made there.

Joyce did not revise this passage again until the mid-1930s when he took up the *transition* pages to make changes, combine episodes, and transform the installments into the final text of *Finnegans Wake*. The intervening decade had seen the steady decline of his daughter's mental health and by 1937 she was permanently institutionalized.[87] In his first set of revisions using the pages of *transition*, Joyce writes two radical changes to the passage. He removes the wonderfully suggestive passage "Count all your quick of my rhythmic ticks." In the intervening years, this playful reference to dancing and to burgeoning sexuality could be re-interpreted as a cruel reference to the repetitive or rhythmic ticks of the schizophrenic. Joyce moves the playful reference to a point later in the passage as "Let me finger their eurhythmytic" (*FW* 147.08) thus emphasizing the sexual and diminishing any possible association with schizophrenic word ticks.[88] He alters the sentence above this deletion to add a more obscure reference to her dancing, changing "Can't you read my dazzled eyes through me true" to "Can't you read my dazzling ones through me true" to evoke the Irish folk song phrase "dancing through and through." He also adds a reference to the identification between father and daughter through their shared eye troubles ("You know I'm tender by my eye") as well as the more self-critical remark, "I just don't care what my thwarters think."

Issy's answer to Shaun's question about love can be read as the author's projected record of Lucia's reaction to her transformation into Issy, a transformation inspired by love that might nonetheless feel damaging to the object of that representation. Evoking his identification with Lucia, Joyce writes of the concerns about eyes and eyesight he shared with his daughter. When his daughter was born, Joyce named her Lucia after the patron saint of light and sight, Santa Lucia. While Lucia was troubled by her strabismus, as he aged, her father suffered from increased optical pain as well as loss of sight. The tenderness also evokes reminders of Issy and Lucia's shared tender youth and the affection or tenderness shared between the strongly identified father and daughter. The repetition of the sound "eye" in the sentence ("I" and "eye") might refer doubly to Issy, who like Lucia sees double and who often repeats her first initial. "I" also refers to the narrator or writer's voice, increasing the sense of identification suggested by the "eye." Retaining the theme of sight (in reading), Issy asks: "Can't you read by dazzling ones through me true?" The daughter asks if she can be read and understood in spite of the dazzling or excessive light, a possible reference to St. Lucia through the association with light. To read truly through Issy might mean to see her source in Lucia. Expanding on the transformation of person into character, Issy suggests: "Pore into me volumes ..." evoking both the precedent volumes, including *Alice's Adventures in Wonderland*, Swift's correspondence, and the legend of Tristan and Iseult, among others, through which Joyce creates her, and also the idea that Lucia is poured into the book, transformed into words ("spell me stark") and represented starkly or directly. This character seems less than concerned about her reception when she says, in the final version, "I just don't care what my thwarters think," dismissing both readers and those who would thwart her. Joyce, on the other hand, might be understood to suffer an instance of troubled conscience about this transformation and whether it adequately accounts for what his daughter ("thwarter") might think.

What are the ethics of this act of transformation of living daughter into written character? Certainly, Joyce's record of Lucia was motivated by love: "transname me loveliness." His transnaming of Lucia as Issy is a less stable act than renaming. The transformation of Lucia into Issy is reciprocal in that she also transforms back into her source; Issy reemerges as Lucia. But transnaming communicates another concern: in transcribing this lovely, does the writer also usurp her identity? In German, usurp is *ubernehmen*, literally overname, perhaps an unethical version of "transnaming." What then are the repercussions of bestowing immortality ("now and here me for all times") by transforming a person into a character? In his first draft, Joyce wrote "now *me* and here me for all times!" (emphasis added). He indicated in this version not only the act of immortalizing through representation, but also the character's wish to be known ("now [know] me") and heard. In the final version, in which he deleted the initial "me" ("now and here me for all times!"), this possibility is crossed by an alternative: that being immortalized might make knowing and hearing impossible as a complex, historical person is reduced to a characterization.

In the final change before publication in the ninth draft of this passage, Joyce adds the sad and tender question that breaks through the genre of the monologue to address the writer directly and to allow Joyce to question the ethics of his representation. He writes: "That I chid you, sweet sir?" There are a number of possible interpretations of this phrase: Are you concerned that I will chide or chastise you? Am I not your child? Do I child you (does the inspiration of Lucia's language and thought give birth to the text)? And finally, did I cheat you, sir, by becoming schizophrenic instead of an artist, as you had hoped for me?

Joyce's revisions in 1937 make it clear that language does not immortalize: Lucia is no longer the "here me," the person inscribed into the manuscript in 1927, because she has been transformed by years of unhappiness and institutionalization. An ethical interpretation of the text designed to match Joyce's emerging ethical representation allows a reader both to acknowledge the version of Lucia (as artist) Joyce inscribed in the text in the 1920s and to register the shifts in textual meaning reflecting her deterioration in the alterations of 1937. Though Lucia could not be immortalized, though her story ended unhappily, the textual production of *Finnegans Wake* tells an alternative story of her father's devotion and admiration and his struggle to rescue his daughter, and also of her vivid imagination, vitality, and charisma. This alternative, textual story contains Joyce's ethical biography of his daughter.

Envoy: to the reader

I began this volume with a love letter that records the realization of James Joyce's ethics in his encounter with his mother in her coffin. In that encounter Joyce recognizes the habitat she provided him, the costs that habitat extracted from her, and the attendant responsibilities arising from her generosity. He writes to Nora of his emerging ethic, in which he would refuse any system that would take another as its victim. That ethic forms the basis for their budding love affair. I'd like to end with another kind of love letter, a letter with no recipient that records Joyce's failed love affair with Amalia Popper and provides another, shadow image of ethics in the form of an abandoned umbrella.

This awkward epistle, *Giacomo Joyce*, is a portrait of the lover who in rejection falls back on the tawdry mechanisms of bigotry: "defending himself against the pain of rejection," Mahaffey argues in *States of Desire*, Joyce adopted "conventionally sexist and anti-Semitic attitudes."[1] But it is also a portrait of recognition, of seeing the ugly potentials of hatred within oneself and accepting responsibilty, of realizing that the thing that makes one discontented or unhappy is not the inadequacy of the other but the failures of the self and further that there are reaches of unknowability within the self that these disappointments reveal.

In *Giacomo Joyce* he records the ultimate lapse in ethics: the abjection of another, the disdain of difference. But Joyce's ethic can also be identified in the shadow of this lapse, in its failures – in other words, where it does not *take place*. Joyce's ethic is not a moral system, a call to the reader for exemplary behavior. *Giacomo Joyce* in its ugliest moments reminds me that Joyce's ethic is one of sympathy – feeling beside, never usurping, never assuming, never taking up my place. While it is the most self-involved and oddly hermetic of his texts it is also the most directly addressed to the reader. Published last among his works, years after his death, it fulfills the function of the envoy in a traditional French ballade – a direct address to the reader to whom the lyric has been dedicated, an inscription of the

reader within the poem as crucial to it, an important personage.[2] Yet
Joyce's actual envoy within *Giacomo Joyce* is strangely cryptic, unreadable,
utopian, impossible, and at the same time, I will argue, ethical: "Envoy:
Love me, love my umbrella."[3]

The notebook is comprised of a series of vignettes, much like his earlier
epiphanies, that record the vacillating motions of unrequited affection
in a series of potent images. The last of these images is of two objects left
behind by the beloved: hat with a red flower, umbrella resting on a piano.
Joyce describes these items as her arms or weapons ("a casque, gules, and
blunt spear on a field, sable"). The piano becomes a kind of battlefield
on which one can see her helmet (or casque) with gules (or red), accompanied by a blunt spear in the guise of an umbrella. His interpretation
of these signs follows: "Envoy: Love me, love my umbrella." The mes-
senger or envoy leaves behind this last message, a direct address to the
reader or patron of the poem: love me, love my weapons, these defensive
implements I use to shield me from harm, an umbrella to protect me
from rain, a hat under which to hide my vulnerable face and hair.

Punning on Joyce's envoy, Derrida writes in the "Envois" to *The Post
Card*, "Love my *ombre, elle* – not me. 'Do you love me?' And you, tell me."[4]
Ombrelle is a parasol, the opposite of Joyce's umbrella in sense if not in
sound, it provides shade from sun rather than shelter from rain. Dividing
the word with a comma, Derrida draws attention to the shade or *ombre*,
the shadow, ghost or revenant which is *elle* – her. The beloved is the shade
of the lover, his opposite and yet inextricably linked to him, the projection
outward of all that he desires and at the same time fears, his shade. In
writing their story, even in the discourse of bigotry, Joyce calls on the
reader to love her: "Love my *ombre, elle* – not me." The representation of
the beloved, precisely in that it is only a shadow, inaccurate and unfair,
provokes sympathy and another form of desire, curiosity. *Giacomo Joyce*
while recording the lapsed ethics of an author's representation, provides
the occasion for the reader's emerging ethic – the opportunity to love
this shadowy representation, to sympathize with her and thus shade her
from the harsh light of an angry presentation.

The notebook's envoy can thus function as an envoy not only from
the beloved to the lover but also from the author to the reader. How can
we as readers understand the directive to love the author's umbrella as we
love him, or in order to love him. The umbrella is his spear when furled.
But when unfurled it may serve as a shield against rain. The umbrella
provides him with a portable habitat like the snail's shell to which he
retreats when threatened. But it is a habitat that can also be a weapon.

The pages that precede record the use of that umbrella, the defenses of bigotry and hatred erected in the face of the threat of disappointed love, rejected affections. But if we are to behave ethically we must recognize the umbrella for what it is and love it and the lover who carries it. The envoy sets out the impossible task of becoming an ethical subject.

For ethics, as I have argued, is impossible; it is utopian. Utopian because it is an impossible dream of perfection and utopian because it takes place in no place precisely so that it will not usurp the place of the other. This is why the love letter, much like the guilty love letter at the heart of *Finnegans Wake*, is the appropriate genre for ethical writing. It takes up no place, always being in circulation, addressed to, responsive to, another.

Notes

INTRODUCTION

1 Richard Ellmann published Yeats's own account of their meeting in his biography of Joyce. At the close of this encounter Joyce asked Yeats his age. "I told him, but I am afraid I said I was a year younger than I am. He said with a sigh, 'I thought as much. I have met you too late. You are too old.'" See Richard Ellmann's *James Joyce* (New York: Oxford University Press, 1959), 103.

2 Describing the process of reading his book, Joyce writes in the *Wake*, "as were it sentenced to be nuzzled over a full trillion times for ever and a night till his noddle sink or swim by that ideal reader suffering from an ideal insomnia...." See James Joyce's *Finnegans Wake*. (New York: Viking, 1939), 120.11–14. (Hereafter referred to as *FW*.)

3 Samuel Beckett makes a similar point when in his essay on *Work in Progress* (See Samuel Beckett et al. *An Exagmination of James Joyce: analysis of the "Work in Progress."* [Paris: Shakespeare and Company, 1929; rpt. New York: Haskell House, 1974] he notes that Joyce's "writing is not *about* something; *it is that something itself*" (14).

4 Sheldon Brivic points out that Mary Joyce was James Joyce's first reader: "His writing began as a discourse to be read to his mother, who was the first audience for his early fiction ... Mark Shechner ... suggests that his work continued to be addressed to his mother after she died...." See Sheldon Brivic's *Joyce's Waking Women: An Introduction to Finnegans Wake* (Madison: The University of Wisconsin Press, 1995), 9.

5 Making this claim, I follow (roughly) the trajectory of Jacques Derrida's work over the past decade in which he has increasingly focused on how his dense textual interpretations give rise to practices of ethics and justice. His early work on Levinasian ethics in "Metaphysics of Violence" has been realized more comprehensively in more recent works such as *The Gift of Death* and *Aporias*. Simon Critchley provides an excellent review of this turn in his *The Ethics of Deconstruction* which traces the ethical implications of early deconstructive criticism and its more explicit manifestations in recent years.

It is useful here also to distinguish my position from that of Martha Nussbaum's influential work on literature and ethics which in many ways runs counter to these positions. She argues in *Love's Knowledge* and elsewhere that literature can be read as a moral philosophy, that narrative encourages "our ability to see and care for particulars, not as representatives of the law, but as what they themselves are: to respond vigorously with sense and emotions before the new; to care deeply about chance happenings in the world, rather than to fortify ourselves against them." See Martha Nussbaum's *Love's Knowledge: Essays on Philosophy and Literature.* (Oxford University Press, 1990), 184. Literature offers Nussbaum the ground against which ethical facilities can be developed.

My emphasis is slightly different. Rather than testing moral vision through ethical dilemmas within the text. I argue that the interpretive facility, that relation between text and reader, itself provides both an ethical dilemma and opportunity.

6 My own technique is modeled on that of the post-structuralist interpreters of Joyce such as Jacques Derrida (particularly in his famous dilation of the single phrase "he war" from *Finnegans Wake*, for example), Margot Norris, Jean-Michel Rabaté Stephan Heath, and Jacques Aubert among many others. My intention is to indicate how this ground-breaking approach introduced over three decades ago continues to open new possibilities for understanding and has particular relevance to engaging Joyce's literary ethic.

7 See James Joyce's *A Portrait of the Artist as a Young Man.* Ed. Chester G. Anderson. (New York: Viking Press, 1968), 205. (Hereafter referred to as *P*) In *Totality and Infinity*, Emmanuel Levinas makes an ethical case which parallels Stephen's esthetic argument. Levinas employs the terms rhetoric and conversation which, it seems, have similar functions to the kinetic and static respectively. "Rhetoric, absent from no discourse, and which philosophical discourse seeks to overcome, resists discourse (or leads to it: pedagogy, demagogy, psychogogy). It approaches the other not to face him, but obliquely – not, to be sure, as a thing, since rhetoric remains conversation, and across all its artifices goes unto the Other [*Autrui*], solicits his yes . . . To renounce the psychagogy, demagogy, pedagogy rhetoric involves is to face the Other (*Autrui*), in a veritable conversation." See Emmanuel Levinas's *Totality and Infinity: And Essay on Exteriority*, trans. Alphonso Lingis (Pittsburgh: Duquesne University Press, 1969), 70. (Hereafter referred to as *TI*). Jill Robbins notes that Levinas understands rhetoric to mean persuasion and "action upon others." Within his ethics, rhetoric indicates the tendency to approach the other at an angle, "approaching him with an agenda." See Jill Robbins's *Altered Reading: Levinas and Literature* (University of Chicago Press, 1999), 17.

8 The Greek etymology of this word "static" also emphasizes dynamic ambivalence rather than paralysis, and was used to describe a state of civil war. In a similar interpretation, Adam Newton describes stasis as a "Paradox of continuous movement." See Adam Newton's *Narrative Ethics* (Cambridge, Massachusetts: Harvard University Press, 1995), 38.

9 Derek Attridge briefly suggests a similar reading of Joyce's ethics in response to Levinas's theory in "Judging Joyce." See especially pages 17–18. He emphasizes, however, that it is difficult to ascribe a "redemptive power"

to the text, in part because its "potential effects are always unpredictable." See Derek Attridge's "Judging Joyce." *Modernism/Modernity* 6.3 (1999): 24. However, if Joyce's texts are to have ethical values, it is precisely because of their profound "otherness," their "refusal to be assimilated to existing cultural norms" (26). Attridge notes that the intense scrutiny and exegetical efforts practiced on these texts over the decades since their publication, have in some ways domesticated this alterity. Though the sheer volume and breadth of scholarship may produce a newly "defamiliarized" reading experience.

10 Homi Bhabha has described the incommensurability of colonial difference, for example, in "Signs Taken For Wonders." He recounts the story of the "vegetarian Bible" which indicates the absolute difference between Indian subjects and their Christian colonizers even as those colonizers attempt to subsume Indian identity using the rhetoric of Christian faith. Joyce extends that difference to gender, class, and sexual orientation among other categories constructing subjectivity.

11 Andrew Gibson provides a lyrical description of the Levinasian other, writing "the other whom I encounter is always radically in excess of what my ego, cognitive powers, consciousness or intuitions would make of her or him. The other always and definitely overflows the frame in which I would seek to enclose the other." Andrew Gibson's *Postmodernity, Ethics and the Novel: From Leavis to Levinas*" (London and New York: Routledge, 1999), 25.

12 Descartes compared the lever with which Archimedes proposed to move the world with the one basic philosophical supposition which, if proven true, would allow the philosopher to acquire all knowledge.

13 Simon Critchley describes Levinas's experiences during World War Two in *The Ethics of Deconstruction*. See Simon Crichley's *The Ethics of Deconstruction* (West Lafayette, Indiana: Purdue University Press, 1999), 281–282. Levinas's own evocation of that experience is eloquent; he dedicates *Otherwise Than Being* to the victims of the Holocaust: "To the memory of those who were closest among the six million assassinated by the National Socialists, and of the millions on millions of all confessions and all nations, victims of the same hatred of the other man, the same anti-Semitism."

14 Emmanuel Levinas, "Difficult Freedom," *The Levinas Reader*, ed. Sean Hand (Oxford: Blackwell, 1989), 257.

15 In this introduction, I often retain Levinas's French *Autrui*, rather than adopting the translated "Other," because it more accurately reflects the absolute transcendence Levinas evokes with this word, and because it will be less easily confused with the Lacanian Other. See footnote 16 for a brief discussion of the relation between the Lacanian and Levinasian Other.

16 Levinas's *Autrui* may be fruitfully compared to Lacan's more familiar concept of the Other. As Hans-Deiter Gondek notes in "Cogito and *Séparation*: Levinas/Lacan," while in Levinas's work the encounter with the *Autrui* constitutes the ethical relationship which is the founding of subjectivity, Lacan's Other represents the moments of extreme foreignness or difference

that are revealed in language. Like Lacan's Other, Levinas's is not necessarily immediately present to the senses; according to Gondek, the encounter with the Other "by no means entails that the face is given to the beholder to see and to read like an open blossom or an open book." See "Cogito and *Séparation*: Lacan/Levinas." *Levinas and Lacan. The Missed Encounter*, ed. Sarah Harasym (Albany: State University of New York Press, 1998), 23.

17 Luce Irigaray, "Questions to Emmanuel Levinas," trans. Margaret Whitford, *Rereading Levinas*, ed. Robert Bernasconi and Simon Critchley (Bloomington: Indiana University Press, 1991), 112–113. Irigaray's ethics, while compelling, may be read as heterocentric in this instance in which she claims that pleasure enjoyed "between the same sex does not result in that immanent ecstasy between the other and myself," and in which she relies on the possibility of procreation to embody the connection found in this pleasure (113).

18 Conceiving of Joyce's "others," I find it helpful to return to Irigaray's *Ethics of Sexual Difference* and more particularly to Stephen Heath's commentary and elaboration of that text. Heath notes that sexual difference cannot be reduced to a simple division between genders, "for the other who differs from me sexually is not just woman or man in the man/woman paradigm, but indeed the other, man or woman, the other to me in sexual difference, whether straight, gay or lesbian.... Sexuality is bound up in sexual difference in more than one paradigm way... an ethics of sexual difference cannot separate itself and sexual difference from race and class. *Not separating them will then increase the urgency of questioning the language and imagination of otherness*... what is needed is for difference to work with the recognition of identities – other identities – *and* with the awareness of the limits, the constraints of identity...." See Stephen Heath's "The Ethics of Sexual Difference," *Discourse* 12.2 (Spring-Summer 1990): 147–148, first emphasis added, second original). Beginning from something like what we call identity politics today, Joyce both recognizes "otherness" and at the same time draws the categories that construct that otherness into question in order to mark the relations of incommensurable difference and incontrovertible connection that are present in each relation of the subject with his or her others.

19 Derek Attridge, "Innovation, Literature, Ethics: Relating to the Other." *PMLA* 114 (1999): 20–31.

20 James Joyce, *Dubliners*, ed. Robert Scholes and A. Walton Litz in consultation with Richard Ellman (New York: Viking Press, 1969), 28. (Hereafter referred to as *D*).

21 James Joyce, *Ulysses* (New York: Vintage-Random, 1986), 12:1430. (Hereafter referred to as *U*).

22 The idea of being responsible to the other in both Levinas's and Joyce's thought should be distinguished from the Christian ethic of loving another as oneself. To treat the other as one treats oneself can potentially mean the submersion of another under the assumptions of similarity. In contrast, both Levinas and Joyce emphasize difference and maintain the ethical imperative of recognizing that difference.

23 Emmanuel Levinas, "The Trace of the Other," trans. Alphonso Lingis, *Deconstruction in Context*, ed. Mark C. Taylor (Chicago and London: University of Chicago Press, 1986), 346.

24 In an interview with Richard Kearney, Levinas notes: "Already in Greek philosophy one can discern traces of the ethical breaking through the ontological, for example in Plato's idea of the 'Good existing beyond Being' *(agathon epekeina tes ousias)*. . . . One can also cite in this connection Descartes' discovery of 'the Idea of the Infinite', which surpasses the finite limits of human nature and the human mind." See Richard Kearney's *Dialogues with Contemporary Continental Thinkers: The Phenomenological Heritage: Paul Ricoeur, Emmanuel Levinas, Herbert Marcuse, Stanislas Breton, Jacques Derrida*, (Manchester University Press, 1984), 61.

25 I return to the relations between national and gendered difference in chapter three.

26 Christine Overall, writing about feminist ethics, makes a similar argument when she notes, "The recognition, or more fundamentally the constitution, of oneself as a self requires the presence of other selves. . . . This means more than the mere acknowledgment of an adversary or the admission of the existence of an object to be subordinated. As Whitbeck puts it, '[R]elationships between people . . . develop through identification and differentiation, through listening and speaking, with *each other*, rather than through struggles to dominate or annihilate the other'" See Christine Overall's "Feminism, Ontology, and 'Other Minds,'" *Feminist Perspectives: Philosophical Essays on Method and Morals*, ed. Lorraine Code, Sheila Mullett, Christine Overall (University of Toronto Press, 1988), 98.

27 Robert Eaglestone, *Ethical Criticism* (Edinburgh University Press, 1997), 152.

28 Eaglestone, *Ethical Criticism*, 99. Levinas is similarly resistant to art in general. In his essay "Reality and its Shadow," which may be read as a reference to the Platonic view of art, Levinas writes: "Does not the function of art lie in not understanding? Does not obscurity provide it with its very element and completion *sui generis*, foreign to dialects and the life of ideas? Will we say that the artist knows and expresses the very obscurity of the real?" See Emmanuel Levinas's "Reality and its Shadow," *The Levinas Reader*, ed. Sean Hand (Oxford: Blackwell, 1989), 131.

29 Andrew Gibson makes a similar argument in *Postmodernity, Ethics and the Novel*. See especially pages 54–55.

30 Eaglestone, *Ethical Criticism*, (135).

31 His approach to literature varied over the course of his career as John Llewelyn has noted in *The Middle Voice of Ecological Conscience*, see especially pages 98–113.

32 Jill Robbins, *Altered Reading: Levinas and Literature*, 91.

33 Drucilla Cornell, *Beyond Accomodation: Ethical Feminism, Deconstruction, and the Law* (New York: Routledge, 1991), xxvii.

34 Emmanuel Levinas, *Time and the Other*, trans. Richard A. Cohen (Pittsburgh: Duquesne University Press, 1987), 88. Having the "opposite meaning"

of consciousness, women by definition would be unable to act as ethical agents. Philosopher Michèle Le Doeuff writes "Lévinas calmly writes that the feminine can have no access to moral existence, in other words to what he regards as best or almost best." She notes also that "when philosophy discusses women, women are not the real subject. But we can still have something to say about it and we do not have to agree to bear the brunt of problems which are nothing to do with us." See Michèle Le Doeuff, *Hipparchia's Choice: An Essay Concerning Women, Philosophy, etc*, trans. Trista Selous (Oxford: Blackwell, 1991), 13.

35 Though Joyce also associates ethics with its literal meaning in the Greek of habitat or dwelling, his description of the relation of the dwelling to the feminine (and indeed the masculine) is radically different. In fact he critiques any masculinity that founds itself by taking a feminine other as an object and ignoring the extent to which she is herself an ethical subject who constructs her habitat rather than merely inhabits it. One illustration of this objection may be found in "A Little Cloud" in which Chandler conflates his wife and child with the inert habitat of his home. He seeks to develop a kind of esthetic subjectivity against the ground of his family as objects. When his wife and child present themselves as other subjects with conscious difference to his assumptions, he resorts to violence. Joyce implies that this violence results from his failure to accept their difference and consciousness. He presents a more potentially ethical resolution to a similar conflict in "The Dead" in which Gabriel's realization of his wife's history and consciousness provides them both with the possibility of renewal, of "going west."

36 Simone de Beauvoir, *The Second Sex*, ed. H. M. Parshley (New York: Knopf, 1952), xvi. In a footnote to Levinas's discussion of the feminine, translator Richard A. Cohen glosses de Beauvoir's criticism of Levinas in her *The Second Sex*. He notes that de Beauvoir accuses Levinas of according "secondary" and "derivative" status to the feminine. Cohen argues that while the issue is crucial, it is "certainly not as simple as de Beauvoir, in this instance, makes it out to be, because for Levinas the other has priority over the subject." See Emmanuel Levinas's *Time and the Other*, trans. Richard A. Cohen (Pittsburgh: Duquesne University Press, 1987), 85. While Levinas cautions that he does not wish to "ignore the legitimate claims of feminism that presupposes all the acquired attainments of civilization," (*ibid* 86) and while the other is indeed granted priority in relation to the subject, his commentary has the strange courtly effect of placing "ladies first." Derrida proposes that Levinas's work on the dwelling and the feminine might be understood as a "*manifeste féministe*." See Jacques Derrida's *Adieu to Emmanuel Levinas*, trans. Pascale-Anne Brault and Michael Naas (Stanford University Press, 1999), 83. But like Simon Critchley, I respectfully admit to difficulty with that reading. See Simon Critchley's *Ethics–Politics–Subjectivity: Essays on Derrida, Levinas and Contemporary French Thought* (London and New York: Verso, 1999), 273. Levinas's support of feminism, in the limited sense in which he defines it ("attainments of civilization"), does not satisfy the charge

de Beauvoir levels that his assumption is of a primary masculine subject who attains ethics in response to the other or feminine as a foil. Even if that foil is granted primacy, responsibility, or even respect, her demand for reciprocity and mutuality is not met. Levinas's theory begs the question: what is a *woman's* ethical subjectivity?

37 De Beauvoir, *The Second Sex*, xvii.

38 Irigaray, "Questions to Emmanuel Levinas," 115.

39 The desire for return to an unaltered home bears a striking resemblance to Levinas's assessment of the Odyssey.

40 See Luce Irigaray's *The Ethics of Sexual Difference*, trans. Carolyn Burke and Gillian C. Gill (Ithaca: Cornell University Press, 1993), 122–123.

41 Irigaray, "Questions to Emmanuel Levinas," 112.

42 While a Kantian ethics focuses primarily on respect for the law and adherence to a universal code of behavior, more postmodern ethical theories influenced by Levinas give precedence to respect for an other in encounters and dilemmas that are essentially undecidable. Ethics in postmodern theory is a dilemma more than it is a code. My own approach also rests on this distinction between morality and ethics, on the dilemma rather than on received code. Adam Newton presents this approach cogently in his *Narrative Ethics* which is indebted to Levinas's philosophy. His literary critical practice seeks to "disrupt the conventionally understood synonymy of the words *moral* and *ethical*" (See Newton's *Narrative Ethics*, 5), locating ethics primarily in the "narrative act," or to use Levinas's terminology, in the "Saying" more than the "Said" (*ibid* 8), and referring to the "radicality and uniqueness of the moral situation itself, a binding claim exercised upon the self by a concrete and singular other whose moral appeal precedes both decision and understanding" (*ibid* 12). Following this logic, Newton notes that a "theory of narrative ethics need not be determined by, nor does it necessarily arise out of, considerations about novels' or their authors' moral or moralizing intentions. As I have said, it is concerned with the intersubjective dynamics of narrative, and their ethical implications, independent of the 'moral paraphrases' which they may invite or which can be ascribed to them" (*ibid* 32–33).

43 Paul Ricouer, *Oneself as Another*, trans. Kathleen Blamey (Chicago and London: University of Chicago Press, 1992), 170.

44 Seyla Benhabib, "The Generalized and the Concrete Other," 274. One possible feminist ethical position on female genital mutilation (FGM) provides an obvious example of an interactive universalist ethics. Such a position might take into account cultural differences which alternately promote or abhor FGM. Recognizing another culture's priorities, a western feminist might advocate the funding of cliterodectomy clinics in the interests of saving women's lives and health through the use of minimally invasive and sterile surgical procedures. At the same time, this same western feminist might *also* condemn FGM as a basic violation of human – and specifically women's – rights.

45 Julia Kristeva, *Desire in Language: A Semiotic Approach to Literature and Art*, ed. Leon Roudiez (New York: Columbia University Press, 1980), 23.

46 See Gayatri Spivak's "Introduction" to *Imaginary Maps* by Mahasweta Devi (Calcutta: Thema, 1993), xxv. I will return to the idea of *aporia* and its relations to the ethical subject in chapter one.

47 Susan Bordo, "The Cartesian Masculinization of Thought," *From Modernism to Postmodernism*, ed. Lawrence Cahoone (Cambridge MA: Blackwell, 1996), 644.

48 Bordo's sympathetic thought should not be confused with the ethics of care discussed in Carol Gilligan's works, such as the admirable *In a Different Voice*, and at the center of debate in feminist ethics in Canada and the United States. I wish to distinguish responsibility to the other from the responsibility to care because of the possible limitations of the latter for feminist thought (limitations which Gilligan herself addresses). More specifically, within a culture in which women are called on as primary domestic and public care-providers, it is wise to be cautious about an uncritical acceptance of care as a model for ethical behavior. Margaret Urban Walker, for example, has asked "whether maternal paradigms, nurturant responsiveness, and a bent toward responsibility for others' needs aren't our oppressive history, not our liberating future, and whether 'women's morality' isn't a familiar ghetto rather than a liberated space." See Margaret Urban Walker, "Moral Understandings: Alternative 'Epistemology' for a Feminist Ethics," *Explorations in Feminist Ethics*, ed. Eve Browning Cole and Susan Coultrap-McQuin (Bloomington: Indiana University Press, 1992), 166.

49 This understanding of "identification" is crucial to my interpretation of James Joyce's relationship with Lucia Joyce as described in chapter four.

50 Kelly Oliver, *Family Values: Subjects between Nature and Culture* (New York: Routledge, 1997), 96.

51 In "French Feminism Revisited," commenting on Levinas's philosophy of the feminine in both *Totality and Infinity* and "Phenomenology of Eros," Gayatri Spivak describes him as "almost comically patriarchal" (See "French Feminism Revisited: Ethics and Politics" in *Feminists Theorize the Political*, ed. Judith Butler and Joan Scott [New York: Routledge, 1992], 76) drawing attention to such phrases as the "forever inviolate virginity of the feminine" (*TI* 258) and "supremely non-public" (*TI* 265). Spivak at the same time pays "respect" to the "grandeur of Levinas's thought," a gesture I feel compelled to replicate, at the same time that, like Spivak, I find myself resisting this "prurient heterosexist, male identified ethics" (*ibid* 77).

52 Drucilla Cornell notes that the emphasis on the mother as a figure through which to formulate an ethical theory, particularly in Julia Kristeva's work, has disturbing implications for feminist practice which has vigorously sought to provide choices concerning maternity for women. "If it is the actual experience of mothering that provides the 'ideal' of a different way of relating to the Other, some women would inevitably be excluded. Feminism, then, would not rely on the experience of women, but on that of mothers." See, Drucilla Cornell's *Beyond Accommodation: Ethical Feminism, Deconstruction, and the Law*, 58. I am in complete agreement with this moment

in Cornell's criticism. It is for this reason that I emphasize, in my own theory, the experience of the fetus, of being born from the womb rather than providing the habitat of the womb. This model is applicable both to men and women, to mothers and to those who chose not to reproduce.

53 Irigaray argues that women are too often understood as mere vessels or habitats. She insists that in sexuality and in pregnancy the body must be envisioned as territory which raises the question of whether the guest is invited or an intruder. Irigaray proposes to make virginity or celibacy (the right to refuse entry) and abortion (the right to refuse an uninvited guest) basic human rights for women. See Whitford's synopsis of this argument in *Luce Irigaray: Philosophy in the Feminine* (London and New York: Routledge, 1991), 160.

54 Julia Kristeva, "Stabat Mater," *The Kristeva Reader*, ed. Toril Moi (New York: Columbia University Press, 1986), 308.

55 One such need, according to Kristeva, is to compensate for the lack inherent in language. "If language is powerless to locate myself for and state myself to the other, I assume–I want to believe – that there is someone who makes up for that weakness. Someone . . . who might make me be by means of borders, separations, vertigos" (*ibid* 321).

56 Kristeva, "Stabat Mater," 322–333 (ellipsis and emphases original).

57 In *Beyond Accomodation*, Drucilla Cornell glosses this discussion in relation to Kristeva's distinction between the semiotic and the symbolic. She notes that within the symbolic system, under the Law of the Father, there is no language for describing the fracture between pregnant mother and fetus. "The 'maternal body,' however, has no designation in the symbolic except as a fantasized unity in which the mother is one with the child. Therefore, it does not express the experience of the maternal body from the position of the pregnant woman, which is not one of unity, but of non-identity with herself and with her child." See Cornell, *Beyond Accommodation*, 41. The difficulty in expressing this fracture or non-identity within the symbolic has serious ramifications for women within ethical and legal systems of justice.

58 Kristeva's own language or style in "Stabat Mater" is designed to disrupt that idealization by registering the experience of pregnancy and mothering in two ways which are presented in parallel in the essay. She describes both her own experience of pregnancy and childbirth and also a theoretical account of the subsuming of the feminine into the maternal in western and Christian cultures. Drucilla Cornell also notes this stylistic experiment writing that the "link between this reconnection with motherhood and the affirmation of the avant-garde writing that disrupts the symbolic through reconnection with the semiotic is embodied in this text." See Cornell, *Beyond Accommodation*, 47.

59 Relying, as she so often does, on biological models and metaphors for addressing philosophical questions, Luce Irigaray is open to charges of essentialism. Irigarary herself addresses such charges explicitly in *Je Tu Nous* by noting: "The difficulties women have in gaining recognition for their social and political rights are rooted in this insufficiently thought out relation between biology and culture. At present, to deny all explanations of a biological

kind – because biology has paradoxically been used to exploit women – is to deny the key to interpreting this exploitation." See Luce Irigaray's *Je Tu Nous: Toward a Culture of Difference*, trans. Alison Martin (New York: Routledge, 1993), 46.

60 Kelly Oliver, *Family Values: Subjects between Nature and Culture*, 102.

61 Hélène Cixous, "The Laugh of the Medusa," *New French Feminisms*, ed. Elaine Marks and Isabelle de Courtivron (New York: Schocken Books, 1981), 251.

62 Lawrence Buell, "Introduction In Pursuit of Ethics" *PMLA* 114.1 (January 1999): 12.

63 Dominic Manganiello's revolutionary book *Joyce's Politics* was one of the first to overturn the myth of Joyce's indifference to politics. Manganiello detailed with careful precision Joyce's political alliances and explicitly-stated preferences as well as the political discussions embedded in his narratives. Vincent Cheng's *Joyce, Race and Empire*, explores the colonial and postcolonial contexts to which Joyce's books are addressed. Joseph Valente's "The Politics of Joyce's Polyphony" in *New Alliances in Joyce Studies* (ed. Bonnie Kime Scott) and *James Joyce and the Problem of Justice* both provide wonderful examples of the emerging trend in Joyce criticism which locates his politics in the immediate realm of his stylistic and linguistic choices. This list is, of course, only partial.

64 Vicki Mahaffey, "Intentional Error: The Paradox of Editing Joyce's *Ulysses*," *Representing Modernist Texts: Editing as Interpretation*, ed. George Bornstein (Ann Arbor: The University of Michigan Press, 1991), 224.

65 Jill Robbins, *Altered Reading: Levinas and Literature*, xxiv.

66 J. Hillis Miller, *The Ethics of Reading: Kant, de Man, Eliot, Trollope, James, and Benjamin* (New York: Columbia University Press, 1987), 4.

67 In *Je Tu Nous* Luce Irigaray writes of the persistence with which men consider women in merely functionary roles. Irigaray also employs the metaphor of the envelope, however in her version, woman is read as envelope with no letter, function without content or consciousness. "Particularly in her role as the mother, 'woman represents the place of man'; she is the 'envelop' by which man delimits himself and, as the mother and man's other, 'woman remains the *place separated from its "own" place.*'" See Luce Irigaray, "Questions to Emmanuel Levinas," 169. Rosalyn Diprose writes in response to Irigaray's metaphor: "Another way to put this is that sexual 'difference' is constituted in such a way that man gains his autonomous identity at the expense of woman. Irigaray's examination of the constitution of sexed identity and difference exposes a structural reason why women's modes of being, particularly motherhood, continue to be excluded from the position of subject of social exchange." See Rosalyn Diprose, *The Bodies of Women: Ethics, Embodiment, and Sexual Difference* (London and New York: Routledge, 1994), 36. In using metaphors of milk and placenta to envision the ethical subject, I hope in part to suggest alternatives to the way in which motherhood has been understood as mere function or envelope and to point to the extent to which the relation to the mother is the foundation of ethical subjectivity.

68 Both Margot Norris and Kimberly Devlin have presented impressive work on the philosophical implications of clothing choices in Joyce's works. See Norris' *Joyce Web* and Devlin's "Pretending in 'Penelope': Masquerade, Mimicry, and Molly Bloom."

69 In "Ethics," Geoffrey Galt Harpham has noted the extent to which ethics evinces a "structural obsession with the relations between apparently opposed terms." See Geoffrey Galt Harpham, "Ethics," *Critical Terms for Literary Study*, ed. Frank Lentricchia and Thomas McLaughlin (University of Chicago Press, 1995), 394. It is that structural obsession with opposition which I am seeking to trace in this chapter both in ethical theory and in ALP's ethical interventions.

CHAPTER ONE

1 Samuel Beckett, *The Unnamable* (London: Calder, 1959), 401–402.

2 In his notes while drafting *Exiles* Joyce writes "All Celtic philosophers seemed to have inclined toward incertitude or skepticism – Hume, Berkeley, Balfour, Bergson." See *James Joyce's Exiles* (New York: Penguin, 1973), 159. Hereafter referred to as *E*.

3 In *Joyce Upon the Void: the Genesis of Doubt*, Jean-Michel Rabaté presents an elegant and complex discussion of the figures and effects of doubt in Joyce's oeuvre.

4 Jacques Derrida, *Aporias*, trans. Thomas Dutoit (Stanford University Press, 1993), 21.

5 See Harpham's excellent history of ethical considerations in recent literary study in *Critical Terms for Literary Study*.

6 Geoffrey Harpham, *Getting It Right: Language, Literature, and Ethics* (University of Chicago Press, 1992), 56.

7 Among the most prominent, and careful, of these critics is Wayne Booth whose *The Company We Keep* regrets that ethical considerations have been, in his view, subjected to "theoretical ostracism."

8 J. Hillis Miller, *The Ethics of Reading*, 10. However, while Miller's ethical criticism is deconstructive in the sense associated with the Yale school of literary criticism, his ethical theory is closer to the certainties of moral philosophy than to the radical break represented by Levinasian and post-Levinasian ethics. Simon Critchley makes a similar argument, noting that "Miller understands ethics in its traditional determination as a region of philosophical inquiry and not in the more radical Levinasian sense." See Simon Critchley, *The Ethics of Deconstruction* (West Lafayette, Indiana: Purdue University Press, 1999), 47.

9 Adam Newton, *Narrative Ethics*, 37.

10 For a reflection on that textual relation see Murray McArthur's "The Example of Joyce: Derrida Reading Joyce." *James Joyce Quarterly*, 32.2 1995: 227–241.

11 Derek Attridge and Daniel Ferrar, *Post-structuralist Joyce: Essays from the French* (Cambridge University Press, 1984), 7–8.

12 Drucilla Cornell, for example, notes of Derrida's deconstructive writing on rigid gender hierarchy: "this intervention is itself explicitly ethical, done in the name of a dream of a new choreography of sexual difference." See Cornell, *Beyond Accommodation*, 18.

13 Phillip Herring also notes the unfinished sentences and fragmentary structures in Joyce's texts which he designates as "gnomonic" and describes as "designed to created mystery." See Phillip Herring, *Joyce's Uncertainty Principle* (Princeton University Press, 1987), x.

14 Jacques Derrida, *Aporia*, 18–19. Andrew Gibson makes a similar point when he defines ethics as the "excess that cannot be known positively within any given system of morality, the aporia that limits any attempt to collapse the good into positive knowledge." See Andrew Gibson, *Postmodernity, Ethics and the Novel*, 16.

15 Jacques Derrida, *Aporias*, 20.

16 My interpretation here contradicts David Fabian's, who argues that the ideal subject is the complete one who has learned to "box his corner" and that the gnomon reaches its "logical geometrical completion" in the figure of the parallelogram. See David R. Fabian, "Joyce's 'The Sisters': Gnomon, Gnomic, Gnome," *Studies in Short Fiction* 5 (1968): 187–189.

17 This definition of the ethical subject as incomplete accords with that of Emmanuel Levinas who argues that the subject emerges from the ethical summons of an other, and that as a result of that dependence on the encounter, the subject is always incomplete.

18 This textbook was among the contents of Joyce's library; the text was stamped J.J. See Richard Ellmann, *The Consciousness of Joyce* (London: Faber and Faber, 1977), 111.

19 Thomas E. Connolly argues that it is Father Flynn who embodies the gnomon in the text because he is incomplete: found wanting in his religious calling, judged mentally incompetent and unable to implement his spiritual office. According to Connolly, Flynn "has become a 'remainder after something else has been removed,' a gnomon." See Thomas E. Connolly, "Joyce's 'The Sisters': A Pennyworth of Snuff," *College English* 27 (1967): 195. I would argue, on the contrary, that Flynn is an absent presence in the text, and a subject who in his spiritual or emotional blindness does not leave himself open to the influence of others nor can he recognize his responsibility. His subjectivity is as boxed in as is the parallelogram absented for a geometrical gnomon. Bernard Benstock concurs with this interpretation of Father Flynn as an absent presence, a ghost. See Benstock, "The Gnomonics of *Dubliners*," *James Joyce Quarterly* 34 (1988): 520.

20 In *The Intimate Enemy*, Ashis Nandy indicates the extent to which the fear of femininity is associated with colonial culture. In an attempt to differentiate between subjects and rulers in an imperial culture, British colonizers commonly ascribed a prevalent femininity in their male subjects. Resisting

colonialism, for many of these men, meant resisting both the feminine within themselves and women as an embodiment of the weakness that allowed them to be colonized.

21 Oscar Wilde expressed the silencing of homosexual desire during his trial when he defined Lord Alfred Douglas's "love that dare not speak its name" as the love of an older man for a younger man. That love is parodied and reduced in the queer old josser's desire for the young boy in which Joyce responds to Wilde not with homophobia but, as Vicki Mahaffey indicates in *States of Desire*, with concern for the combined idealization of and exploitation of youth evidenced in Wilde's relations with rent boys. The silencing of "queer" desires, as Ed Cohen indicates, has a lengthy history in Christian cultures. "The Latin designation for sodomy was *crime non nominandum inter christanos* – the crime not to be named among Christians. See Ed Cohen, *Talk on the Wilde Side: Towards a Genealogy of a Discourse on Male Sexualities* (New York: Routledge, 1993), 240. Cohen also notes that "sodomy had been defined in ecclesiastical terms as one of the gravest sins against divine law whose name alone proved such an affront to God that it was often named only as the unnamable" (*ibid* 103).

22 Bernard Benstock associates the gnomon (or no man) with emasculation throughout *Dubliners*. See Benstock, "The Gnomonics of *Dubliners*," 537–538.

23 I discuss Anna Livia Plurabelle as "geomater" in relation to ethical subjectivities in chapter three.

24 David Weir notes that the ellipses in *Dubliners* are structural and narrative as well as grammatical. Discussing Eveline's aborted departure from Dublin, he writes of the ellipses between the opening passage in her father's home and ending section at the North Wall: "our attention is directed to the ommission [of a narrative transition between the two parts] by a row of dots or ellipses marks. This narrative omission seems highly functional: just as the narrative omits the journey from the room to the dock, so Eveline declines to continue that journey by refusing to board the ship with Frank. . . . We can say that Eveline reenacts an activity of the narrative itself by going blank at the moment of the expected journey, or we can say that the static Eveline has influenced the narrative in that it has appropriated her inability to move at precisely the juncture of the story where a physical action necessarily occurs." See David Weir, "Gnomon is an Island: Euclid and Bruno in Joyce's Narrative Practice," *James Joyce Quarterly* 28 (Winter 1991): 345 (ellipses added).

25 In invoking this call to the other for justice as an ethical event, I am echoing James McMichael's nuanced definition of justice which is both impossible and necessary. McMichael defines justice as the case each subject has with an other. "Justice is impossible if only because there is too little time for me to hear every person's case, each case needing to be heard anew with each change in the person's need. It would spare me much displeasure if I could quietly wish for justice as a utopia: but justice is more than utopian

for the person who wants it since wanting it is a restlessness for which there can be no time at the end of political history that any utopia presupposes." My concept of ethics is very close to McMichael's idea of justice which he defines in opposition to sentimentality. If *"the sentimentalist is he who would enjoy without incurring the immense debtorship for a thing done"* (*U* 9:550–951) (as Stephen defines it, cribbing from George Meredith's *The Ordeal of Richard Feveral*, page 180), justice is the recognition of debts owed. "My understanding of that debtorship begins when I recognize *Ulysses* as the testament of a person who wants justice, as most persons do. Justice, as I understand it, is a situation in which every person has a case with all persons. A person *is* a case in the sense that he calls for help in meeting his needs. Help can come, though only if he *has* a case, only if another person hears his call and responds to it unsentimentally. *Ulysses* is such a call. Joyce's case with me in *Ulysses* is that he wants to be "with any as any with any" (*U* 17:68), which he can be only if every person has a case with all persons." See James McMichael, *Ulysses and Justice* (Princeton University Press, 1991), 8.

26 It is worth noting that Levinas's *maurvaise conscience* is radically different from Nietzsche's more familiar *"resentiment"* as bad conscience as described in *On the Genealogy of Morals*.

27 Emmanuel Levinas, "Ethics as First Philosophy," *The Levinas Reader*, ed. Sean Hand (Oxford: Blackwell, 1989), 82. Levinasian and indeed Joycean ethics are profoundly utopian in the sense of taking place in the no place. Andrew Gibson notes that ethics "in itself is a function of imperfection or – in a term of Cornell's . . . – 'inadequation.' It is precisely their insistence on inadequation that makes ethical feminism and deconstruction utopian." See Gibson, *Postmodernity, Ethics and the Novel*, 175. For Joyce, as for Cornell and other feminist ethicists I have been discussing, ethics is always an effort in excess, it can never be achieved but nonetheless defines the subject in his or her striving for and toward the other.

28 Jacques Derrida, *Aporias*, 21.

29 Arthur Power, *Conversations with James Joyce* (New York: Barnes and Noble, 1974), 35. Clive Hart points out that while Joyce is indebted to Ibsen in constructing both *Exiles* and *Portrait*, Joyce's play should not be read strictly as a realist work nor solely in the tradition of Ibsen's "well-made" play. Rather, the play adopts the *style indirect libre* techniques innovated in *Portrait* and *Dubliners* and as such, "the dramatic tone need not be the dramatist's. Nor of course entirely that of the characters: the idiom of *Exiles* is curiously poised between the two, leaving the characters and their actions half real, half reinterpreted with a critical ironic voice." Clive Hart, "The Language of *Exiles*," *Coping with Joyce: Essays from the Copenhagen Symposium*, ed. Morris Beja and Shari Benstock (Columbus: Ohio State University Press, 1989), 124.

30 In using this word, liberated, I am adapting Richard's own term "I have allowed you complete *liberty* – and allow you it still . . . " (*E*, emphasis added, 65) to define his relational experiment with Bertha.

31 Joyce provides evidence of either interpretation of her decision (to stay or not to stay with Robert), littering Act 3 with textual cues that stimulate our curiosity. For example, Bertha offers to reveal the events of the previous evening for Richard's benefit, which if her morality is purely conventional would indicate her chastity. Robert in his turn asks her: "Were you mine in that sacred night of love?" (*E* 137), indicating that some act of love licensing his sense of ownership has taken place. Bertha, responding to Robert, tells him "Remember your dream of me. You dreamed that I was yours last night . . ." (*E* 138) without clarifying if that dream coincides with events.

32 See "Women on the Market" in Luce Irigaray's *This Sex Which is Not One* and "The Traffic in Women" by Gayle Rubin in *Toward an Anthropology of Women.*

33 James McMichael, *Ulysses and Justice*, 21.

34 Joseph Valente explains this dilemma: "She has found that his liberal-rational species of freedom, a freedom from restraints and commitments, shaped within and suited to historically masculine spheres of activity and interest, belies the concrete feeling of emotional dependency that the resulting isolation instills in her. . . ." See Joseph Valente, *James Joyce and the Problem of Justice: Negotiating Sexual and Colonial Difference* (Cambridge University Press, 1995), 162.

35 Emmanuel Levinas, "The Other in Proust," *Proper Names*, trans. Michael B. Smith (Stanford University Press, 1996), 104.

36 Jacques Derrida, *Aporias*, 32.

37 Other characters seem particularly compelled to confess their condition to Beatrice. Zack Bowen indicates the prevalence of the confessional mode throughout the play, assessing the "lines of dialogue consumed by confessions," which he argues indicate Joyce's insufficient distance from the guilt of the "Cosgrave affair" at the time of *Exiles*'s composition. But the confessional mode may also be an indication of responsibility, the necessity of claiming one's own fault in the face of the other.

38 Beatrice is not without desires of her own, her desire for Richard is implied by her correspondence with him. But her desire is more akin to what Levinas and others (Deleuze and Guattari, most notably) have described as a desire of plenitude. "Desire is the need of him who has no more needs. We can recognize it in the desire for an other who is another [*autrui*], neither my enemy . . . nor my complement. . . . This desire for another, which is our very sociality, is not a simple relationship with a being where . . . the other is converted into the same." See Emmanuel Levinas, *Trace of the Other*, 350. While Beatrice is certainly not without needs, she does not map those needs onto another by projecting them as a version of herself. She accepts Richard in his otherness in an act of ethical interpretation.

39 Luce Irigaray, *Speculum of the Other Woman*, trans. Gillian C. Gill (Ithaca: Cornell University Press, 1985), 133.

40 Margaret Whitford, *Luce Irigaray: Philosophy in the Feminine* (London and New York: Routledge, 1991), 157.

41 Attridge writes that "innovative mental acts produce lasting alterations in the subjectivity that achieves them: once I have articulated the new thoughts that I had dimly apprehended, my thinking will never be entirely the same again. If that new articulation becomes public, with the disarticulation of settled modes of thought that made it possible (and thus that made it possible), it may alter cognitive frameworks across a wider domain, allowing further acts of creativity in other minds." See Derek Attridge's "Innovation, Literature, Ethics: Relating to the Other," *PMLA* 114 (January 1999): 22–23.

CHAPTER TWO

1 Throughout this chapter, I make the assumption, shared by most Joyce scholars, that the Stephen Dedalus described in childhood and adolescence in *A Portrait of the Artist as a Young Man* is the same Stephen Dedalus described as an adult in *Ulysses*.

2 Lorraine Code, *Epistemic Responsibility* (Hanover: University Press of New England, 1987), 3.

3 Jacques Derrida, *The Gift of Death*, trans. David Wills (University of Chicago Press, 1995), 25.

4 Margaret Whitford, *Luce Irigaray: Philosophy in the Feminine*, 149.

5 The relationship between coined money and sovereign power is made explicit in the "Cyclops" episode.

> But he, the young chief of the O'Bergan's, could ill brook to be outdone in generous deeds but gave therefor with gracious gesture a testoon of costliest bronze. Thereon embossed in excellent smithwork was seen the image of a queen of regal port, scion of the house of Brunswick, Victoria her name, Her Most Excellent Majesty, by grace of God of the United Kingdom of Great Britain and Ireland and of the British dominions beyond the sea, queen, defender of the faith, Empress of India, even she, who bore rule, a victress over many peoples, the wellbeloved, for they knew and loved her from the rising of the sun to the going down thereof, the pale, the dark, the ruddy and the ethiop. (*U* 12:290–299)

> The image on this coin is that of Queen Victoria, under whose rule British colonialism enjoyed its greatest expansion. This passage draws on the relationship between the image of Victoria and the imperial victories consolidated by the widening circulation of her currency. Victoria's coin yokes the idea of sovereign authority and imperial control to the circulation of her currency in colonial territories.

6 In *Portrait* Stephen excuses his unorthodox behavior by telling Davin, "– This race and this country and this life produced me. . . . I shall express myself as I am" (*P* 203). While Stephen is aware of the extent to which he is produced by his national context, Joyce implies that he is, in turn, responsible to it.

7 Margaret Urban Walker, "Moral Understandings: Alternative 'Epistemology' for a Feminist Ethics," 166.

8 Louis Althusser, "Ideology and the Ideological State Apparatuses (Notes toward an Investigation)," *Lenin and Philosophy and Other Essays*, trans. Ben Brewster (New York: Monthly Review Press, 1971), 143.

9 Althusser postulates that while the ideological impositions of such institutions as schools, churches, or hospitals are not immediately evident, participants are indoctrinated through the rote practices of those institutions. Stephen's resistance to the Roman Catholic Church derives from assumptions similar to those of Althusser: to participate in the practices of the ideological institution is to be interpolated into that ideology.

10 For examinations of Stephen's misogyny see Judith Spector's "On Defining a Sexual Aesthetic: A Portrait of the Artist as Sexual Antagonist" and Suzette Henke's "Stephen Dedalus and Women: A Portrait of the Artist as a Young Misogynist.'

11 At times Stephen's ethics are perhaps more compatible with Foucault's definition of ethics as "care for the self" than Levinas's as "responsibility to the other." Foucault notes that care for the self as he outlines it in his *History of Sexuality* (especially in volume three) "has truly permeated all ethical thought" in which individual liberty within the framework of a disciplined practice of care was considered the basis of ethical behavior. See Michel Foucault's "The Ethic of Care for the Self as a Practice of Freedom," trans. J. D. Gauthier, S.J., *The Final Foucault*, ed. James Bernauer and David Rasmussen (Cambridge, Mass.: MIT Press, 1988), 4. However, Foucault emphasizes that care for the self results in care for others: "the assumption of all this morality was that the one who cared for himself correctly found himself, by that very fact, in a measure to behave correctly in relationship to others and for others" (*ibid* 7).

12 In this imagined interaction between Stephen's poetry and Emma's reception of it, the reader might see a precursor to the interactions between Richard and Beatrice in *Exiles*, and the extent to which Joyce insistently figures the artist's muse equally as a reader and a critic, a partner in the creation of meaning.

13 Stephen is frequently guilty of submitting women to this objectifying gaze. As Margot Norris points out his encounter with the bird-girl may be read as a kind of repetition or revision of Gabriel's conversion of his wife into a symbol when she stands on the staircase in "The Dead," listening to "distant music." Norris notes also that his esthetic preoccupations rest on his mother's unacknowledged labor as she irons the family's clothes, while he reads his paper on esthetics, and assembles his second-hand clothes so that he can retreat into the esthetic, preoccupations of his "silence, exile, and cunning." Margot Norris, *Joyce's Web* (Austin: University of Texas Press, 1992), 141.

14 Lipking writes: "When Milton appointed Lycidas 'the Genius of the shore,' he was staking a claim for his nation as well as his poem. The spirit who guards the coast will cast a long shadow of British influence across the Irish Sea, translating the martyrdom of one poor soul into an opportunity for a

new English poet to tame the flood and take his rightful place." Lawrence Lipking, "The Genius of the Shore: Lycida, Adamastor, and the Poetics of Nationalism," *PMLA* 111 (March 1996): 205.

15 This Biblical citation is from the King James version.

16 Slavoj Zizek, *The Sublime Object of Ideology* (London: Verso, 1989), 80.

17 In making this comment on May Dedalus' recognition of difference, I am drawing on Julia Kristeva's theory in "Stabat Mater," in which she insists on a mother's awareness of the otherness in pregnancy and her concurrent nurturing of that difference, and also on May Dedalus's rich support of her son's intellectual life, a life denied her by the accident of gender.

18 Kristeva's original title for "Stabat Mater," discussed in my introduction, was "*Heréthique de l'amour*" and was published under that title in *Tel Quel* in 1977. She renamed the essay when she included it in *Tales of Love*. For an extensive discussion of Kristeva's *heréthique* in relation to her political philosophy, see Marilyn Edelstein's "Toward a Feminist Postmodern Poléthique."

19 Marilyn Edelstein, "Towards a Feminist Postmodern Poléthique: Kristeva on Ethics and Politics," *Ethics, Politics, and Difference in Julia Kristeva's Writing*, ed. Kelly Oliver (New York: Routledge, 1993), 196.

20 Stephen's status as an Irish errand boy may justify, by punning association, the errant method he engages as a subject of Erin under English rule.

21 This connection is emphasized further when Stephen compares Deasy's letter to the Irish people with the Biblical epistle to the Hebrews.

22 Examples of such mistakes include: the French aid that came too late to assist Irish rebels in 1798, the marital errancy that brought down Parnell, the Easter rising that had to be rescheduled for the Monday following Easter, and so on.

23 Stephen also "teaches" in the National Library when he explains his theory about Hamlet to the other men assembled there. But in this encounter he is less concerned with pedagogy than with shoring up his own intellectual reputation. The results, while more pyrotechnic, are less ethically effective. He fails to consider the possible responsibility entailed by his epistemological intervention. Though, in disowning the theory when he leaves the room he presents his listeners with a dilemma and at the same time promotes the kind of ambivalence that has made learning possible in this classroom. However, it is easier for Stephen to assume responsibility when his audience is made up, presumably, of impressionable children.

24 Commenting also on Stephen's pedagogy in *Ulysses*, Patrick McGee notes that while, in his awkwardness, Stephen apparently fails as a teacher "in any normative sense," he does make it possible for his students to learn by exploiting the "linguistic accident" in Armstrong's attempt to identify Pyrrhus. Patrick McGee, "Joyce's Pedagogy: *Ulysses* and *Finnegans Wake*," *Coping with Joyce: Essays from the Copenhagen Symposium*, ed. Morris Beja and Shari Benstock (Columbus: Ohio State University Press, 1989), 207. "In other words, Stephen, whatever his intention, teaches his students that understanding involves more than effacing words in order to grasp a referent" (*ibid* 209).

25 Stephen's pedagogical practice may not seem methodical, relying as it does on error and mistake. But as Luce Irigaray notes in *This Sex Which is Not One*, one definition of "method" is "detour, fraud, and artifice." Luce Irigaray, *This Sex Which Is Not One*, trans. Catherine Porter, (Ithaca: Cornell University Press, 1977), 150. Blanchot in *The Writing of Disaster* makes a similar case in characterizing Plato's etymology of *alètheia*, or truth, as an "errant course, the straying of the gods." Maurice Blanchot, *The Writing of Disaster*, trans. Ann Smock (Lincoln: Nebraska University Press, 1995), 74. This erroneous practice is characteristic not only of Stephen's teaching, but of Joyce's method in writing *Ulysses*. Modeling his fiction on Homer's *Odyssey*, Joyce enlisted Odysseus' precedent of wandering and of the use of fraud and artifice as a method of returning home.

26 For more on Columbanus, see Alban Butler's *Lives of Saints*.

27 Margaret Urban Walker also argues that ethics rely on an individualized perception: "acute and unimpeded perception of particular human beings" is "the condition of adequate moral response." Margaret Urban Walker, "Moral Understandings: Alternative 'Epistemology' for a Feminist Ethics," 166. Sara Ruddick relies on some of the qualities of maternity for her model of ethical behavior which involves (as Walker summarizes) "acceptance of another's separate consciousness making its own sense of the world; recognition of the common humanity of the other's familiar longings and impulses; surrendering expectations of repeatability in order to follow the distinct trajectory of a particular life" (*ibid* 167). Ruddick's maternal model coincides with Stephen's reliance on *amor matris* to understand his ethical responsibility.

28 I am grateful to Betsy Wice for this wonderful insight offered during a seminar on *Ulysses* which I had the privilege to teach at the Rosenbach Museum and Library in Philadelphia.

29 Sympathy and empathy are, of course, not used in this specific sense in common parlance in which they may be perceived as indistinguishable, or in which empathy might be understood to exhibit greater kindness, to have a higher value. In making this distinction I draw both on the etymological roots of each word (in which sympathy indicates "suffering," *pathos* and "before," *sym* and empathy indicates "suffering," *pathos* and "within" or "under," *em*), and also the philosophical sense in which Susan Bordo and Stanley Cavell both use the word sympathy, in which the separation between self and other in feeling for another is emphasized.

30 Stanley Cavell, *Must We Mean What We Say?* (Cambridge University Press, 1976), 253.

31 Edith Wyschogrod writes that "the ethical body in its susceptibility to wounding, to outrage and hurt, is a brake or restraint upon the self prior to action even to deliberation and challenges of self-righteousness.... [the body] can now be seen in its dual function as a proscription against harming the other and as placing oneself at the disposal of the other. No longer an isolated consciousness nor even a being in the world, the body of the body-subject has become the body of ethics." Edith Wyschogrod, "Toward a Postmodern

Ethics: Corporeality and Alterity," *Ethics and Aesthetics: The Moral Turn of Postmodernism*, ed. Gerhard Hoffmann and Alfred Hornung. (Heidelberg: Universitatsverlag, 1996), 66–67.

32 Emmanuel Levinas, *Otherwise than Being: or, Beyond Essence*, trans. Alphonso Lingis (Pittsburgh: Duquesne University Press, 1998), 64. Hereafter referred to as *OTB*.

33 Simon Critchley, *The Ethics of Deconstruction*, 285 (emphasis original).

34 Levinas discusses the ethical implications of Berkeley's theories of sensation in *Otherwise than Being* (62–63).

35 Stephen's pedagogical approach is akin to Sigmund Freud's analysis of the relations between mistakes in speech and the unconscious in what has come to be called the 'Freudian slip': a slip of the tongue reveals a variant unconscious association embedded in the intended statement. Stephen makes a practice of understanding speech in the way Freud suggests: he notes the vagaries or slips in authoritative pronouncements and in doing so exposes the larger implications of limited statement. In Joyce's writing the slip in language provides greater access to moments of unconscious disruption of intention. The indicative lapse, which Stephen interprets to uncover unconscious motivations, becomes the symptom in Joyce's artistic practice. In his writing, the mistake is uncovered, emphasized, pronounced, and converted into method. This errant method becomes even more evident in Stephen's conversation with Deasy. For further discussion on error as method in Joyce's work see Vicki Mahaffey's "Intentional Error."

36 Jacques Derrida, *The Gift of Death*, 26.

37 It must be emphasized that orthodoxy does not always exclude choice. Rather, the heretical implications of choice are underscored in Joyce's texts in response to a particular moment in Catholic history, a moment in which (as "Grace" hilariously illustrates) the relatively new doctrine of Papal infallibility had a chilling effect on theological innovation.

38 Jacques Derrida writes "The heterogeneity that we have identified between the exercise of responsibility and its theoretical or even doctrinal thematization, is also, surely, what ties responsibility to *heresy*, to the *hairesis* as choice, election, preference, inclination, bias, that is, decision; but also as a school (philosophical, religious, literary) that corresponds to that bias; and finally heresy in the sense fixed in the vocabulary of the Catholic Church and made more general since, namely, departure from a doctrine, difference within and difference from the officially and publicly stated doctrine and the institutional community that is governed by it. Now, to the extent that this heresy always marks a difference or departure, keeping itself apart from what is publicly or commonly declared, it isn't only, in its very possibility, the essential condition of responsibility; paradoxically, it also destines responsibility to the resistance or dissidence of a type of secrecy." Jacques Derrida, *The Gift of Death*, 26. While it would be possible for an individual to choose freely to adhere to an orthodox belief or to act in accordance with accepted

doctrine, those choices and acts, thought seemingly orthodox would still, according to Derrida's definition, be considered heretical. The expectation of an authoritarian structure is that belief will be immediate and without question. The act of choosing itself, whether it is to adhere or resist, would be considered a form of heresy. Stephen's Jesuitical training in doubt indicates a fissure in the church's authority. To be compliant with his Jesuit education, to obey that authority, Stephan must register and explore his own doubts, thus resisting the general theological authority of the church.

39 Mr. Tate's accusation is echoed by Stephan's school fellows who accuse him of heresy not only in his essay but in his love of Byron's unorthodox poetry. Stephen experiences something like a martyrdom for his own heresy in admiring Byron when the other boys beat him to force an admission of Byron's errancy. In this incident Stephen learns that he prefers heresy and heterodoxy to obedience and orthodoxy (which he associates with the poet laureate, Tennyson).

40 In defining Deasy's morality, I draw on Margaret Urban Walker's definition of conventional moral philosophy, which seems particularly appropriate to the schoolmaster's thought; she writes that contemporary "philosophical practice still largely views ethics as the search for moral knowledge, and moral knowledge as comprising universal moral formulae and the theoretical justification of these." Margaret Urban Walker, "Moral Understandings: Alternative 'Epistemology for a Feminist Ethics," 165.

41 Marc Shell, studying the metaphoric use of money in the languages of philosophy and literature, notes that the "exchange value of the earliest coins derived wholly from the material substance (electrum) of the ingots of which the coins were made and not from the inscriptions stamped into these ingots. The eventual development of coins whose politically authorized inscriptions were inadequate to the weights and purities of the ingots into which the inscriptions were stamped precipitated awareness of the quandaries about the relationship between face value (intellectual currency) and substantial value (material currency)." See Marc Shell, *Money, Language, and Thought: Literary and Philosophical Economies from the Medieval to the Modern Era* (Berkeley: University of California Press, 1982), 1.

42 Ralph Waldo Emerson, *The Selected Writings* (New York: Random House, 1940), 17 (emphasis added).

43 Friedrich Nietzsche, "On Truth and Lying in an Extra-Moral Sense" (1873), *Friedrich Nietzsche on Rhetoric and Language*, trans. & ed. Sander L. Gilman, Carole Blair, and David Parent (Oxford University Press, 1989), 250.

44 Jacques Derrida, "White Mythologies," 217 (emphasis original).

45 According to both Shell and Derrida, philosophical texts express a distrust of metaphorical language through (another metaphoric) comparison of figurative language with coins. Derrida notes that metaphor requires a detour through symbolic associations to attain its signification, and that movement of thought through metaphor may threaten loss of intended meaning.

"Metaphor, therefore, is determined by philosophy as a provisional loss of meaning, an economy of the proper without irreparable damage, a certain inevitable detour, but also a history with its sight set on, and within the horizon of, the circular reappropriation of literal, proper meaning. This is why the philosophical evaluation of metaphor has always been ambiguous: metaphor is dangerous and foreign . . ." (*ibid* 270). Emerson, in his reliance on nature as a model, and his preference for simplicity, conveys a similar suspicion of devious language. It is precisely the danger of metaphor, however, that attracts Joyce. The detour of signification through the intricacies of metaphorical comparison promises an accumulation of errant associations that more than compensates for the threatened loss of intentionally. Joyce enters the tradition of philosophical discourse on metaphor and money by investing in the potential of detour, which for him promises accretion and gain. Or, as he expresses it in *Ulysses*, "the longest way round is the shortest way home." This heretical economics may explain, in part, why Stephen is always in debt and why Leopold and Molly Bloom are characteristically generous with money. Each, in a singular way, resists an orthodox economy in which coin stands for particular value or right to ownership.

46 See Don Gifford and Robert J. Seidman, *Ulysses Annotated: Notes for James Joyce's Ulysses*, 2nd edn. (Berkely: University of California Press, 1988), 34.

47 R. F. Foster, *Modern Ireland: 1600–1972* (London: Penguin Books, 1988), 141.

48 James II was not the only royal to use the sovereign in this way. According to Marc Shell, coinage was a common method for asserting sovereignty. For example, Constantine the Great saw a vision of a flaming cross with the legend "by this conquer" before a decisive battle. "The legend soon appeared, as HOC SIGNO VICTOR ERIS ("you will be victorious through this") impressed into designed coins . . ." (Shell, 99).

49 Don Gifford and Robert J. Seidman, *Ulysses Annotated: Notes for James Joyce's Ulysses*, 34. Archaeological digs in Ireland (whose findings are in the collection of the Irish National Museum in Dublin) have revealed the literal powers of the Irish bog to preserve Ireland's treasures. These excavations have uncovered objects dating to the Viking occupation which were buried, for safekeeping, in the bogs of Ireland where few invaders would look for treasure. The pieces are literal treasures in that they are made often from precious metals; but they are also treasures for the lush source of historical information they provide.

50 A spooner is another word for a toady or sycophant. The presence of these souvenir spoons in Deasy's collection may indicate his unquestioning allegiance to power.

51 Stephen's monthly wage would have amounted to about ninety dollars according to a "direct and rough" translation of 1904 Irish pounds into contemporary US dollars, or at approximately four hundred dollars based on *Thom's Official Directory of the United Kingdom of Great Britain and Ireland* (published in 1904) which lists market prices for staple foods that can be compared to

current values. See Don Gifford and Robert J. Seidman, *Ulysses Annotated: Notes for James Joyce's Ulysses*, 7. The modesty of his salary provides a more obvious reason for his pervasive debts, however, his habit of buying drinks for friends and giving charity to acquaintances undermines this explanation as sole interpretation.

52 According to Daniel Moshenberg, Stephen's attitude toward money corresponds to his desire for autonomy. Disrupting the systems that uphold the colonial sovereign's coins promises the acquisition of individual sovereignty. "... Stephen believes in the power of debt: 'The problem,' says Stephan, 'is to get money' (*U* 1.497). The problem is to get one's sovereignty." Daniel Moshenberg, "The Capital Couple: Speculating on 'Ulysses'" *James Joyce Quarterly* 25 (Spring 1988): 334.

53 Stephen's rebuttal provides a model for interpreting Deasy's other quotation. "If youth but knew" is only part of Henri Estienne's often-quoted adage in *Les Prémices* which reads in full: "*Si jeunesse savait, si vieillesse pouvait*" or "if youth but knew, if age but could." While Deasy indicts Stephen's youthful inexperience, he also unconsciously reveals his own aged impotence.

54 "– the strangers, says the citizen. Our own fault. We let them in. We brought them in. The adulteress and her paramour brought the Saxon robbers here.... A dishonored wife, says the citizen, that's what's the cause of all our misfortunes" (*U* 12:1156–1164).

55 "– I just wanted to say, he said. Ireland, they say, has the honour of being the only country which never persecuted the jews. Do you know that? No. And do you know why?

"He frowned sternly on the bright air.

"– Why, sir? Stephen asked, beginning to smile.

"– Because she never let them in, Mr Deasy said solemnly." (*U* 2:437–442).

56 Stephen indicates in this question, "[w]ho has not?", his own culpability in "sins" of racial and gender hatred. And while *Ulysses* charts his ethical practice, it also reflects his lapses.

57 Richard Ellmann, *James Joyce*, 326–327.

58 See Don Gifford and Robert J. Seidman, *Ulysses Annotated: Notes for James Joyce's Ulysses*, 33.

59 See R.F. Foster, *Modern Ireland*, 14 and Joseph Lee, *The Modernisation of Irish Society: 1848–1918* (Dublin: Gill and MacMillan, 1973), 10.

60 Close to the end of the day and of *Ulysses*, Stephen inquires about the publication of Deasy's letter in the *Telegraph*: "– Is that first epistle to the Hebrews, he asked as soon as his bottom jaw would let him, in? Text: open thy mouth and put thy foot in it" (*U* 16:1268–1269). Stephen's reference to Deasy's letter as an epistle to the Hebrews recalls the schoolmaster's erroneous joke that the Jews were never allowed into Ireland (*U* 2:437–442). Stephen's inquiry implies that Deasy's letter, addressed to the Irish populace, is a letter written to the Hebrews; all the Irish, in effect, are Jews. The Biblical letter to the Hebrews is addressed to an early Judeo-Christian community and warns against a reversion to Judaism by arguing that the new covenant

through Jesus makes obsolete the covenant with God through Moses. This epistle to the Hebrews advocates obedience to the authority of God based on the Word. Stephen's comment on the letter to the Hebrews reiterates many of the issues that vexed the encounter between teacher and schoolmaster. The Biblical letter's emphasis on the conflicting authorities that call upon the Christian community echoes the double authority of the Roman and English imperial orders. The reference also evokes complex connections throughout *Ulysses* between the Irish and the Jews as disenfranchised populations.

61 Margaret Urban Walker, "Moral Understandings: Alternative 'Epistemology' for a Feminist Ethics," 169–170.

62 The paper money proves useless not only because it is thoroughly inscribed by the economic authority that releases it and leaves no blank space for Stephen's notes, but also because it is money that Stephen already owes to a number of lenders.

63 Readers familiar with Irish literature would note another source for this poem. Douglas Hyde translated a traditional Irish poem as "My Grief on the Sea," and it contains language similar to Stephen's. "And my love came behind me – / He came from the South; / His breast to my bosom, / His mouth to my mouth." Stephen's adaptation of Hyde's sentimental poem changes the subject from romance to death and parasitism, leaving the impression that he resists not only Deasy's bovine imperial sympathies but also the romantic nationalism frequently expressed in Hyde's writing.

CHAPTER THREE

1 Geoffrey Galt Harpham has noted the extent to which ethics evinces a "structural obsession with the relations between apparently opposed terms." Geoffrey Galt Harpham, "Ethics," 394. It is that structural obsession with opposition which I am seeking to trace in this chapter both in ethical theory and in ALP's ethical interventions.

2 Drucilla Cornell notes that many versions of psychoanalytic theory propose that "separation from the mother must take place if individuation is to be achieved . . . that the mother must be abjected in order for the subject to be." In the face of these theories, Cornell notes that "psychic laws of culture are ethical rather than simply descriptive" as such they "seek to articulate a form of the person that is normatively desirable." Rather than merely describing a pre-existing tendency to separation, psychoanalytic theory mandates it as a necessary step in normative development. An ethical alternative might allow for a more complex relation of responsibility such as I have been describing in the ethical disposition of self in relation to an other.

3 Declan Kiberd makes a similar argument concerning the interdependence of Irish and English identities under colonialism in *Inventing Ireland* in which he observes: "Ireland was . . . patented as not-England, a place whose peoples

were, in many important ways, the very antitheses of their new rulers from overseas.... From the later sixteenth century, ... the English have presented themselves to the world as controlled, refined and rooted; and so it suited them to find the Irish hot-headed, rude and nomadic, the perfect foil to set off their own virtues." Declan Kiberd, *Inventing Ireland*, (Cambridge: Harvard University Press, 1995), 9.

4 John Bishop notes a similar rivalry between the two washerwomen in the Anna Livia section. See John Bishop, *Joyce's Book of the Dark, Finnegans Wake*, (Madison: University of Wisconsin Press, 1986), 350–351.

5 Simon Critchley also claims that the "ethical relation to the other" is the "condition of possibility" for both justice and politics. See especially pages 183–185. He goes on to define politics as *"the art of response to the singular demand of the other*, a demand that arises in a particular context – although the infinite demand cannot simple be reduced to its context...." See Simon Critchley, *Ethics, Politics, Subjectivity*, 276. Derrida's *Politics of Friendship* explores the possibility for a political justice based on friendship, but the friendship he proposes to call *aimance* must defy a tradition of such bonds based on androcentrism, fraternalism, and patriarchy.

6 Kiberd points out that it has been the role of poets in Ireland, from the beginning of recorded history, to provide a political conscience. He notes a trend in Irish poetry that insisted on constructing a native identity to counterpoint the stereotypes of barbarity imposed on the Irish by British representations.

7 See especially W.B. Yeats's "The Celtic Element in Literature" and "Ireland and the Arts" and Lady Augusta Gregory's "Ireland, Real and Ideal" for examples of this discourse.

8 Kimberly J. Devlin also notes the intersubjective structures of identity in *Finnegans Wake*. However, using a Lacanian model, she sees the subject structured in his or her self-consciousness before the gaze of another rather than experiencing responsibility in the encounter with the face of another. "What we confront in the *Wake* is the subject's image of himself as he imagines he appears to the other I/eyes, to alien subjectivities. The human enthrallment to the gaze, in short, is a technical as well as a thematic concern in the *Wake*, a concern vividly dramatized in the book's idiosyncratic but revealing narrative form." See Kimberly Devlin, "See Ourselves as Others See Us': Joyce's Look at the Eye of the Other," *PMLA* 104.5 (1989): 889.

9 While Levinas himself does not capitalize these words, the Saying and the Said, I follow the procedure of his respondents who use the capital letters to distinguish these terms from ordinary usage.

10 Andrew Gibson, *Postmodernity, Ethics and the Novel: From Leavis to Levinas*, 137.

11 I borrow this example from Simon Critchley's *The Ethics of Deconstruction*, 287.

12 Levinas writes: "The correlation of the saying and the said, that is, the subordination of saying to the said, to the linguistic system and to ontology,

is the price that manifestation demands. In language qua said everything is conveyed before us, be it at the price of betrayal" (*OTB* 6).

13 See Robert Bernasconi and Simon Critchley, eds, *Rereading Levinas* (London: Athlone Press, 1991), 178.

14 Simon Critchley, *The Ethics of Deconstruction*, 8.

15 In *Reauthorizing Joyce*, Vicki Mahaffey notes that Joyce adopts this Homeric textile mutability in Molly's mutable "text styles."

16 Both Molly and ALP speak in monologues which may at first seem to undermine my claim that theirs is ethical saying, which would require an other to whom the subject is responsible in the saying, an other to whom the subject speaks. These monologues are structurally defined, however, by the presence of and responsibility to an other: the reader.

17 Stephen Heath, "Ambioviolences: Notes for Reading Joyce," *Post-structuralist Joyce: Essays from the French*, ed. Derek Attridge and Daniel Ferrar (Cambridge University Press, 1984), 39.

18 Robert Eaglestone, *Ethical Criticism*, 153.

19 Levinas describes the ethical Saying in scriptural language, writing that the "first saying is to be sure but a word. But the word is God." Emmanuel Levinas, "Language and Proximity," *Collected Philosophical Papers*, trans. Alphonso Lingis (Pittsburgh: Duquesne University Press, 1998), 126.

20 There is a rich theoretical discussion in Joyce studies concerning the altered interpretative demands *Finnegans Wake* places on readers. Jean-Michel Rabaté, for example, employs the metaphor of a machine to describe the *Wake*'s "theoretical functioning." See Jean-Michel Rabaté, "Lapsus ex machina," *Poststructuralist Joyce*, ed. Derek Attridge (Cambridge University Press), 98. Bruns notes that reading the *Wake* "can no longer be conceived as an analytic process." See Gerald Bruns "The otherness of Words: Joyce, Bakhtin, Heidegger," *Postmodernism – Philosophy and the Arts*, ed. Hugh J. Silverman (New York and London: Routledge, 1990), 127. Citing Jacques Lacan's seminar work on Joyce, McCarthy describes the text as *lalangue*, which is irreducible and heterogeneous, that which *langue* excludes. He notes that this last text "is a fine example (in fact, the ultimate example) of what semioticians have called the *open*, or *plural*, text.... The open text ... gives the impression of being deliberately incomplete, of having 'gaps' which elicit a response from the reader who must fill in those gaps...." Patrick McCarthy, "A Warping Process: Reading *Finnegans Wake*," *Joyce Centenary Essays*, ed. Richard F. Peterson, Alan M. Cohn, and Edmund L. Epstein (Carbondale: Southern Illinois University Press, 1983), 49. I would emphasize that the openness of the text, while experienced often by readers as a kind of sadism, especially when the text is *Finnegans Wake*, is an ethical gesture to the reader's own knowledge, imagination, and creativity. Joyce describes his responsibility to the reader, his acknowledgment of the reader's presence, and his concerns about the difficulty he is imposing on us throughout the text. And as McCarthy concludes, "Joyce and his readers are ultimately partners ... " (*ibid* 54).

21 I use the term "erasure" with Jacques Derrida's argument from *Of Grammatology* in mind.

22 Efforts to locate Bruno's presence and influence in *Finnegans Wake* began before the book's publication with Beckett's "Dante . . . Bruno. Vico . . . Joyce." Atherton lists Bruno among the structural books consulted in the text's production, but speculates that Joyce would not have read Bruno carefully or extensively. See James S. Atherton, *The Books at the Wake: A Study of Literary Allusions in James Joyce's Finnegans Wake* (New York: Viking Press, 1960), 37. Though most critical emphasis has been on the theory of coincident opposites, Gino Moliterno traces the possible influence of "Bruno's own nightpiece, the riotous, ribald, *cinquecento* comedy," *Candelaio*. See Gino Moliterno, "The Candlebearer at the *Wake*: Bruno's Candelaio in Joyce's Book of the Dark," *Comparative Literature Studies* 30.3 (1993): 270. It is not only in *Finnegans Wake* that Joyce relies on Bruno's philosophy in structuring his own texts. Michael Seidel notes the connection between Bruno's *Spaccio del bestia trionfante* and *Ulysses*, concentrating especially on the patterns of wandering and return. See Michael Seidel's *Epic Geography: James Joyce's Ulysses* (Princeton University Press, 1976), 55–56. Robert Newman also draws on this Bruno text in tracing the astrological references in *Ulysses* as exemplars in the coincidence of contraries explored also among Joyce's characters in the novel.

23 Joyce paraphrases here a footnote to Bruno in Samuel Taylor Coleridge's essay XIII of *The Friend* (ed. Barbara E. Rooke, Princeton University Press, 1969, 94). "Every power in nature and in spirit must evolve an opposite, as the sole means and condition of its manifestation: and all opposition is a tendency to re-union." Coleridge goes on to write: "This is the universal Law of Polarity of essential Dualism, first promulgated by Heraclitus, 2000 years afterwards republished, and made the foundation both of Logic, of Physics, and of Metaphysics by Giordano Bruno. The Principle may be thus expressed. The *Identity* of Thesis and Antithesis is the substance of all *Being*: their *Opposition* the condition of all *Existence*, or Being manifested; and every *Thing* or Phaenomenon is the Exponent of a Synthesis as long as the opposite energies are retained in that Synthesis. Thus Water is neither Oxygen nor Hydrogen, nor yet is it a commixture of both; but the Syntheis or Indifference of the two: and as long as the copula endures, by which it becomes Water, or rather which alone *is* Water, it is not less a *simple* Body than either of the imaginary Elements, improperly called its Ingredients or Components. . . ." I quote Coleridge's treatment of Bruno at length in order to draw attention to his example of water as the substance which best exemplifies the coincidence of opposites.

24 It is also this hierarchy of difference which Susan Bordo attributes to metaphysics in "The Cartesian Masculinization of Thought." She suggests the sympathetic model as an ethical alternative to metaphysical thought based on the dominance of one arbitrary category over its opposite.

25 Jean-Michel Rabaté, "Bruno No, Bruno Si: Note on a Contradiction in Joyce." *James Joyce Quarterly* 27 (1989): 36.

26 The fluid mechanics which inform the writing of *Finnegans Wake* do not emanate specifically and solely from the voice or writing of ALP. Rather, there is an aggregation of disruptive influences in the language of the *Wake* around the figures for ALP. It is because of ALP's association, by way of the river, with fluidity, and because of the disruptions performed in and by water, that I link this perceptual and creative method with ALP, not because this character is responsible in any naturalistic fashion for the stylistic innovations in the text.

27 John Bishop notes that the sound of the river is echoed or produced by the sound of the bloodstream rushing in the dreamer's ear, a sound that Joyce's contemporaries Havelock Ellis and Sigmund Freud speculated may be one source or catalyst for dreams. See John Bishop, *Joyce's Book of the Dark*, *Finnegans Wake*, 347–348. Fluidity, then, is associated with the unconscious and its patterns of thought. Those patterns may also, as Bishop argues, illuminate (as it were) the obscurity of the text which relies on a stylistics inspired by unconscious association.

28 Translation: "the fact that the whole of the river flows safely, with a clear stream, and that those things which were to have been on the bank would later be in the bed; finally, that everything recognizes itself through something opposite and that the stream is embraced by rival banks." See Roland McHugh, *Annotations to Finnegans Wake* (Baltimore: The Johns Hopkins University Press, 1980), 287.

29 Gilles Deleuze and Felix Guattari, *A Thousand Plateaus*, trans. Brian Masumi (Minneapolis: University of Minnesota Press, 1983), 25.

30 Luce Irigaray, *This Sex Which Is Not One*, 111.

31 Kimberly Devlin discusses the dialectic of subjectivity in the monologue. She points out that "The larger representation of the female as speaking or writing subject, on the one hand, and as viewed or discussed object, on the other, may reflect the dreamer's attempt to envision this 'other' point of view, countered by a recognition of its inaccessibility, its remoteness." See Kimberly Devlin's "ALP's Final Monologue in *Finnegans Wake*: The Dialectical Logic of Joyce's Dream Text," *Coping with Joyce*, ed. Morris Beja and Shari Benstock (Columbus: Ohio State University Press, 1989), 232. Devlin reviews and refutes the argument made by Shari Benstock, Cliver Hart, and Margot Norris, among others, that ALP's final monologue occurs after the dream and beyond the imagination whose unconscious narrates the rest of the *Wake*.

32 Suzette Henke, *James Joyce and The Politics of Desire* (New York: Routledge, 1990), 41.

33 Stephen Conlin and John de Courcy, *Anna Liffey: The River of Dublin* (Dublin: The O'Brien Press, 1988), 11.

34 Roy F. Foster, *Modern Ireland*, 3.

35 Vince Cheng's *Joyce, Race, and Empire* (Cambridge University Press, 1995) details the extent of this colonial insistence on difference with an extensive discussion of the "othering" of the Irish by English discourse and representation. See especially his introduction (pp. 15–74).

36 For a comprehensive discussion of rumor in relation to postcolonial history see Gayatri Spivak's "Subaltern Studies: Deconstructing Historiography" from *In Other Worlds*.

37 The word splicing derives from the practice of joining together rope pieces by unraveling and then interweaving two strands. The word is also applied to the filmic technique of montage which involves cutting apart segments of film in order to join together different shots.

38 Sheldon Brivik also notes the interlacing of the domestic and political in ALP's monologue. He describes the development of subjectivity as dependent on the other in more Lacanian terms, reflecting that dialectic in national terms as well: "Just as ALP's personality has been defined by paternal intervention, so nationality is formed by foreign incursion.... And the Irish personality was formed by English invasions, which gave the Irish such fundamental components as their ordinary language and their rebelliousness.... The universality of such patterns is indicated by remembering that the English personality, often thought of as pure, was formed earlier by ... invasions." See Sheldon Brivic, *Joyce's Waking Women: An Introduction to Finnegans Wake* (Madison: The University of Wisconsin Press, 1995), 107.

39 I use the term "mimicry" here with reference to Homi Bhabha's concept elaborated in "Of Mimicry and Man" from *The Location of Culture* in which he describes the complex camouflage effect of opposition in colonial culture such that the dominant or invading culture both describes the native's inherent (and presumably inferior) difference and, at the same time, demands conformity to the colonizer's ("civilized") example. Bhabha describes how that mimicry might itself be used as a method for liberation if the colonized subject returns the gaze of colonizer, embodies the stereotype, and produces a destabilizing suspicion or fear that undermines colonial control.

40 I refer once again here to theories proposed by Ashis Nandy in *The Intimate Enemy: Loss and Recovery of Self under Colonialism* in which he argues that the process of colonization entails a certain "feminizing" of colonized populations. They are represented with the attributes and characteristics usually associated with women. Because those feminine attributes are perceived as a form of degradation, the complication of gender difference becomes a salient means for examining colonial difference.

41 John Bormanis makes a stronger claim for the relations between gender subversion and decolonization in Joyce's texts suggesting that "sexual subversion and the disruption of patriarchal genealogies and discourses are both necessary and parallel steps in the liberation of women and colonized peoples." See John Bormanis, "Lilith on the Liffey: Gender, Rebellion, and Anticolonialism in *Finnegans Wake*," *James Joyce Quarterly* 34.4 (1997): 489. My own reading is, perhaps, less optimistic about the liberating potentials of subversion.

42 Imagining the colonial situation through an abusive marital bond recognizes the real damage inflicted on the subjected partner in the relationship. But Joyce's examination of both versions of domination shifts the emphasis

from victimization to complicity. He has noted, for example, that colonial rule fosters self-betrayal in the indigenous population, making Ireland a partner in her own domination. Though that complicity is passive and unconscious, it is nonetheless troubling.

43 By drawing attention to power shifts in this marriage, I do not intend to imply that these *changes* are equivalent *exchanges* or that the partners merely switch roles within a stable hierarchy. Rather, I wish to indicate that the power hierarchy itself is constantly changing, evolving, and solidifying into new patterns as the figures within it alter.

44 For a more complete treatment of the Grace O'Malley myth in *Finnegans Wake* see Vicki Mahaffey, '"Fantastic Histories': Nomadology and Female Piracy in *Finnegans Wake*," in *Joyce and History*, ed. Mark Wallager, Victor Luftig, and Robert Spoo (Ann Arbor: University of Michigan, 1996), 157–176.

45 I am indebted in this interpretation to Jacques Aubert's technique in addressing the first word in *Finnegans Wake*, "riverrun." Jacques Aubert, "riverrun," *Post-structuralist Joyce: Essays from the French*, ed. Derek Attridge, and Daniel Ferrar (Cambridge University Press, 1984), 69–79.

CHAPTER FOUR

1 Virginia Woolf, *Between the Acts*, (London: Harcourt Brace and Company, 1941), 185.

2 This letter was sent during the "phoney war" when there was little actual military activity between France and Germany, but the threat of invasion from a much stronger army nonetheless motivated the mobilization of French forces along the Maginot line.

3 James Joyce, Letter to Lucie Noel Léon, Monday, 4 September 1939, Joyce/Léon Papers, National Library of Ireland, Dublin, Ireland.

4 James Joyce, Letter to Paul Léon, 11 September 1939, Joyce/Léon Papers, National Library of Ireland, Dublin, Ireland.

5 According to Ellmann, Brauchbar was a Swiss businessman who had studied English with Joyce during the Great War. Joyce worked with him to aid Jewish refugees in World War Two. See *Letters of James Joyce*. Vol II, ed. Richard Ellmann (New York: Viking Press, 1966), 405.

6 Ellmann translates the letter: "My daughter is with her *maison de santé* near S. Nazaire, hence deep in the occupied zone on the dangerous coast – and this in spite of everything I had tried to do in advance to assure her tranquillity." See *Letters of James Joyce*. Vol II, ed. Richard Ellmann (New York: Viking Press, 1966), 405.

7 Brenda Maddox, *Nora: The Real Life of Molly Bloom* (Boston: Houghton Mifflin, 1988), 347.

8 It is important to note that I entirely agree with Carol Shloss that it is impossible, years later, to confirm the diagnosis of schizophrenia ascribed to Lucia Joyce. Understanding of the disease was in its infancy when she was committed to the asylum, our understanding of the emotional condition

has advanced in the intervening years such that a contemporary clinician might describe Lucia in entirely different terms. It is no longer clear whether her institutionalization would be necessary under contemporary conditions, nor if her disturbances can be ascribed solely to organic or environmental causes or to ills produced by the treatments themselves. Therefore, when I use the term schizophrenia, I refer to the explanation her family was given, to their own available information on her condition, and to the beliefs this diagnosis would have promoted at the time. Shloss is among the first to indicate the tragedy and possible injustice of Lucia's situation, a tragedy I hope to underscore in the following pages.

9 Carol Shloss, "*Finnegans Wake* and the Daughter's Body," *Abiko Quarterly with James Joyce Studies* 9 (1997–1998): 118.

10 Shari Benstock, "Nightletters: Woman's Writing in the Wake," *Critical Essays on James Joyce*, ed. Bernard Benstock (Boston: G.K. Hall & Co., 1985), 223.

11 Ellmann notes in his biography that Joyce "did not disavow guilt; he embraced it eagerly." See Richard Ellmann's *James Joyce*, 650.

12 Philip Kuberski, "The Joycean Gaze: Lucia in the I of the Father," *Sub-Stance* 14 (1985): 62.

13 Finn Fordham, "*Finnegans Wake* and the Dance," *Abiko Quarterly with James Joyce Studies* 9 (1997–1998): 12.

14 Adam Newton describes a similar concern for narrative ethics more generally when he writes of the "small but still momentous distance that lies between person and character, or character and caricature, the gains, losses, and risks taken up when selves represent or are represented by others." See Adam Newton's *Narrative Ethics*, 18.

15 Andrew Gibson registers these same dilemmas in the ethical practice of representation. See especially his discussion of Conrad's *Heart of Darkness* (Andrew Gibson, *Postmodernity, Ethics and the Novel*, 54–65).

16 Stephen Heath, "Ambioviolences: Notes for Reading Joyce," 149.

17 Heath notes three senses of the term representation as it has been commonly understood: "an imaging (the representation of this or that), an argumentation (this or that is represented to those who receive it), a deputation (the representation is representative, it offers a common position and stands in for those who fashion and receive it, as something of their truth)." When imaging and argumentation are carried into deputation, the result is an "appropriate assumption of the common position that is crucial and the crucial point of critical concern." In this form the representation allows two crucial lapses: the assumption of the universal subject standing in for all others represented or the defeated "seduction of global simulacratization" (*ibid* 149). In the latter case the difficulties of representing another become an excuse for ignoring the ethical responsibility to include the other in representation.

18 Richard Ellmann, *Ulysses on the Liffey* (New York: Oxford University Press, 1972), 79.

19 It is important to remember that Issy is not the only character in the *Wake* capable of splitting into other versions of her self. The twins, Shem and Shaun, for example, appear in separate episodes as the Ondt and the Gracehopper

and the Mookse and the Gripes, among others. The two parents express versions of themselves in their children: HCE becomes Shem and Shaun, ALP becomes Issy. However, Issy is notable in her tendency to split into *multiple* characters *at one time*. She becomes the *seven* rainbow girls, the *several* Maggies and Jinnies.

20 My glosses are derived from Roland McHugh's *Annotations to Finnegans Wake* (Baltimore: The Johns Hopkins University Press, 1980), 260.

21 Joyce's investment in his daughter's artistry is justified by the range and proficiency of her talents. She was an imaginative and capable painter (University College London, for example, has photographs of an extraordinary, privately-owned painting by Lucia Joyce among the Lidderdale papers) and illustrator (as evidenced by her work on the Chaucer Lettrines). Her abilities as a dancer and choreographer are testified to in a *Paris Times* article which notes the variety and scope of her current projects: "The other day she arranged the dances to 'Le Pont d'Or,' an *operette-bouffe* by Emile Fernandez.... She has danced at [the *Comédie des Champs-Elysées*] twice with the members of 'Les Six'.... She has danced at the Theatre du Vieux-Colombier and in Brussels." See "On the Left Bank," *The Paris Times*, March 14, 1928, No. 1371: A7.

22 As Shari Benstock notes "Biddy has turned the letter into 'literature' (112.27) by piecing together the evidence she has dug up and, like a good critic, has come up with a 'reading' of the letter (or some bits of it) that bears little – if any – resemblance to the original document." See Shari Benstock's "The Genuine Christine: Psychodynamics of Issy," *Women in Joyce*, ed. Suzette Henke & Elaine Unkeless (Urbana: University of Illinois Press, 1982), 185.

23 David Hayman, "Genetic Criticism and Joyce: An Introduction," *Genetic Joyce. European Joyce Studies* 5 (1994): 6.

24 R.J. Schork makes a perhaps greater claim for the technique, though in the same vein as Hayman's description, when he writes that genetic interpretation allows the reader to "detect the blurred traces left by Joyce's imagination." R.J. Schork, "By Jingo: Genetic Criticism of *Finnegans Wake*," *Joyce Studies Annual* 5 (1994): 106.

25 Daniel Ferrar and Michael Groden, "Post-Genetic Joyce," *Romantic Review* 86 (1995): 509.

26 Jean Michel Rabaté, "Pound, Joyce and Eco: Modernism and the 'Ideal Genetic Reader,'" *Romanic Review* 86.3 (May 1995): 495.

27 In chapter two I also noted the importance of error in Stephen's teaching method evoked in his statement "A man of genius makes no mistakes. His errors are volitional and are the portals of discovery."

28 Richard Ellmann, *James Joyce*, 649.

29 The Chaucer Lettrines were the only project on which Joyce and Lucia actually collaborated. She had been working on a decorative alphabet on her own and Joyce searched for an application for her beautiful designs. "At last he hit upon the notion of using her letters in *A Chaucer* ABC, which was published with a preface by Louis Gillet in 1936" (*ibid* 658). *A Chaucer ABC* is based

on Geoffrey Chaucer's translation of an old French poem in which each stanza begins with a letter in alphabetical order. Joseph Valente has noted the importance of these *lettrines* to Joyce's conception of his own project: "the *lettrine* serves as a metaphor for the link between Lucia's impact on Joyce's creativity, which he everywhere associates with transgression and lapse, and Lucia's own graphic role in marking that impact. Indeed, Joyce's belief in the correlation between Lucia's progression on her *lettrines* and his progression on the *Wake* provides direct biographical support for such a reading." See Joseph Valente's *James Joyce and the Problem of Justice: Negotiating Sexual and Colonial Difference* (Cambridge University Press, 1995), 122.

30 Jerome McGann, "Composition as Explanation (of Modern and Postmodern Poetries)," *Cultural Artifacts and the Production of Meaning: The Page, the Image, and the Body*, ed. Margaret J.M. Ezell & Katherine O'Brien O'Keeffe (Ann Arbor: The University of Michigan Press, 1994), 122.

31 Philip Kuberski, "The Joycean Gaze: Lucia in the I of the Father," 49.

32 Gilles Deleuze and Felix Guattari, *Anti-Oedipus*, trans. Robert Hurley, Mark Seem, and Helen R. Lane (Minneapolis: University of Minnesota Press, 1983), 282.

33 For Deleuze and Guattari, the schizo's response to the social field and his or her revolutionary processing of stimuli are alternatives to the dominant, neurotic oedipalization expected of subjects in a capitalist social economy. Though borrowing their terminology, I am not making precisely the same point. Lucia and James Joyce seem to have been fully engaged in the struggles of identification inherent in the oedipal family dynamic. Their shared schizoid processing as artists did not provide either of them with an alternative to the perils or pleasures of this strong identification. Nor do I believe that the family dynamic was a "cause" of Lucia's difficulty.

34 *Letters of James Joyce*, 366.

35 Margaret McBride represents a version of this argument in "Finnegans Wake: The Issue of Issy's schizophrenia" in which she argues that Issy's role in *Finnegans Wake* increased as the text developed from first draft to finished version and that she is ultimately figured as the narrator. McBride argues, therefore, that the text is not a rendering of a dream so much as a mimicry of schizophrenic phantasmagoria. She notes that Jung described schizophrenia as a "waking dream" and also remarked on the connections between Joyce's writing and the mental disorder. See Margaret McBride's "Finnegans Wake: The Issue of Issy's Schizophrenia," *Joyce Studies Annual* 7 (1996): 148.

36 Richard Ellmann, *James Joyce*, 692.

37 Michael Robbins, *Experiences of Schizophrenia: An Integration of the Personal, Scientific, and Therapeutic* (London: The Guilford Press, 1993), 2.

38 Cheryl Herr has described the disturbed family dynamics that Joyce himself may have held responsible for his daughter's disturbance. For example, Nora Barnacle was sometimes violent in her child-rearing practices, and in spite of his abhorrence of violence toward children (a position he articulates

clearly in "Counterparts"), James Joyce did not necessarily intervene. Herr argues that "even though relatively little physical and emotional violence may be evident in the received standard narrative of Lucia's childhood, rather little overt violence is required to deform a sensitive and gifted child." See Cheryl Herr, "Fathers, Daughters, Anxiety, and Fiction," *Discontented Discourses: Feminism / Textual Intervention / Psychoanalysis*, ed. Marleen S. Barr & Richard Feldstein. (Urbana: University of Illinois Press, 1989), 194.

39 Michael Robbins, *Experiences of Schizophrenia: An Integration of the Personal, Scientific, and Therapeutic*, 2.

40 *DSM-IV: Diagnostic and Statistical Manual of Mental Disorders*, 4th edn. (Washington, DC: American Psychiatric Association, 1994), 280.

41 Michael Robbins, *Experiences of Schizophrenia: An Integration of the Personal, Scientific, and Therapeutic*, 14.

42 An example of this dissociation is evident in Lucia's response to her father's death: "What is he doing under the ground, that idiot? When will he decide to come out? He's watching us all the time." (See Richard Ellmann's *James Joyce*, 743). This oddly humorous response is remarkably at odds with the genuine grieving revealed in dream journals she kept later in her life in which she refers to nightmares about his death. In letters to Nora Barnacle's niece Bozena Delimata as late as 1973, her longing for her father is still evident. On May 7, 1973 she writes that her father is in heaven along with her mother and that she still misses them. On July 11, 1973 she writes again with her curious mixture of humor and bathos, asking Delimata to pray for her and for her small knees. She remembers that her father also had small knees and wonders what she can do for him now. Yet on January 13, 1974 she seems to have forgotten that her parents are dead. She writes that she is very worried about them and asks for help. In this letter she describes herself as "mad," and longs to be sent to Ireland. For more on Lucia Joyce's late correspondence and dream journal housed at the University of Texas, see David Hayman's "Shadow of His Mind: The Papers of Lucia Joyce."

43 Quoted in Margaret McBride's "*Finnegans Wake*: The Issue of Issy's Schizophrenia," 155–156.

44 Michael Robbins, *Experiences of Schizophrenia: An Integration of the Personal, Scientific, and Therapeutic*, 14.

45 Michael Robbins, *Experiences of Schizophrenia: An Integration of the Personal, Scientific, and Therapeutic*, 21. See also *DSM-IV: Diagnostic and Statistical Manual of Mental Disorders*, 282.

46 Michael Robbins, *Experiences of Schizophrenia: An Integration of the Personal, Scientific, and Therapeutic*, 98.

47 Michael Robbins, *Experiences of Schizophrenia: An Integration of the Personal, Scientific, and Therapeutic*, 98. According to the DSM IV: "The first-degree biological relatives of individuals with Schizophrenia have a risk for Schizophrenia that is about 10 times greater than that of the general population. Concordance rates for Schizophrenia are higher in monozygotic twins

than in dizygotic twins. . . . Although much evidence suggests the importance of genetic factors in the etiology of Schizophrenia, the existence of a substantial discordance rate in monozygotic twins also indicates the importance of environmental factors" (DSM IV, 283).

48 Peter L. Giovacchini, *Schizophrenia and Primitive Mental States: Structural Collapse and Creativity* (London: Jason Aronson Inc. 1997), 7.

49 Robert Polhemus notes that Joyce researched historic and mythic versions of the love between older men and younger women in presenting the love between HCE and Issy. He lists among his examples: Lot and his daughters, Dante and Beatrice Portinari, Swift, Stella and Vanessa, Charles Dodgson, Alice Liddell and Isa Bowman, Morton Prince and Christine Beauchamp, and the Daddy Browning and Peaches scandal among others. See Robert Polhemus's "Dantellising Peaches and Miching Daddy, the Gushy Old Goof: The Browning Case and Finnegans Wake," *Joyce Studies Annual* 5 (1994): 81.

50 Molly Bloom thinks of "Wardeb Daly" or Warden Daly at the end of her monologue when she remembers how many times she and Bloom have moved (or wandered) and also contemplates the bed she's lying in, which her father gave them and which came from Gibraltar. Her musings associate sexuality and wandering or moving, an association that might signal punishment for the original sin of sexual knowledge, just as Joyce associated the wandering of his family with Lucia's "madness" and the possibility of his strong identification with her as a form of sexual sin like incest.

51 In dating the drafts and revisions of Joyce's manuscript I rely entirely on the scholarship of the *Archives*; their exhaustive investigation of the *Wake* in progress has yielded unusually reliable manuscript dating.

52 A reader may also be reminded of Eve, who in Milton's *Paradise Lost*, prefers her own reflected image to the real partner she is assigned, Adam.

53 Originally "mere" (in English) meant not "nothing more than" but "nothing less than," thus mere and mearest are both opposite and the same. *Mere* may also be read as the French for mother, indicating ALP as one of Issy's possible doubles.

54 Following her engagement to Alex Ponisovsky in 1932, Lucia herself retreated to an extreme form of inwardness, entering a catatonic state, and lying inert on the Léon's sofa. See Richard Ellmann's *James Joyce*, 650.

55 See Alice Miller's *The Drama of the Gifted Child* on the importance of "healthy narcissism."

56 Ovid, *The Metamorphosis of Ovid*, trans. David R. Slavitt (Baltimore: Johns Hopkins University Press, 1994), III. 390–392. Hereafter cited as "Ovid."

57 Maurice Blanchot, *The Writing of Disaster*, trans. Ann Smock (Lincoln: Nebraska University Press, 1995), 127. Blanchot, who was a close friend of Levinas's, may well have been evoking the latter's ethical theory in this reference to the other.

58 Quoted in Anne-Emmanuelle Berger's "The Latest Word from Echo," *New Literary History* 27.4 (1996): 634.

59 Anne-Emmanuelle Berger, "The Latest Word from Echo," 636.

60 See Judith Greenberg's "The Echo of Trauma and the Trauma of Echo" for a sensitive discussion of the figuring of grief in Ovid's myth.

61 Sigmund Freud, "On Narcissism," *The Standard Edition of the Complete Psychological Works of Sigmund Freud*, ed. James Strachey (London: Hogarth Press, 1966), 88.

62 Sigmund Freud, "Letter to an American Mother," (1935). *American Journal of Psychiatry*, 107 (1951): 786.

63 Sigmund Freud, *Introductory Lectures on Psychoanalysis*, trans. James Strachey (New York: Norton & Company, 1966), 426.

64 Michael Warner, "Homo-Narcissism; or Heterosexuality," *Engendering Men*, ed. Joseph A. Boone & Michael Cadden (New York: Routledge, 1990), 202.

65 For Lacan, the evidence of the mirror stage refutes Rene Descartes's "*cogito*," ("It is an experience that leads us to oppose any philosophy directly issuing from the *Cogito*," precisely in its implications concerning the relation between self and other. See Jacques Lacan's, *Écrit*, trans. Alan Sheridan (New York: W. W. Norton & Company, 1977), 1. In Descartes' theory, knowledge and understanding are validated through interior contemplation; understanding of the outside world attained through the senses is fraught with error and deception. Lacan, on the other hand, notes that in the mirror stage, the subject constitutes his or her self through an image of the self seen in the outside world (the mirror reflection); that image provides reliable information about the separation and interaction between interior and exterior that constitutes the subject. Lacan's version of knowledge, then, is ethical, according to the principles I have laid out in defining epistemological ethics in chapter two, in that it is developed in relation to and with responsibility for an other.

66 At this moment, Lacan argues, the child becomes a symbolic subject "objectified in the dialectic of identification with the other." See Jacques Lacan's *Ecrits*, 2. The sense of the self attained in the mirror stage emerges before the later alterations in which the subject will understand herself in a dialectical relation to her others, and before she has a language through which to assert herself as stable and total by using words such as "*I*". At the same time, recognizing the mirror image is profoundly alienating for the child. The image in the mirror is an "Ideal-I." While this form in the mirror "situates the agency of the ego" and allows the child to identify herself as acting, congruently, the child's sense of self is located in a fiction or representation contrary to her real experience, which is much more partial, fragmented, and "turbulent" than the image in the mirror. The sense of self as experienced is always at odds with the primordial *I* she developed in front of the mirror. The "*Gestalt*," the exteriorized image in the mirror, "symbolizes the mental permanence of the *I*, at the same time that it prefigures its alienating destination. . . . " See Jacques Lacan's *Écrit*, 2.

67 Carol Shloss has uncovered extensive evidence of Lucia's love affairs with other women. Among the sources she cites are: 1) the "Anamnese von Fraulein Lucia Joyce," which was a psychiatric interview that Paul Léon and James Joyce participated in at the Burgholzli (in Zurich) during their

attempts to find treatment for Lucia. The doctor records Lucia's previous lesbian relationship with one of her nurses. (2) In an interview with Lucia's close woman friend Zdenka Podhajsky, a young Czech dancer, Richard Ellmann learned that Podhajsky was greeted by Lucia on her return from Paris sometime before 1930 with the excited information that Lucia was now a lesbian. A more exhaustive account of Lucia's sexuality will be presented in Shloss's forthcoming biography of Lucia Joyce.

68 Carol Mavor, "Dream-Rushes: Lewis Carroll's Photographs of the Little Girl," *The Girl's Own: Cultural Histories of the Anglo-American Girl, 1830–1915*, ed. Claudia Nelson and Lynne Vallone (Athens: University of Georgia Press, 1994), 189.

69 For more on St. Cecelia, see Alban Butler's *Lives of Saints*, ed. Carl Horstmann (Millwood NY: Kraus 1987).

70 Irigaray expresses these concepts in poetic language that nearly rivals that of Joyce when making his own similar point, she writes: "*How can I be distinguished from her? Only if I keep on pushing through to the other side, if I'm always beyond, because on this side the screen of their projections, on this* plane *of their representations, I can't live. I'm stuck, paralyzed by all those images, words, fantasies. . . . So either I don't have any* "self," *or else I have a multitude of* "selves" *appropriated by them, for them, according to their needs or desires. . . . Well, I can say this much about my identity: I have my father's name. . . .*" See Luce Irigaray's *This Sex Which is Not One*, 17. Responding to these shifting projections, Alice must herself be capable of transformation in order that she might alternately meet and evade the paternal expectations. Accepting her father's name, but with reservations, Irigaray's Alice is interpolated into the Lacanian "Law of the Father." But because identity is for her the displaced image in the mirror, the father's name which identifies her is also at a distance. Joyce explores this same ambivalent locus in placing his girl figure before the mirror: how does he inscribe her in the law of the father, a law he questions in writing this last text, by inscribing her under his name?

71 Luce Irigaray, *This Sex which Is Not One*, 10.

72 Ann Cvetkovich, "Sexual Trauma/Queer Memory: Incest, Lesbianism, and Therapeutic Culture," *GLQ* 2 (1995): 356.

73 Davis makes these remarks in an interview with Liz Galst, "Overcoming Silence: Lesbians Lead the Recovery Movement for Survivors of Child Sexual Abuse," *Advocate* 3 (December 1991): 62–63.

74 Ann Cvetkovich, "Sexual Trauma/Queer Memory: Incest, Lesbianism, and Therapeutic Culture," 357.

75 Jen Shelton notes that in *Finnegans Wake* Joyce traverses some of the same territory that concerned Freud as he made the transition from the (poorly named) seduction theory to the Oedipal complex. However, Joyce resists Freud's later conclusions concerning the girl's complicity in seduction, exposing "this construct as a sham." Rather, "Joyce offers a narrative/counternarrative text that contests Freud's version of family relations, suggesting a version that is more closely allied with the victim of incest than

with the perpetrator of it." See Jen Shelton's "Issy's Footnote: Disruptive Narrative and the Discursive Structure of Incest in *Finnegans Wake*," *ELH* 66.1 (1999): 213.

76 Shari Benstock offers a nuanced reading of Issy's dream: "The daughter's desire to expose her father by disclosing his sin . . . is also her effort to recover an elusive piece of information about her own past, to read the transcript of her unconscious, to discover her presence in the father's dream." See Shari Benstock's "Nightletters: Woman's Writing in the *Wake*," 225.

77 Jeffrey Masson provides a very controversial history of Freud's transition from the seduction theory to the Oedipal model. For more on the questions around Freud's writing on incest in a literary context see Cvetkovich and Bernheimer.

78 Joyce's worst fears and ugliest presumptions about himself, his art, and his treatment of his daughter are realized in Philip Kuberski's response to *Finnegans Wake*: "The author's alienated object of incestuous desire, both the daughter's place and the narcissistic place of the author, finds a domain for its sustenance and development in *Finnegans Wake*, a book that appropriates the theme of incest in terms of incestuous art – a discourse shirking re-sponsibilities of representation and repression, self-absorbed, self-reflective, self-engendered. Such a discourse invites the semblance of the unconscious, dream, nonsense, and schizophrenia." See Philip Kuberski's "The Joycean Gaze: Lucia in the I of the Father," 55.

79 Cheryl Herr, "Fathers, Daughters, Anxiety, and Fiction," 196.

80 Joseph Valente, *James Joyce and the Problem of Justice*, 102.

81 Shari Benstock notes the literary sources for identification and differentiation contained in this passage. "The literary setting of this scene is taken from *Swift's Journal to Stella*, the psychological background from Morton Prince's case history of Christine Beauchamp in *The Dissociation of Personality*. Both of these works describe clandestine writings between lovers/enemies who employ petnames and pseudonyms to hide identities and exchange roles as the writers and receivers of letters. The alliance of Self and Other in the writing act is a collaboration that breeds both narcissistic love and hate." See Shari Benstock's "Nightletters: Woman's Writing in the *Wake*," 226.

82 Richard Ellmann, *James Joyce*, 663.

83 See John Gordon's "Notes on Issy" and W.Y. Tindall's *Reader's Guide to Finnegans Wake* respectively for discussions of this passage.

84 Carol Shloss promotes a similar reading of the text when she suggests that readers "understand Lucia to be the interlocutor as well as one of the subjects of this book." See Carol Shloss's "*Finnegans Wake* and the Daughter's Body," 131. Crossing the position of subject with that of interlocuter is one of the ways in which Joyce undermines traditional representation to present an ethical alternative.

85 For further information on Lucia's dance career, see Finn Fordham's "*Finnegans Wake* and the Dance," 30–31, Richard Ellmann's *James Joyce*, 612, and Bonnie Kime Scott's *Joyce and Feminism* (London: The Harvester

Press, 1984), 79. Shloss notes the extent to which Lucia's physical language of the dance was the language she employed to express her distress during the years of her "madness." She also observes that given her love of movement, her artistic expression through dance, the institutional constraint of her body in "treatment" was particularly cruel: "Anyone whose sentient life is reduced and supervised in these humiliating ways must experience pain; but for dancers, whose bodies are their most eloquent vehicle for expression, physical constraint is a literal ex-communication." See Carol Shloss's "*Finnegans Wake* and the Daughter's Body," 119.

86 *The Paris Times* notes on March 14, 1928: "When [Lucia Joyce] reaches her full capacity for rhythmic dancing, James Joyce may yet be known as his daughter's father."

87 Richard Ellmann, *James Joyce*, 686.

88 Eurythmics were a "new, highly reactionary method of dance practiced in Nazi Germany." See Finn Fordham's "*Finnegans Wake* and the Dance," 32. Lucia's own dance was more influenced by the theories of the school "Ballets Rhythme et Couleur," as Bonnie Kime Scott indicates in *Joyce and Feminism* 79.

ENVOY: TO THE READER

1 Vicki Mahaffey, *States of Desire* (New York and Oxford: Oxford University Press, 1998), 149.

2 The envoy is generally placed at the end of a poem, traditionally a French ballade, and is addressed to a person of importance, often the person who commissioned the poem and is therefore, conceivably, the poem's first reader.

3 James Joyce, *Giacomo Joyce* (London: Faber & Faber, 1968), 16.

4 Jacques Derrida, *The Post Card*, trans. Alan Bass (University of Chicago Press, 1987), 239.

Bibliography

The Bible. Authorized King James Version. The New Scofield Reference Bible. Ed. Ci.I. Scofield, D.D. (New York: Oxford University Press, 1967).

Althusser, Louis. "Ideology and the Ideological State Apparatuses (Notes toward an Investigation)." *Lenin and Philosophy and Other Essays*. Trans. Ben Brewster. (New York: Monthly Review Press, 1971).

Atherton, James S. *The Books at the Wake: A Study of Literary Allusions in James Joyce's Finnegans Wake*. (New York: Viking Press, 1960).

Attridge, Derek, ed. *The Cambridge Companion to James Joyce*. (Cambridge University Press, 1990).

Attridge, Derek, ed. "Innovation, Literature, Ethics: Relating to the Other." *PMLA* 114 (January 1999): 20–31.

Attridge, Derek, ed. "Judging Joyce." *Modernism/Modernity* 6.3 (1999): 15–32.

Attridge, Derek and Daniel Ferrar. *Post-structuralist Joyce: Essays from the French*. (Cambridge University Press, 1984).

Aubert, Jacques. "riverrun." *Post-structuralist Joyce: Essays from the French*. Ed. Derek Attridge and Daniel Ferrar. (Cambridge University Press, 1984), 69–79.

Barthes, Roland. "The Death of the Author." *Twentieth Century Literary Theory: A Reader*. Ed. K. M. Newton (New York: St. Martins 1997), 120–123.

Bass, Ellen and Laura Davis. *The Courage to Heal: A Guide for Women Survivors of Child Sexual Abuse*. (New York: Perenial Library, 1988).

de Beauvoir, Simone. *The Second Sex*. Ed. H. M. Parshley. (New York: Knopf, 1952).

Beckett, Samuel, et al. *An Exagmination of James Joyce: Analysis of the "Work in Progress."* (Paris: Shakespeare and Company, 1929); rpt. (New York: Haskell House, 1974).

Beckett, Samuel, et al. *The Unnamable*. (London: Calder, 1959).

Benhabib, Seyla. Situating the Self. Gender, Community and Postmodernism in Contemporary Ethics. (New York: Routledge, 1992), 153.

Benstock, Bernard. "The L.S.d of Dubliners." *Twentieth Century Literature* 34 (1988): 191–210.

Benstock, Bernard. *The Seventh of Joyce*. (Bloomington: Indiana University Press, 1982).

Benstock, Bernard. "The Gnomonics of Dubliners." *James Joyce Quarterly* 34 (1988): 519–538.

Benstock, Shari. "Nightletters: Woman's Writing in the Wake." *Critical Essays on James Joyce*. Ed. Bernard Benstock. (Boston: G. K. Hall & Co., 1985), 221–233.

Benstock, Shari. "The Genuine Christine: Psychodynamics of Issy." *Women in Joyce*. Ed. Suzette Henke and Elaine Unkeless. (Urbana: University of Illinois Press, 1982), 169–196.

Berger, Anne-Emmanuelle. "The Latest Word from Echo." *New Literary History* 27.4 (1996): 621–640.

Bernasconi, Robert and Simon Critchley, eds. *Rereading Levinas*. (London: Athlone Press, 1991), 162–189.

Bernheimer, Charles and Claire Kahane, Ed. *In Dora's Case: Freud–Hysteria–Feminism*. (New York: Columbia University Press, 1985).

Bhabha, Homi. *The Location of Culture*. (New York: Routledge, 1994).

Bishop, John. *Joyce's Book of the Dark, Finnegans Wake*. (Madison: University of Wisconsin Press, 1986).

Blanchot, Maurice. *The Writing of Disaster*. Trans. Ann Smock (Lincoln: Nebraska University Press, 1995).

Bloom, Harold. *The Anxiety of Influence*. (New York: Oxford University Press, 1973).

Booth, Wayne C. *The Company We Keep: An Ethics of Fiction*. (Berkeley and London: University of California Press, 1988).

Boland, Eavan. "Anna Liffey." *In A Time of Violence*. (New York & London: W. W. Norton and Company, 1994).

Bordo, Susan. "The Cartesian Masculinization of Thought." *From Modernism to Postmodernism*. Ed. Lawrence Cahoone. (Cambridge, MA: Blackwell, 1996), 638–664.

Bormanis, John. "Lilith on the Liffey: Gender, Rebellion, and Anticolonialism in *Finnegans Wake*." *James Joyce Quarterly* 34.4 (1997): 489–503.

Bowen, Zack. "*Exiles*: The Confessional Mode." *James Joyce Quarterly* 29.3 (1992): 581–591.

Brivic, Sheldon. *Joyce's Waking Women: An Introduction to Finnegans Wake*. (Madison: The University of Wisconsin Press, 1995).

Bruns, Gerald. "The Otherness of Words: Joyce, Bakhtin, Heidegger." *Postmodernism–Philosophy and the Arts*. Ed. Hugh J. Silverman. (New York and London: Routledge, 1990), 120–136.

Buell, Lawrence. "Introduction In Pursuit of Ethics." *PMLA* 114.1 (January 1999): 7–17.

Butler, Alban. *Lives of Saints*. Ed. Carl Horstmann. (Millwood NY: Kraus, 1987).

Carroll, Lewis. *Alice in Wonderland*. Illus. John Tenniel. (New York: Scholastic, 1989).

Cavell, Stanley. *Must We Mean What We Say?* (Cambridge University Press, 1976).

Cheng, Vincent J. "Stephen Dedalus and the Black Panther Vampire." *James Joyce Quarterly*. 24 (1987): 161–176.

Cheng, Vincent J. *Joyce, Race, and Empire*. (Cambridge University Press, 1995).

Cixous, Helene. "Sorties." *The Newly Born Woman*. Helene Cixous and Catherine Clement. Trans. Betsy Wing. (Minneapolis: University of Minnesota Press, 1986), 63–132.

Cixous, Helene. "The Laugh of the Medusa." *New French Feminisms*. Ed. Elaine Marks and Isabelle de Courtivron. (New York: Schocken Books, 1981).

Code, Lorraine. *Epistemic Responsibility*. (Hanover: University Press of New England, 1987).

Cohen, Ed. *Talk on the Wilde Side: Towards a Genealogy of a Discourse on Male Sexualities*. (New York: Routledge, 1993).

Coleridge, Samuel Taylor. *The Friend*. Ed. Barbara E. Rooke. (Princeton University Press, 1969).

Connolly, Thomas E. "Joyce's 'The Sisters': A Pennyworth of Snuff." *College English* 27 (1967): 189–195.

Conlin, Stephen and John de Courcy. *Anna Liffey: The River of Dublin*. (Dublin: The O'Brien Press, 1988).

Cornell, Drucilla. *Beyond Accommodation: Ethical Feminism, Deconstruction, and the Law*. (New York: Routledge, 1991).

Critchley, Simon. *The Ethics of Deconstruction*. (West Lafayette, Indiana: Purdue University Press, 1999).

Critchley, Simon. *Ethics–Politics–Subjectivity: Essays on Derrida, Levinas and Contemporary French Thought*. (London and New York: Verso, 1999).

Cvetkovich, Ann. "Sexual Trauma / Queer Memory: Incest, Lesbianism, and Therapeutic Culture." *GLQ* 2 (1995): 351–377.

Deleuze, Gilles and Felix Guattari. *Anti-Oedipus*. Trans. Robert Hurley, Mark Seem, and Helen R. Lane. (Minneapolis: University of Minnesota Press, 1983).

Deleuze, Gilles and Felix Guattari. *A Thousand Plateaus*. Trans. Brian Masumi. (Minneapolis: University of Minnesota Press, 1983).

Deleuze, Gilles and Claire Parnet. *Dialogues*. Trans. Hugh Tomlinson and Barbara Habberjam. (New York: Columbia University Press, 1987).

Derrida, Jacques. *Adieu to Emmanuel Levinas*. Trans. Pascale-Anne Brault and Michael Naas. (Stanford University Press, 1999).

Derrida, Jacques. *Aporias*. Trans. Thomas Dutoit. (Stanford University Press, 1993).

Derrida, Jacques. *Dissemination*. Trans. Barbara Johnson. (The University of Chicago Press, 1981).

Derrida, Jacques. *The Gift of Death*. Trans. David Wills. (The University of Chicago Press, 1995).

Derrida, Jacques. *Limited, Inc*. (Evanston, IL: Northwestern University Press, 1988).

Derrida, Jacques. "Living On: Borderlines." *Deconstruction and Criticism*. Trans. James Hulbert. (New York: Continuum, 1990), 75–176.

Derrida, Jacques. *The Politics of Friendship*. (London & New York: Verso, 1997).

Derrida, Jacques. *The Post Card*. Trans. Alan Bass. (University of Chicago Press, 1987).

Derrida, Jacques. "Des Tours de Babel." *Difference and Translation*. Ed. and trans. Joseph Graham. (Ithaca: Cornell University Press, 1985), 165–248.

Derrida, Jacques. "Violence and Metaphysics." *Writing and Difference*. Trans. Alan Bass. (London: Routledge, 1978), 79–183.

Derrida, Jacques. *Writing and Difference*. Trans. Alan Bass. (University of Chicago Press, 1978).

Descartes, Rene. *Discourse on Method and Meditations on First Philosophy*. Trans. Desmond M. Clarke. (London: Penguin, 1998).

Devlin, Kimberly. "ALP's Final Monologue in *Finnegans Wake*: The Dialectical Logic of Joyce's Dream Text." *Coping with Joyce*. Ed. Morris Beja and Shari Benstock. (Columbus: Ohio State University Press, 1989).

Devlin, Kimberly. "Pretending in 'Penelope': Masquerade, Mimicry, and Molly Bloom." *Novel* 25 (1991): 71–89.

Devlin, Kimberly. "'See Ourselves as Others See Us': Joyce's Look at the Eye of the Other." *PMLA* 104 (5), 1989: 882–893.

Diprose, Rosalyn. *The Bodies of Women: Ethics, Embodiment, and Sexual Difference*. (London & New York: Routledge, 1994).

DSM-IV: Diagnostic and Statistical Manual of Mental Disorders, 4th edn. (Washington, DC: American Psychiatric Association, 1994).

Eaglestone, Robert. *Ethical Criticism*. (Edinburgh University Press, 1997).

Eco, Umberto. *Opera Aperta*. (Milano: T. Bompiani, 1962).

Edelstein, Marilyn. "Towards a Feminist Postmodern Poléthique: Kristeva on Ethics and Politics." *Ethics, Politics, and Difference in Julia Kristeva's Writing*. Ed. Kelly Oliver. (New York: Routledge, 1993), 196–214.

Ellmann, Richard. *James Joyce*. (New York: Oxford University Press, 1959).

Ellmann, Richard. *The Consciousness of Joyce*. (London: Faber and Faber, 1977).

Ellmann, Richard. *Ulysses on the Liffey*. (New York: Oxford University Press, 1972).

Emerson, Ralph Waldo. *The Selected Writings*. (New York: Random House, 1940).

Fabian, David R. "Joyce's 'The Sisters': Gnomon, Gnomic, Gnome." *Studies in Short Fiction* 5 (1968): 187–189.

Ferrar, Daniel and Michael Groden. "Post-Genetic Joyce." *Romanic Review* 86 (1995): 501–512.

Fordham, Finn. "*Finnegans Wake* and the Dance." *Abiko Quarterly with James Joyce Studies* 9 (1997–1998): 12–41.

Foster, R. F. *Modern Ireland: 1600–1972*. (London: Penguin Books, 1988).

Foucault, Michel. "The Ethic of Care for the Self as a Practice of Freedom." Trans. J. D. Gauthier, S. J. *The Final Foucault*. Ed. James Bernauer and David Rasmussen. (Cambridge, Massachusetts: MIT Press, 1988), 1–20.

Freil, Brian. *Translations*. (New York: Samuel French, Inc.: 1981).

Freud, Sigmund. *Introductory Lectures on Psychoanalysis*. Trans. James Strachey. (New York: Norton & Company, 1966).

Freud, Sigmund. "On Narcissism." *The Standard Edition of the Complete Psychological Works of Sigmund Freud*. Ed. James Strachey. (London: Hogarth Press, 1966).

Freud, Sigmund. "Letter to an American Mother" (1935). *American Journal of Psychiatry* 107 (1951): 786.

Galst, Liz. "Overcoming Silence: Lesbians Lead the Recovery Movement for Survivors of Child Sexual Abuse." *Advocate* 3 (December 1991): 62–63.

Gibson, Andrew. *Postmodernity, Ethics and the Novel: From Leavis to Levinas.* (London and New York: Routledge, 1999).

Gifford, Don and Robert J. Seidman. *Ulysses Annotated: Notes for James Joyce's Ulysses.* 2nd edn. (Berkeley: University of California Press, 1988).

Gillespie, Michael Patrick. *Reading the Book of Himself: Narrative Strategies in the Works of James Joyce.* (Columbus: Ohio State University Press, 1989).

Gilligan, Carol. *In a Different Voice: Psychological Theory and Women's Development.* (Cambridge, Mass: Harvard University Press, 1982).

Giovacchini, Peter L. *Schizophrenia and Primitive Mental States: Structural Collapse and Creativity.* (London: Jason Aronson Inc. 1997).

Glasheen, Adeline. "Finnegans Wake and the Girls from Boston, Mass.," *Hudson Review* 7 (Spring, 1954).

Gondek, Hans-Dieter. "Cogito and *Séparation*: Lacan/Levinas." *Levinas and Lacan. The Missed Encounter.* Ed. Sarah Harasym. (Albany: State University of New York Press, 1998).

Gordon, John. "Notes on Issy." *A Wake Newslitter.* 7 (1982): 1–17.

Goux, Jean-Joseph. *Symbolic Economies: After Marx and Freud.* Trans. Jennifer Curtiss Gage. (Ithaca: Cornell University Press, 1990).

Greenberg, Judith. "The Echo of Trauma and the Trauma of Echo." *American Imago* 55.3 (1998): 319–347.

Gregory, Augusta. *Selected Writings.* (London: Penguin Books, 1995).

Hall, H. S. and F. H. Stevens. *A Textbook of Euclid's Elements for the Use of Schools.* Second edn. (London: Macmillan, 1892).

Harpham, Geoffrey Galt. "Ethics." *Critical Terms for Literary Study.* Ed. Frank Lentricchia and Thomas McLaughlin. (University of Chicago Press, 1995).

Harpham, Geoffrey Galt. *Getting It Right: Language, Literature, and Ethics.* (University of Chicago Press, 1992).

Hart, Clive. "The Language of *Exiles*." *Coping with Joyce: Essays from the Copenhagen Symposium.* Ed. Morris Beja and Shari Benstock. (Columbus: Ohio State University Press, 1989), 123–136.

Hart, Clive. *Structure and Motif in Finnegans Wake.* (Chicago: Northwestern University Press, 1962).

Hayman, David. "Genetic Criticism and Joyce: An Introduction." *Genetic Joyce. European Joyce Studies* 5 (1994): 1–21.

Hayman, David. "Shadow of His Mind: The Papers of Lucia Joyce." *Joyce in Texas.* Ed. David Oliphant and Thomas Zigal. (Austin: University of Texas Press, 1983).

Heath, Stephen. "Ambioviolences: Notes for Reading Joyce." *Post-structuralist Joyce: Essays from the French.* Ed. Derek Attridge and Daniel Ferrar. (Cambridge University Press, 1984), 31–66.

Heath, Stephen. "The Ethics of Sexual Difference." *Discourse* 12(2), Spring–Summer 1990: 128–153.

Henke, Suzette. "Stephen Dedalus and Women: A Portrait of the Artist as a Young Misogynist." *Women in Joyce*. Ed. Suzette Henke and Elaine Unkeless. (Urbana: University of Illinois Press, 1982).

Henke, Suzette. *James Joyce and The Politics of Desire*. (New York: Routledge, 1990).

Herr, Cheryl. "Fathers, Daughters, Anxiety, and Fiction." *Discontented Discourses: Feminism/Textual Intervention/Psychoanalyis*. Ed. Marleen S. Barr and Richard Feldstein. (Urbana: University of Illinois Press, 1989), 173–207.

Herring, Phillip. *Joyce's Uncertainty Principle*. (Princeton University Press, 1987).

Irigaray, Luce. *The Ethics of Sexual Difference*. Trans. Carolyn Burke and Gillian C. Gill. (Ithaca: Cornell University Press, 1993).

Irigaray, Luce. *Je Tu Nous: Toward a Culture of Difference*. Trans. Alison Martin. (New York: Routledge, 1993).

Irigaray, Luce. "Questions to Emmanuel Levinas." Trans. Margaret Whitford. *Rereading Levinas*. Ed. Robert Bernasconi and Simon Critchley. (Bloomington: Indiana University Press, 1991).

Irigaray, Luce. *Speculum of the Other Woman*. Trans. Gillian C. Gill. (Ithaca: Cornell University Press, 1985).

Irigaray, Luce. *This Sex Which Is Not One*. Trans. Catherine Porter. (Ithaca, New York: Cornell University Press, 1977).

Joyce, James. *The Critical Writings of James Joyce*. Ed. Ellsworth Mason and Richard Ellmann. (New York: Viking Press, 1959).

Joyce, James. *Dubliners*. Ed. Robert Scholes and A. Walton Litz in consultation with Richard Ellmann. (New York: Viking Press, 1969).

Joyce, James. *Exiles*. (New York: Penguin, 1973).

Joyce, James. *Finnegans Wake*. (New York: Viking, 1939).

Joyce, James. *Giacomo Joyce*. (London: Faber & Faber, 1968).

Joyce, James. *James Joyce Archive*. Ed. Danis Rose, David Hayman, John O'Hanlon and Michael Groden. (New York: Garland, 1978).

Joyce, James. Letter to Lucie Noel Léon. 4 September 1939. Joyce/Léon Papers. (National Library of Ireland, Dublin, Ireland).

Joyce, James. Letter to Paul Léon. 11 September 1939. Joyce/Léon Papers. (National Library of Ireland, Dublin, Ireland).

Joyce, James. *Letters of James Joyce*. Vol I. Ed. Stuart Gilbert. (New York: Viking Press, 1957); reissued with corrections, 1966. Vols. II and III. Ed. Richard Ellmann. (New York: Viking Press, 1966).

Joyce, James. *A Portrait of the Artist as a Young Man*. Ed. Chester G. Anderson. (New York: Viking Press, 1968).

Joyce, James. *Stephen Hero*. Ed. John J. Slocum and Herbert Cahoon. (New York: New Directions, 1944, 1963).

Joyce, James. *Ulysses*. (New York: Vintage-Random, 1986).

Joyce, Lucia. Letters to Bozena Delimata. May 7, 1973, July 11, 1973, and January 13, 1974. Lucia Joyce Archive. Harry Ransom Center. University of Texas, Austin, Texas.

Kearney, Richard. *Dialogues with Contemporary Continental Thinkers: the Phenomenological Heritage: Paul Ricoeur, Emmanuel Levinas, Herbert Marcuse, Stanislas Breton, Jacques Derrida,* (Manchester University Press, 1984).

Kiberd, Declan. *Inventing Ireland.* (Cambridge: Harvard University Press, 1995).

Kristeva, Julia. *Desire in Language: A Semiotic Approach to Literature and Art.* Ed. Leon Roudiez. (New York: Columbia University Press, 1980).

Kristeva, Julia. *Powers of Horror: An Essay on Abjection.* Trans. Leon S. Roudiez. (New York: Columbia University Press, 1982).

Kristeva, Julia. "Stabat Mater." *The Kristeva Reader.* Ed. Toril Moi. (New York: Columbia University Press, 1986).

Kuberski, Philip. "The Joycean Gaze: Lucia in the I of the Father." *Sub-Stance.* 14 (1985): 49–66.

Lacan, Jacques. *Écrit.* Trans. Alan Sheridan. (New York: W. W. Norton & Company, 1977).

Le Doeuff, Michèle. *Hipparchia's Choice: An Essay Concerning Women, Philosophy, etc.* Trans. Trista Selous. (Oxford: Blackwell, 1991).

Lee, Joseph. *The Modernisation of Irish Society: 1848–1918.* (Dublin: Gill and MacMillan, 1973).

Levinas, Emmanuel. "Difficult Freedom" and "Ethics as First Philosophy." *The Levinas Reader.* Ed. Sean Hand. (Oxford: Blackwell, 1989).

Levinas, Emmanuel. "Language and Proximity." *Collected Philosophical Papers.* Trans. Alphonso Lingis. (Pittsburgh, Duquesne University Press, 1998).

Levinas, Emmanuel. "The Other in Proust" *Proper Names.* Trans. Michael B. Smith. (Stanford University Press, 1996).

Levinas, Emmanuel. *Otherwise than Being: or, Beyond Essence.* Trans. Alphonso Lingis. (Pittsburgh: Duquesne University Press, 1998).

Levinas, Emmanuel. "Reality and Its Shadow." *The Levinas Reader.* Ed. Sean Hand (Oxford: Blackwell, 1989).

Levinas, Emmanuel. *Time and the Other.* Trans. Richard A. Cohen. (Pittsburgh: Duquesne University Press, 1987).

Levinas, Emmanuel. *Totality and Infinity: And Essay on Exteriority.* Trans. Alphonso Lingis. (Pittsburgh: Duquesne University Press, 1969).

Levinas, Emmanuel. "The Trace of the Other." Trans. Alphonso Lingis. *Deconstruction in Context.* Ed. Mark C. Taylor. (Chicago and London: University of Chicago Press, 1986), 345–359.

Lipking, Lawrence. "The Genius of the Shore: Lycida, Adamastor, and the Poetics of Nationalism." *PMLA* 111 (March 1996): 205–221.

Llewelyn, John. *The Middle Voice of Ecological Conscience.* (New York: St. Martin's Press, 1991).

Lyons, F. S. L. *Ireland Since the Famine.* (London: Weidenfeld and Nicolson, 1971).

Maddox, Brenda. *Nora: The Real Life of Molly Bloom.* (Boston: Houghton Mifflin, 1988).

Mahaffey, Vicki. "Intentional Error: The Paradox of Editing Joyce's Ulysses." *Representing Modernist Texts: Editing as Interpretation.* Ed. George Bornstein. (Ann Arbor: University of Michigan Press, 1991), 171–192.

Mahaffey, Vicki. "'Fantastic Histories': Nomadology and Female Piracy in *Finnegans Wake.*" *Joyce and History.* Ed. Mark Wallager, Victor Luftig, and Robert Spoo. (Ann Arbor: University of Michigan Press, 1996), 157–176.

Mahaffey, Vicki. *Reauthorizing Joyce.* (New York: Cambridge University Press, 1988).

Mahaffey, Vicki. *States of Desire.* (New York and Oxford: Oxford University Press, 1998).

Manganiello, Dominick. *Joyce's Politics.* (London: Routledge & Kegan Paul, 1980).

Manganiello, Dominick. "The Politics of the Unpolitical in Joyce's Fictions." *James Joyce Quarterly* 25 (1992): 241–258.

Masson, J. Moussaieff. *The Assault on Truth: Freud's Suppression of the Seduction Theory.* (New York: Farrar, Straus and Giroux, 1984).

Mavor, Carol. "Dream-Rushes: Lewis Carroll's Photographs of the Little Girl." *The Girl's Own: Cultural Histories of the Anglo-American Girl, 1830–1915.* Ed. Claudia Nelson and Lynne Vallone. (Athens: University of Georgia Press, 1994).

McBride, Margaret. "Finnegans Wake: The Issue of Issy's Schizophrenia." *Joyce Studies Annual* 7 (1996): 145–175.

McCarthy, Patrick A. "A Warping Process: Reading *Finnegans Wake.*" *Joyce Centenary Essays.* Ed. Richard F. Peterson, Alan M. Cohn, and Edmund L. Epstein. (Carbondale: Southern Illinois University Press, 1983), 47–57.

McGann, Jerome. "Composition as Explanation (of Modern and Postmodern Poetries)." *Cultural Artifacts and the Production of Meaning: The Page, the Image, and the Body.* Ed. Margaret J. M. Ezell and Katherine O'Brien O'Keeffe. (Ann Arbor: University of Michigan Press, 1994).

McGee, Patrick. "Joyce's Pedagogy: *Ulysses* and *Finnegans Wake.*" *Coping with Joyce: Essays from the Copenhagen Symposium.* Ed. Morris Beja and Shari Benstock. (Columbus: Ohio State University Press, 1989), 206–219.

McHugh, Roland. *Annotations to Finnegans Wake.* (Baltimore: Johns Hopkins University Press, 1980).

McMichael, James. *Ulysses and Justice.* (Princeton University Press, 1991).

Meredith, George. *The Ordeal of Richard Feveral.* (New York: Scribner's, 1917).

Miller, Alice. *The Drama of the Gifted Child: The Search for the True Self.* Trans. Ruth Ward. (New York: Basic Books, 1997).

Miller, J. Hillis. *The Ethics of Reading: Kant, de Man, Eliot, Trollope, James, and Benjamin.* (New York: Columbia University Press, 1987).

Moliterno, Gino. "The Candlebearer at the *Wake*: Bruno's Candelaio in Joyce's Book of the Dark." *Comparative Literature Studies.* 1993 (30.3): 269–294.

Moshenberg, Daniel. "The Capital Couple: Speculating on 'Ulysses.'" *James Joyce Quarterly* 25 (Spring 1988): 333–347.

Nandy, Ashis. *The Intimate Enemy: Loss and Recovery of Self under Colonialism.* (Delhi: Oxford University Press, 1983).

Newman, Robert. "Bloom and the Beast: Joyce's Use of Bruno's Astrological Allegory." *New Alliances in Joyce Studies.* Scott, Bonnie Kime (ed.). (Newark: University of Delaware Press, 1988), 210–218.

Newton, Adam. *Narrative Ethics.* (Cambridge, Mass.: Harvard University Press, 1995).

Nietzsche, Friedrich. "On Truth and Lying in an Extra-moral Sense." (1873) *Friedrich Nietzsche on Rhetoric and Language.* Trans. and ed. Sander L. Gilman, Carole Blair, and David Parent. (Oxford University Press, 1989), 246–257.

Norris, Margot. *The Decentered Universe of Finnegans Wake: A Structuralist Analysis.* (Baltimore: Johns Hopkins University Press, 1976).

Norris, Margot. *Joyce's Web.* (Austin: University of Texas Press, 1992).

Norris, Margot. "The Last Chapter of 'Finnegans Wake': Stephen Finds His Mother." *James Joyce Quarterly* 25 (1987): 11–30.

Nussbaum, Martha. *Love's Knowledge: Essays on Philosophy and Literature.* (Oxford University Press, 1990).

Oliver, Kelly. *Family Values: Subjects between Nature and Culture.* (New York: Routledge, 1997).

"On the Left Bank." *The Paris Times.* March 14, 1928, No. 1371: A7.

Overall, Christine. "Feminism, Ontology, and 'Other Minds.'" *Feminist Perspectives: Philosophical Essays on Method and Morals.* Eds. Lorraine Code, Sheila Mullett, Christine Overall. (Toronto: University of Toronto Press, 1988).

Ovid. *The Metamorphosis of Ovid.* Trans. David R. Slavitt. (Baltimore: Johns Hopkins University Press, 1994).

Polhemus, Robert M. "Dantellising Peaches and Miching Daddy, the Gushy Old Goof: The Browning Case and Finnegans Wake." *Joyce Studies Annual* 5 (1994): 75–103.

Power, Arthur. *Conversations with James Joyce.* (New York: Barnes and Noble, 1974).

Prince, Morton. *The Dissociation of Personality: A Biographical Study in Abnormal Psychology.* (New York: Longmans, Green, and Co., 1906).

Rabaté, Jean Michel. "Back to Beria! Genetic Joyce and Eco's 'Ideal Readers.'" *European Joyce Studies* 5: 65–83.

Rabaté, Jean Michel. "Bruno No, Bruno Si: Note on a Contradiction in Joyce." *James Joyce Quarterly* 27 (1989): 31–39.

Rabaté, Jean Michel. *James Joyce, Authorized Reader.* (Baltimore: Johns Hopkins University Press, 1991).

Rabaté, Jean Michel. *Joyce Upon the Void: the Genesis of Doubt.* (New York: St. Martin's Press, 1991).

Rabaté, Jean Michel. "Lapsus Ex Machina." *Post-Structuralist Joyce: Essays from the French.* Ed. Derek Attridge. (Cambridge University Press, 79–102).

Rabaté, Jean Michel. "Pound, Joyce and Eco: Modernism and the 'Ideal Genetic Reader.'" *Romanic Review* May 1995, 86 (3): 485–500.

Ricouer, Paul. *Oneself as Another.* Trans. Kathleen Blamey. (Chicago and London: University of Chicago Press, 1992).

Robbins, Jill. *Altered Reading: Levinas and Literature*. (University of Chicago Press, 1999).

Robbins, Michael. *Experiences of Schizophrenia: An Integration of the Personal, Scientific, and Therapeutic*. (London: The Guilford Press, 1993).

Rubin, Gayle. "The Traffic in Women." *Toward an Anthropology of Women*. Ed. Rayna R. Reiter. (New York: Monthly Review Press, 1975).

de Saussure, Ferdinand. *Course in General Linguistics*. Ed. Charles Bally, Albert Sechehaye, and Albert Riedlinger. Trans. Roy Harris. (London: Duckworth, 1983).

Schork, R. J. "By Jingo: Genetic Criticism of *Finnegans Wake*." *Joyce Studies Annual* 5 (1994): 104–127.

Scott, Bonnie Kime. *Joyce and Feminism*. (London: The Harvester Press, 1984).

Seidel, Michael. *Epic Geography: James Joyce's Ulysses*. (Princeton University Press, 1976).

Shell, Marc. *Money, Language, and Thought: Literary and Philosophical Economies from the Medieval to the Modern Era*. (Berkeley: University of California Press, 1982).

Shelton, Jen. "Issy's Footnote: Disruptive Narrative and the Discursive Structure of Incest in *Finnegans Wake*." *ELH* 66.1 (1999): 203–221.

Shloss, Carol. "*Finnegans Wake* and the Daughter's Body." *Abiko Quarterly with James Joyce Studies* 9 (1997–1998): 118–137.

Spector, Judith A. "On Defining a Sexual Aesthetic: A Portrait of the Artist as Sexual Antagonist." *Midwest Quarterly* 26 (1984): 81–94.

Spivak, Gayatri Chakravorty. *In Other Worlds: Essays in Cultural Politics*. (New York: Methuen, 1987).

Spivak, Gayatri Chakravorty. "French Feminism Revisited: Ethics and Politics." *Feminists Theorize the Poltical*. Ed. Judith Butler and Joan Scott. (New York: Routledge, 1992), 54–85.

Spivak, Gayatri Chakravorty. "Introduction." *Imaginary Maps*. By Mahasweta Devi. (Calcutta: Thema, 1993).

Tindall, W. Y. *A Reader's Guide to Finnegans Wake*. (New York: Farrar, Straus, & Giroux, 1969).

Valente, Joseph. "The Politics of Joyce's Polyphony." *New Alliances in Joyce Studies*. Ed. Bonnie Kime Scott. (Newark: University of Delaware Press, 1988), 56–72.

Valente, Joseph. *James Joyce and the Problem of Justice: Negotiating Sexual and Colonial Difference*. (Cambridge University Press, 1995).

Walker, Margaret Urban. "Moral Understandings: Alternative 'Epistemology' for a Feminist Ethics." *Explorations in Feminist Ethics*. Ed. Eve Browning Cole and Susan Coultrap-McQuin. (Bloomington: Indiana University Press, 1992).

Wallager, Mark, Victor Luftig, and Robert Spoo (ed). *Joyce and History*. (Ann Arbor: University of Michigan Press, 1996).

Warner, Michael. "Homo-Narcissism; or Heterosexuality." *Engendering Men*. Ed. Joseph A. Boone and Michael Cadden. (New York: Routledge, 1990).

Weir, David. "Gnomon is an Island: Euclid and Bruno in Joyce's Narrative Practice." *James Joyce Quarterly* 28 (Winter 1991): 343–360.

Whitford, Margaret. *Luce Irigaray: Philosophy in the Feminine.* (London and New York: Routledge, 1991).

Wimsatt , W. K. and Monroe Beardsley. *The Verbal Icon: Studies in the Meaning of Poetry.* (Lexington: University of Kentucky Press, 1954).

Woolf, Virginia. *Between the Acts.* (London: Harcourt Brace and Company, 1941).

Wyschogrod, Edith. "Toward a Postmodern Ethics: Corporeality and Alterity." *Ethics and Aesthetics: The Moral Turn of Postmodernism.* Ed. Gerhard Hoffmann and Alfred Hornung. (Heidelberg: Universitatsverlag, 1996), 53–67.

Yeats, W. B. *The Collected Poems.* Ed. Richard J. Finneran. (New York: Scribner Paperback Poetry, 1996).

Yeats, W. B. *Essays and Introductions.* (New York: Macmillan, 1961).

Yeats, W. B. *A Vision.* (New York: Macmillan, 1956).

Zizek, Slavoj. *The Sublime Object of Ideology.* (London: Verso, 1989).

Index

1515728R00108

Printed in Germany
by Amazon Distribution
GmbH, Leipzig